D0120912

STAGE SOURCE BOOK
PROPS
Gill Davies

STAGE SOURCE BOOK
PROPS
Gill Davies

A & C Black ▪ London

First published 2004 by
A & C Black Publishers Limited
Alderman House
37 Soho Square
London W1D 3QZ

www.acblack.com

ISBN 0-7136-6584-X

CIP catalogue records for this book are available from the British Library and the Library of Congress.

Stage Source Book PROPS
was conceived, edited and designed by
Playne Books Limited
Chapel House
Trefin, Haverfordwest
Pembrokeshire SA62 5AU
United Kingdom

Author
© Gill Davies 2004

Research and editorial assistants
Vivienne Prior
Chris Skinner

Designers and illustrators
Richard Cotton
David Playne
Jade Stott

Typeset in Glypha

Printed in China

Introduction

The success of every company and of each production will depend upon attention to detail. To make or gather together props that look authentic requires a good deal of research, especially if the setting is historic. Many different sources will need to be tapped.

The aim of **Stage Source Book: Props** is to simplify this gathering of information by bringing it all together into one volume, thus eliminating numerous visits to the library and the need to beg, borrow – or buy – countless works of reference, and then decipher the contents.

The book covers specific periods of time, from Ancient Egypt and the Romans to the 1990s, as well as specialist settings like farms, the wild west, shops and fairy tales. Over 1,200 clear, simple drawings and several photographs capture the essence of each setting – from furniture and tableware to toys and weapons – with guidelines on size and colour. The emphasis varies from one period to another, as appropriate, and sometimes includes special features, such as Egyptian hieroglyphics and Elizabethan ornament.

Obviously, while some fashionable settings are a pure reflection of their period, some basic items, like the campfire, may be repeated in several centuries – and many homes accumulate items from earlier times to become a conglomerate mix. Much depends on the characters and the play's intent. The most important aim is never to include an item not yet invented or designed!

With examples of plays from each category, plus useful background information on theatre development, major events and daily life, I do hope the book will prove a valuable source of information – and inspiration.

The research has been fascinating and, as a director and props 'grafter', trying to get it right for over thirty years, staggering back from the library with heavy piles of books balanced under my chin, I wish I had written this **Stage Source Book** series long ago!

Gill Davies

Contents

5   **Introduction**

Props for historical settings

8   **Ancient Egypt**
Age of the Pharoahs:
3000-30 BC

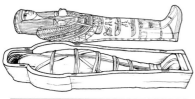

15   **Ancient Greece**
The birthplace of theatre:
780-323 BC

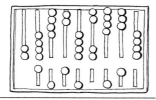

21   **Ancient Rome**
Imperial growth:
753 BC – 324 AD

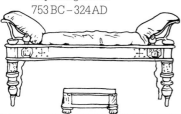

28   **The Dark Ages**
Invaders and raiders:
500-1000 AD

35   **The Middle Ages**
The Gothic period:
1000-1500

40   **1500-1599**
The age of Shakespeare

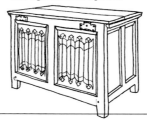

47   **1600-1699**
Puritanism versus opulence

54   **1700-1799**
The age of revolutions

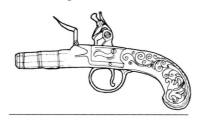

61   **1800-1839**
Heroes and heroines

67   **1840-1869**
Imperialism and industry

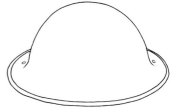

74   **1870-1899**
The thrust for change

81   **1900-1919**
The world marches to war

88   **1920-1939**
The jazz age

94   **The 1940s**
War, austerity and escapism

Contents

99   1950s
We've never had it so good!

104   1960s
The swinging decade

109   1970s
Riding high

114   1980s-1990s
Towards the new
millennium

Props for special settings

119   Gardens

124   Wild West

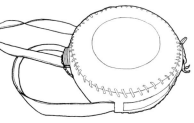

128   Biblical

132   Fairy tale and pantomime

135   The Orient

135   Institutions:
Religious settings, hospitals
and schools

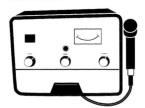

140   Shopping and offices

142   Hotels, pubs
and restaurants

144   Farms and cottages

147   Grand homes
Palaces, castles, stately homes
and mansions

150   Periods and styles review

152   Bibliography

153   Useful Addresses

154   Index

Ancient Egypt

Age of the Pharoahs: 3000-30 BC

From its earliest history to the birth of
Christ, and diplomatic relations with the
Romans, Ancient Egypt 's rich vibrant
culture developed far ahead of her
European counterparts – and has provided
a colourful setting for many a film and play.

Performance

There were no specific theatres but the Egyptians did perform religious and ritualistic pageants, satires, myths, plays and dance. They used backdrops and a wide variety of musical instruments – string harps, lyres, lutes, drums, flutes, clarinets, pipes, trumpets, oboes, rattles, tambourines, bells and cymbals.

Plays set in Ancient Egypt:

Aida – Elton John and Leann Rimes

Aida – An opera by Verdi

Antony and Cleopatra – William Shakespeare

Caesar and Cleopatra – George Bernard Shaw

Firstborn – Christopher Fry

Joseph and His Amazing Technicolour Dreamcoat – Tim Rice and Andrew Lloyd Webber

And set in more recent times . . .
Death on the Nile – Agatha Christie

Lifestyle

Lfe revolved around the Nile and the fertile land along its banks. The yearly flooding enriched the soil and brought good harvests. Only when the Nile did not rise high enough to water the fields, was there famine. Wages were paid in wheat, fish, vegetables, oils, wood for fuel, pottery and clothing. Copper tools included axes, saws, chisels and drills. While temples and tombs were built from stone, farmers, field hands, craftsmen and scribes built mud-brick homes. Pharaohs too, lived in mud-brick palaces – albeit on a grand scale.

Food and drink

Wheat and barley were used to make bread and beer (the basic diet of rich and poor alike) at home, in palaces or temple kitchens. Grain was ground between stones, mixed into dough with water, shaped into loaves and baked in a clay oven. Dates or honey could be added to make cakes.

Beer (more popular than water) was made at the same time, by adding partly-baked bread to water and leaving this to ferment before straining into jars. It was so coarse it might be drunk through a syphon . Fruit drinks were popular and the rich drank wine made from trodden grapes, squeezed in a cloth. Wine was stored in pottery jars with labels that indicated the vineyard and date.

People enjoyed dried and fresh fruit (pomegranates, dates and figs), lettuces, cucumbers, spring onions, fish, eggs, milk, yoghurt and cheese as well as almonds and sesame seeds. Soups contained peas, beans, lentils, leeks and onions. Herbs and spices added flavour; sesame and olive oils were used in cooking.

Meat was roasted over an open fire but only the wealthy regularly enjoyed beef, lamb, goat, venison, pork, duck, geese, quail and pigeon. The poor caught rabbits, hares and wild birds. Women and girls prepared packed lunches for men and boys to take to work or school. Food was served on trays or baskets resting on stands, rather than tables. There were no plates; people ate with their fingers. Drink was served in cups of pottery, faience or gold.

Gold

Gold was seen as a mystical material because it stayed looking new, even if buried for years; associated with the sun and everlasting life, it was given to neighbouring rulers to ensure a friendly relationship. It was believed that the gods were made of gold and gold masks protected dead royalty. A main source was Nubia (nub is the ancient Egyptian word for gold), where it was mined from mountains deep in the desert – by the army, or convicted criminals. As dust, nuggets or rings, it was carried back to the cities where royal goldsmiths turned it into statues and jewellery or beat it into incredibly fine 0.005mm leaf.

Letters

Papyrus paper was expensive so short letters were often written on flakes of limestone or broken pottery shards. Scarab seals and clay sealings are used. Royal letters to foreign rulers were inscribed on clay tablets. In the Graeco-Roman period, letters, invitations and tax demands were often written on wooden boards. Meanwhile, letters to the gods were delivered to temples while those to the dead were posted in or near tombs.

Coffins and tombs

Many Old Kingdom coffins were shaped like houses or palaces because people thought the dead person would live there in the afterlife. Often, a pair of eyes were painted on the east side of the coffin so that the dead could see out.

Leisure

Pastimes depicted in the tombs include hunting, wrestling and boxing, playing board games, banqueting, music and dancing. 600 musicians played simultaneously at a concert in 250 BC.

Ancient Egypt

Home and furnishings

The Egyptians slept in beds but instead of pillows, they used headrests made of stone, ivory or wood. Sheets were of linen.

They had small tables and stools. Some stools were cross-legged and had cushions stuffed with feathers. There were gilded and inlaid chairs, jewel caskets, wig boxes, candlesticks, flower vases, gold and silver tableware and vessels made of alabaster, glass, faience and pottery. Wooden storage chests contained utensils or jewellery.

Wood was used for shelving and stone for column bases, steps, drainage systems and bathrooms. Brick walls were plastered and exteriors painted white. Interior walls and floors were often painted in vivid colours – as well as ceilings, doorways, windows and balconies.

Decoration and inlays included:
- Stylized bullheads, leaping calves
- plants, flowers, and spiral vines
- birds and feathers
- gods and amulets
- colored, gilded and glazed tiles.

Craftsmen in royal workshops worked directly under the king's instructions to create superb furniture and exquisite household items. In the palace, the pharaoh's decorated throne was raised on a dais, with steps leading up to it.

Jewellery and personal items

As well as fine gold pieces, simple necklaces and bracelets were made from pierced stones and shells. There was highly skilled engraving and inlaying on rings, bracelets, necklaces, and amulets.

Faience ware, usually in blue-green or turquoise glass, was also popular.

Most items were stored in chests or caskets. Cosmetics were popular and many cosmetic spoons, kohl tubes, mirrors, tweezers, and perfume bottles have been discovered.

Historic background

7000-3000 BC
Nomadic tribes settle on Nile banks.

3000 BC
King Narmer unites Upper Egypt (Aswan to Cairo) and Lower Egypt (Nile Delta) into one kingdom; founding of state, administration, and calendar; invention of a script.

3100 BC
Hieroglyphic script used.

2900-2600 BC
Great Pyramids built at Giza.

2055 BC
Mentuhotep II gains control .

2000 BC
Karnak Temple begun; Egyptians control Nubia.

1600 BC
Ahmose unifies the country.

1500 BC
Hatshepsut is pharaoh.

1400 BC
Tutankhamun becomes pharaoh.

1274 BC
Ramesses II fights Battle of Kadesh.

1100 BC
Upper and Lower Egypt split.

945-730 BC
Libyans rule Egypt.

800-728 BC
Nubian king Piy conquers Egypt.

700-671 BC
Assyrians attack Egypt.

600-525 BC
Persians conquer Egypt.

400-332 BC
Alexander the Great conquers Egypt and founds Alexandria.

300 BC
Alexandrian Museum and Library.

289 BC
Ptolemy II builds lighthouse at Alexandria.

30 BC
Cleopatra VII, the last Egyptian queen, dies. Egypt a Roman province.

300 AD
Last use of hieroglyphic writing.

394-640 AD
Egypt ruled by Byzantine Constantinople.

600-642 AD
Egypt conquered by Arabs.

640 AD
Expulsion of Byzantines: Egypt a province of caliph kingdom.

900-969 AD
Cairo founded; casing blocks stripped off Giza pyramids.

Ancient Egypt

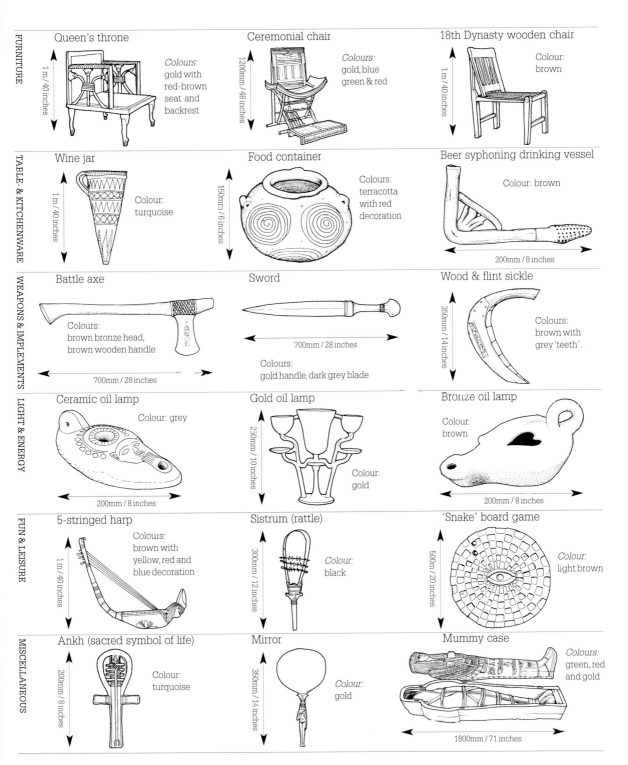

FURNITURE

Queen's throne
1 m / 40 inches
Colours: gold with red-brown seat and backrest

Ceremonial chair
1200mm / 48 inches
Colours: gold, blue green & red

18th Dynasty wooden chair
1 m / 40 inches
Colour: brown

TABLE & KITCHENWARE

Wine jar
1 m / 40 inches
Colour: turquoise

Food container
150mm / 6 inches
Colours: terracotta with red decoration

Beer syphoning drinking vessel
Colour: brown
200mm / 8 inches

WEAPONS & IMPLEMENTS

Battle axe
Colours: brown bronze head, brown wooden handle
700mm / 28 inches

Sword
700mm / 28 inches
Colours: gold handle, dark grey blade

Wood & flint sickle
350mm / 14 inches
Colours: brown with grey 'teeth'.

LIGHT & ENERGY

Ceramic oil lamp
Colour: grey
200mm / 8 inches

Gold oil lamp
250mm / 10 inches
Colour: gold

Bronze oil lamp
Colour: brown
200mm / 8 inches

FUN & LEISURE

5-stringed harp
1 m / 40 inches
Colours: brown with yellow, red and blue decoration

Sistrum (rattle)
300mm / 12 inches
Colour: black

'Snake' board game
500m / 20 inches
Colour: light brown

MISCELLANEOUS

Ankh (sacred symbol of life)
200mm / 8 inches
Colour: turquoise

Mirror
350mm / 14 inches
Colour: gold

Mummy case
Colours: green, red and gold
1800mm / 71 inches

11

Ancient Egypt

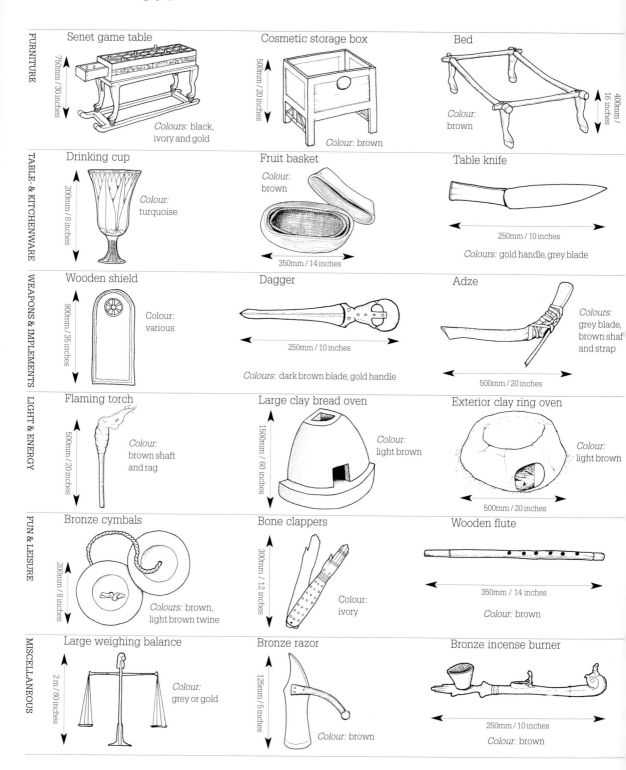

FURNITURE

Senet game table

750mm / 30 inches

Colours: black, ivory and gold

Cosmetic storage box

500mm / 20 inches

Colour: brown

Bed

400mm / 16 inches

Colour: brown

TABLE- & KITCHENWARE

Drinking cup

200mm / 8 inches

Colour: turquoise

Fruit basket

Colour: brown

350mm / 14 inches

Table knife

250mm / 10 inches

Colours: gold handle, grey blade

WEAPONS & IMPLEMENTS

Wooden shield

900mm / 35 inches

Colour: various

Dagger

250mm / 10 inches

Colours: dark brown blade, gold handle

Adze

Colours: grey blade, brown shaf and strap

500mm / 20 inches

LIGHT & ENERGY

Flaming torch

500mm / 20 inches

Colour: brown shaft and rag

Large clay bread oven

1500mm / 60 inches

Colour: light brown

Exterior clay ring oven

Colour: light brown

500mm / 20 inches

FUN & LEISURE

Bronze cymbals

200mm / 8 inches

Colours: brown, light brown twine

Bone clappers

300mm / 12 inches

Colour: ivory

Wooden flute

350mm / 14 inches

Colour: brown

MISCELLANEOUS

Large weighing balance

2 m / 80 inches

Colour: grey or gold

Bronze razor

125mm / 5 inches

Colour: brown

Bronze incense burner

250mm / 10 inches

Colour: brown

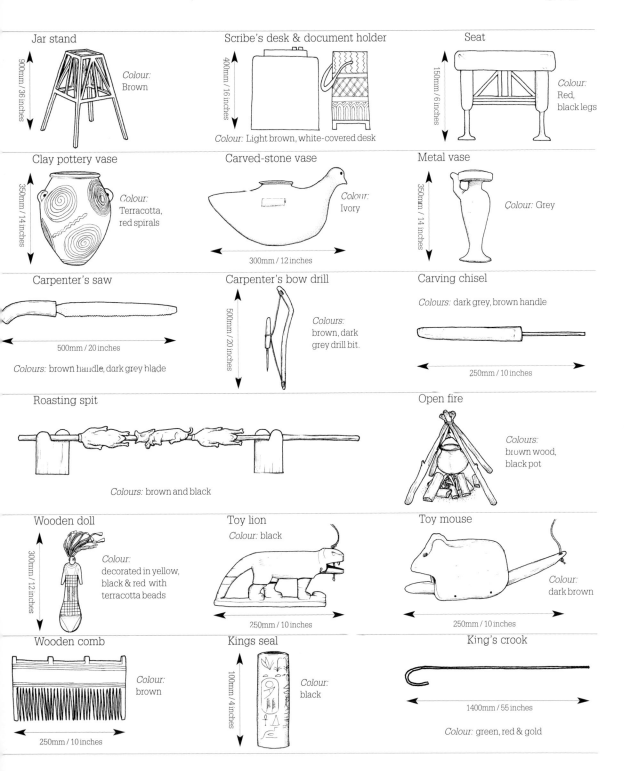

Jar stand

900mm / 36 inches

Colour:
Brown

Scribe's desk & document holder

400mm / 16 inches

Colour: Light brown, white-covered desk

Seat

150mm / 6 inches

Colour:
Red,
black legs

Clay pottery vase

350mm / 14 inches

Colour:
Terracotta,
red spirals

Carved-stone vase

300mm / 12 inches

Colour:
Ivory

Metal vase

350mm / 14 inches

Colour: Grey

Carpenter's saw

500mm / 20 inches

Colours: brown handle, dark grey blade

Carpenter's bow drill

500mm / 20 inches

Colours:
brown, dark
grey drill bit.

Carving chisel

Colours: dark grey, brown handle

250mm / 10 inches

Roasting spit

Colours: brown and black

Open fire

Colours:
brown wood,
black pot

Wooden doll

300mm / 12 inches

Colour:
decorated in yellow,
black & red with
terracotta beads

Toy lion

Colour: black

250mm / 10 inches

Toy mouse

250mm / 10 inches

Colour:
dark brown

Wooden comb

Colour:
brown

250mm / 10 inches

Kings seal

100mm / 4 inches

Colour:
black

King's crook

1400mm / 55 inches

Colour: green, red & gold

Ancient Egypt

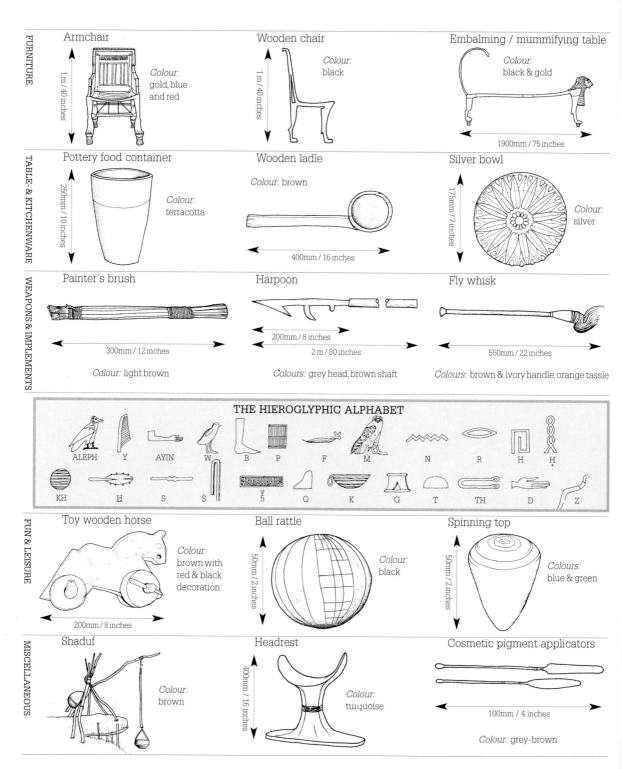

FURNITURE

Armchair
1m / 40 inches
Colour: gold, blue and red

Wooden chair
1m / 40 inches
Colour: black

Embalming / mummifying table
Colour: black & gold
1900mm / 75 inches

TABLE- & KITCHENWARE

Pottery food container
250mm / 10 inches
Colour: terracotta

Wooden ladle
Colour: brown
400mm / 16 inches

Silver bowl
175mm / 7 inches
Colour: silver

WEAPONS & IMPLEMENTS

Painter's brush
300mm / 12 inches
Colour: light brown

Harpoon
200mm / 8 inches
2m / 80 inches
Colours: grey head, brown shaft

Fly whisk
550mm / 22 inches
Colours: brown & ivory handle, orange tassle

THE HIEROGLYPHIC ALPHABET

ALEPH   Y   AYIN   W   B   P   F   M   N   R   H   H.

KH   H   S   Ś   V/5   Q   K   G   T   TH   D   Z

FUN & LEISURE

Toy wooden horse
Colour: brown with red & black decoration
200mm / 8 inches

Ball rattle
50mm / 2 inches
Colour: black

Spinning top
50mm / 2 inches
Colours: blue & green

MISCELLANEOUS

Shaduf
Colour: brown

Headrest
400mm / 16 inches
Colour: turquoise

Cosmetic pigment applicators
100mm / 4 inches
Colour: grey-brown

Ancient Greece

The birthplace of theatre: 780-323 BC

This period runs from the Archaic period to
the death of Alexander the Great.
Ancient Greece was the launchpad of
Western theatre. Philosopher Aristotle
claimed that theatre began with hymns to the
god Dionysus at the annual spring festival.

Backdrop to Ancient Greece

The first theatres

The earliest theater design was based on the threshing circle, used for separating wheat from chaff. The arenas were vast, with multiple entrances. Set into the hillside, their natural contours provided fine acoustics and visibility. The theatre of Dionysus, the most celebrated in classical Athens, was set on a slope below the Acropolis. Initially audiences stood or sat on the ground. Later, wooden or stone benches were raised on the hillside. Some theatres could hold up to 20,000 and became the prototypes for amphitheatres and sports arenas.

By the 5th century BC, a chorus and leader chanted lines. The chorus danced, sang, made sound effects and played musical instruments such as a lyre or pipe. They performed in the 'orchestra', not on a raised stage. The main actors (initially just one speaking actor and later, three) portrayed mythical and historical characters, at first in an empty space but later in front of a rectangular structure where simple scene building represented settings. Actors changed costumes in dressing rooms set into the buildings of this backdrop façade. Stage machinery was sometimes used but scenes of war or violence usually took place offstage. Performances were in daylight – actors held up an oil lantern to show when night had fallen.

Masks denoted character, emotion or sex (only men performed). The concept of realistic characters only developed later as powerful playwrights emerged. In the 6th century BC, Thespis became both the first dramatist and first real actor and his name gave rise to the term thespian. Other playwrights included tragedians, Aeschylus and Sophocles, in whose works the role of the chorus grew as the focal point between characters. It was Euripides (480-406 BC) who introduced a naturalistic approach. Comedy playwrights included Aristophanes (448-380 BC) and Menander (342-292 BC) who used topical humour and satire. Tragedy reached a peak when Greek society was at its height; comedy became most popular during its decline.

Original Ancient Greek plays

The Bacchae – Euripides

Lysistrata – Aristophanies

Medea – Euripides

Oedipus at Colonus – Sophocles

Oedipus the King – Sophocles

The Trojan Women – Euripedes

More recent plays include:

Goodbye Iphigenia – George MacEwan Green

Love of the Nightingale – Timberlake Wertenbaker

A Phoenix too Frequent – Christopher Fry

Rape of the Belt – Benn W Levy

Troilus and Cressida – William Shakespeare

Lifestyle: homelife

Most men worked in business or farming. At home, the role of husband was protected by legislation. Men were treated with great respect and relaxed on couches, to be fed and entertained by slaves while the women might join them, sitting on a chair, if no guests were present. Usually the women and children ate and slept in another room. Women were not allowed to go to the Olympics, or into the marketplace or city streets. Their most important role, after maternal duties, was the running of the household – whether managing slaves or doing it all themselves – or working in the fields. Whether citizens, freeborn or slaves, women had no political voice and lived under the control of men.

Under Athenian law, sons inherited from their fathers and (usually aged about 30) married a girl aged about 16. In Athens marriage was optional; In Sparta it was obligatory. The wedding ceremony usually took place during a full moon in January. The bride had a ceremonial bath, and wore a veil – removed only when she went to her husband's house. In Sparta, the bride was abducted and left alone, in the dark, on a pile of bamboo, dressed in men's clothing and with her hair cut short. Her bridegroom visited her after celebrating with his friends.

Ancient Greek art and drama depicts women on pottery and in literature – cleaning, spinning and weaving, cooking, and supervising slaves. Girls helped to cook, weave and clean. They learned ancient songs and dances and participated in religious festivals. A few were taught to read and write by their mothers.

Boys went to school from 6 to 16 years old and learned to read, write the alphabet and use an abacus; they also had lessons in poetry, music, gymnastics – wrestling, running, jumping, and javelin throwing. Army recruits started training at 7 and joined the army when 20 years old.

Athens was dusty, ill-supplied with water and the houses were used only for eating and sleeping. Furniture was sparse but elegant with sofas or recliners for resting and eating, fine chairs with or without a back, three or four-leg tables, used for carrying and displaying food and beds made of stretched canvas stripes that supported a mattress.

Food and drink

The day began when the sun rose. The first meal was bread dipped in neat wine, and sometimes olives. A substantial but plain lunch was eaten in the afternoon. The main evening meal included bread, fish (sometimes meat) olives, onions, lentils and fruit. Athenians cared more about socializing and exchanging ideas than food. In Sparta, they ate communal dinners, supplemented by wine and good conversation. Plato, Xenophone and Plutarch were inspired by this and developed the Symposium, gathering to drink and hold philosophical and political conversations. Reclining on sofas, barefoot, they ate with their fingers, cleaned their palates with bread, and drank an aromatic wine followed by wine mixed with water in krater pots.

Dress and hygiene

Caring for body and appearance – and exercising – was seen as an important duty. Bathing was in public baths or at home in clay bathtubs (rectangular, with an elevated place where they could rest, and no hole for emptying the water). Smaller, round wooden or clay pots were used for freshening up and for washing children. Special chalk (not soap) was used. Athenians would just clean faces and hands in the morning and wash fully in the evening, before eating. Visits to the barber for haircuts, beard and moustache trimming, manicure and pedicure were also social occasions. Athenian women wore wigs and make-up on special occasions; they coloured their faces and braided and dyed their hair (usually fair) or bound it with a fillet. They plucked unwanted hair or used a razor. Spartans believed in hard physical exercise and the women were forbidden cosmetic adornment. Most went barefoot, even in the streets, but sometimes they wore simple sandals attached by thongs.

Entertainment and leisure

There were some sixty days of state celebrations per year in Athens. A visit to the Gymnasium, Lyceum or Academy was a social opportunity, as were visits to the baths. The Athenian public baths were not elaborate, and usually provided only cold water. Popular activities included cat and dog fighting, cockfights, games with coins or beans, 'five lines' played with dice, festivals, sports and theatrical performances.

Historic background

780 - 560 BC
Greek colonies set up.

776 BC
First Olympiad.

753 BC
Legend claims Rome founded.

621 BC
Athens ruled by an oligarchy. A code of laws establishes death as punishment for all crimes.

580-489 BC
Pythagoras.

663 BC
Assyrian Empire peaks.

660 BC
Empire of Japan begins.

525 BC
Persians conquer Egypt.

509 BC
Roman Republic founded.

508 BC
Athenian democracy established.

499 BC
Greek city states revolt in Asia Minor against Persian rule.

490 BC
Greeks defeat Persians at Marathon.

431-404 BC
Peloponnesian War between Athens and Sparta.

429-347 BC
Plato.

429 BC
Hippocrates, who began Hippocratic Oath, survives plague that kills over a third of the population of Athens.

399 BC
Death of Socrates.

395 - 387 BC
Corinthian War.

390 BC
Celts sack Rome.

332 BC
Alexander the Great conquers Egypt.

323 BC
Death of Alexander the Great.

300 BC
Greek mathematician Euclid sets out principals of geometry.

Ancient Greece

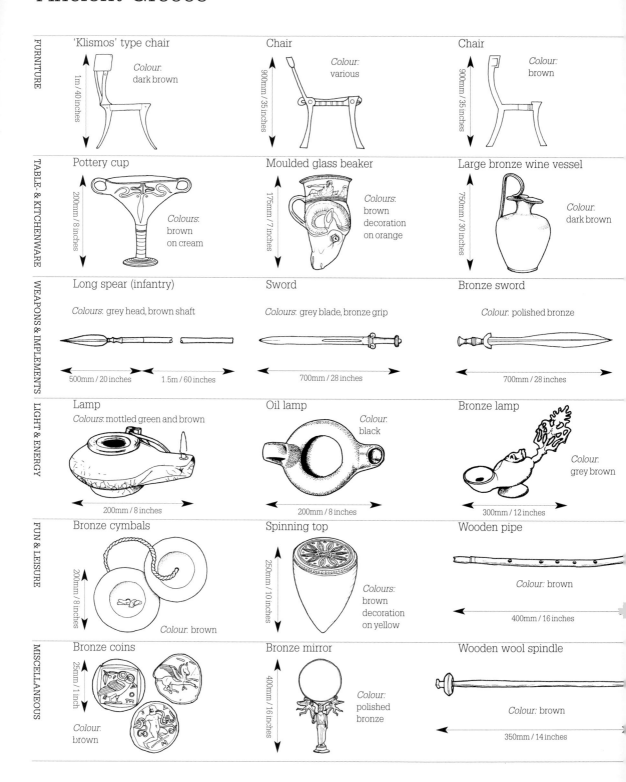

FURNITURE

'Klismos' type chair
1m / 40 inches
Colour: dark brown

Chair
900mm / 35 inches
Colour: various

Chair
900mm / 35 inches
Colour: brown

TABLE- & KITCHENWARE

Pottery cup
200mm / 8 inches
Colours: brown on cream

Moulded glass beaker
175mm / 7 inches
Colours: brown decoration on orange

Large bronze wine vessel
750mm / 30 inches
Colour: dark brown

WEAPONS & IMPLEMENTS

Long spear (infantry)
Colours: grey head, brown shaft
500mm / 20 inches
1.5m / 60 inches

Sword
Colours: grey blade, bronze grip
700mm / 28 inches

Bronze sword
Colour: polished bronze
700mm / 28 inches

LIGHT & ENERGY

Lamp
Colours: mottled green and brown
200mm / 8 inches

Oil lamp
Colour: black
200mm / 8 inches

Bronze lamp
Colour: grey brown
300mm / 12 inches

FUN & LEISURE

Bronze cymbals
200mm / 8 inches
Colour: brown

Spinning top
250mm / 10 inches
Colours: brown decoration on yellow

Wooden pipe
Colour: brown
400mm / 16 inches

MISCELLANEOUS

Bronze coins
25mm / 1 inch
Colour: brown

Bronze mirror
400mm / 16 inches
Colour: polished bronze

Wooden wool spindle
Colour: brown
350mm / 14 inches

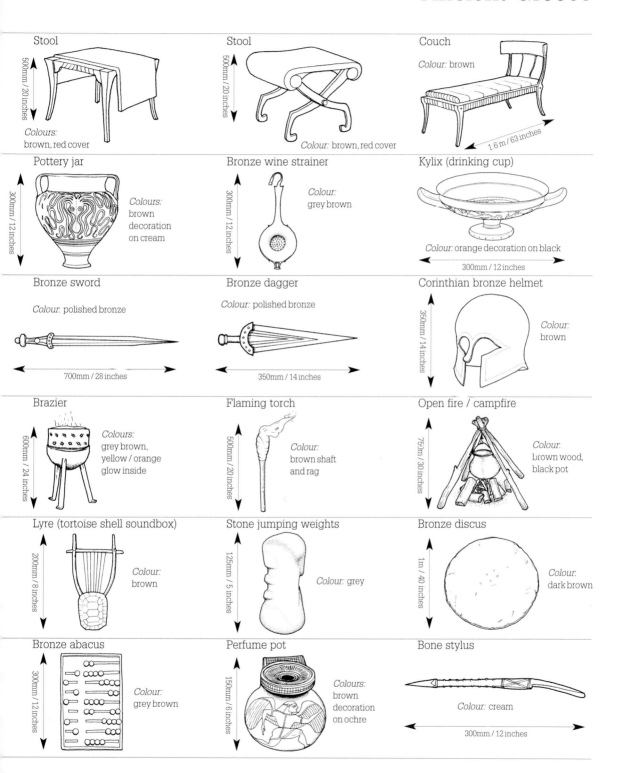

Stool

500mm / 20 inches

Colours:
brown, red cover

Stool

500mm / 20 inches

Colour: brown, red cover

Couch

Colour: brown

1.6 m / 63 inches

Pottery jar

300mm / 12 inches

Colours:
brown
decoration
on cream

Bronze wine strainer

300mm / 12 inches

Colour:
grey brown

Kylix (drinking cup)

Colour: orange decoration on black

300mm / 12 inches

Bronze sword

Colour: polished bronze

700mm / 28 inches

Bronze dagger

Colour: polished bronze

350mm / 14 inches

Corinthian bronze helmet

350mm / 14 inches

Colour:
brown

Brazier

600mm / 24 inches

Colours:
grey brown,
yellow / orange
glow inside

Flaming torch

500mm / 20 inches

Colour:
brown shaft
and rag

Open fire / campfire

75cm / 30 inches

Colour:
brown wood,
black pot

Lyre (tortoise shell soundbox)

200mm / 8 inches

Colour:
brown

Stone jumping weights

125mm / 5 inches

Colour: grey

Bronze discus

1m / 40 inches

Colour:
dark brown

Bronze abacus

300mm / 12 inches

Colour:
grey brown

Perfume pot

150mm / 6 inches

Colours:
brown
decoration
on ochre

Bone stylus

Colour: cream

300mm / 12 inches

Ancient Greece

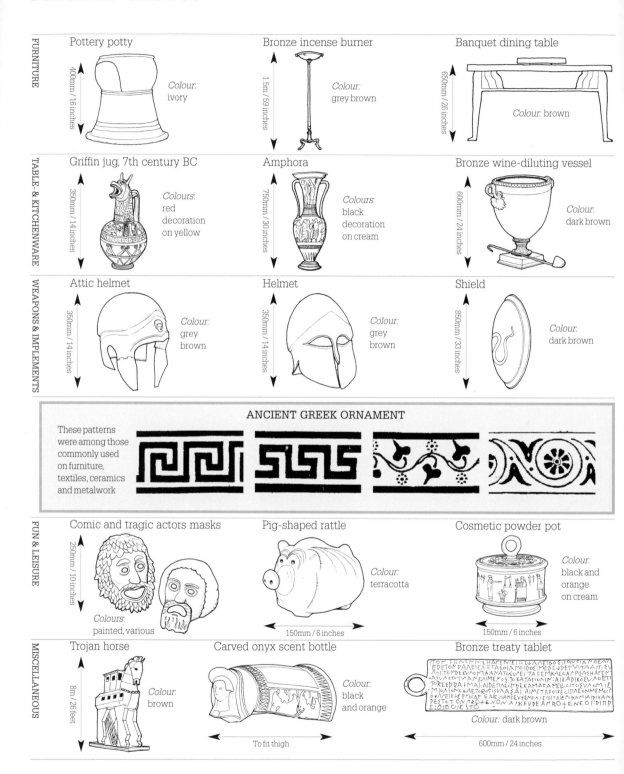

FURNITURE

Pottery potty
400mm / 16 inches
Colour: ivory

Bronze incense burner
1.5m / 59 inches
Colour: grey brown

Banquet dining table
650mm / 26 inches
Colour: brown

TABLE- & KITCHENWARE

Griffin jug, 7th century BC
350mm / 14 inches
Colours: red decoration on yellow

Amphora
750mm / 30 inches
Colours: black decoration on cream

Bronze wine-diluting vessel
600mm / 24 inches
Colour: dark brown

WEAPONS & IMPLEMENTS

Attic helmet
350mm / 14 inches
Colour: grey brown

Helmet
350mm / 14 inches
Colour: grey brown

Shield
850mm / 33 inches
Colour: dark brown

ANCIENT GREEK ORNAMENT

These patterns were among those commonly used on furniture, textiles, ceramics and metalwork

FUN & LEISURE

Comic and tragic actors masks
250mm / 10 inches
Colours: painted, various

Pig-shaped rattle
Colour: terracotta
150mm / 6 inches

Cosmetic powder pot
Colour: black and orange on cream
150mm / 6 inches

MISCELLANEOUS

Trojan horse
8m / 26 feet
Colour: brown

Carved onyx scent bottle
Colour: black and orange
To fit thigh

Bronze treaty tablet
Colour: dark brown
600mm / 24 inches

Ancient Rome

Imperial growth: 753 BC - 324 AD

From its reputed beginnings in 753 BC, the Empire grew for nearly 1,000 years but was in decline by 200 AD. Although the Romans adopted many Greek traditions, they were realists – not idealists. Excellent builders, they created a network of roads all leading to Rome, the busy heart of the empire.

Backdrop to Ancient Rome

Theatre in Ancient Rome

Plays by Plautus, Terence, and Seneca survive today. Terence (190-159 BC) introduced the subplot, and Plautus (c. 250-184 BC) greater humour. Soon outrageous farce and slapstick were popular, although serious plays were still recited.

By 400 BC, painting depicted sets. In time, raised stages arrived with temporary narrow wooden platforms about 30 metres (100 ft) long and stage house with openings for entrances. Later this was decorated with columns, statues, niches, and porticoes, and covered by a roof. Scenery was described as tragic (palatial columns), comic (homely dwellings), or satyric (landscape).

The first permanent stone theatre was built by Pompeius in 55-52 BC. A front curtain dropped into a slot at the beginning of a performance and was raised at the end. Roman actors wore contemporary garments and masks depicting multiple roles.

The Colosseum held 45,000 spectators. Many amphitheatres were of concrete, faced with stone. The Circus Maximus, used for chariot racing and made famous in *Ben Hur*, could seat 250,000. Gladiator fights, chariot races, music, dance, boxing, and battles were staged – sometimes against wild animals. Amphitheatres could be flooded for mock battles at sea or to show victims being fed to hungry crocodiles.

By AD 354, there was entertainment on over 100 festival days per year. Strolling players performed too, on simple timber platforms raised on posts. Meanwhile, as Christianity began to spread, the bawdier aspects meant that playacting became sinful in the eyes of the Church. Moreover, the arena was associated with the martyrdom and pagan rituals. Roman theatre declined as the Empire expanded and the last recorded performance in Rome was in 533 AD.

Plays set in Ancient Rome – or involving the Romans – include:

Antony and Cleopatra – William Shakespeare

Britannicus – Racine

Caesar and Cleopatra – George Bernard Shaw

Coriolanus – William Shakespeare

A Funny Thing Happened on the Way to the Forum – Stephen Sondheim, Burt Shevelove and Larry Gelbart

Julius Caesar – William Shakespeare

The Roman Actor – Philip Massinger

Trial of Lucullus – Bertolt Brecht

Food and drink

Slaves cooked and cut up the food as there were no forks or knives. The Romans ate with their fingers or used spoons, and freshened up afterwards with a damp towel.

For breakfast, there was bread dipped in wine, or with olives, cheese or raisins. The upper classes also had fresh meat, fish, fruits and vegetables, and sweetened food with honey. Luncheon at 11 am was bread, salad, olives, cheese, fruit, nuts, and cold meat. Supper was simple – porridge made of vegetables, or fish, bread, olives, and occasional meat.

The table was in the atrium and the family sat on stools. Often children waited on their parents. Later, a separate dining room was used and couches replaced benches or stools. The rich had elaborate dinner parties. Women and children ate separately, sitting on chairs, while men drank wine, and relaxed on couches around the table. They might be entertained by dancing girls or a play. At first, wine was a male privilege; if a wife had alcohol, she might be beaten.

Clothing and appearance

Early Romans wore togas but in time, only senators wore these. Tunics were of cool linen in summer and warm wool in winter. Soldiers had chainmail and scale armor plates on a linen or leather backing, plus leather armour. Outdoor shoes were leather. Indoors, women wore brightly coloured shoes which were sometimes decorated with pearls.

A single ring was usually the only jewellery worn by men but some sported a dozen. Women used highly polished metal mirrors and wore ornate necklaces, earrings, pins, pearls, bracelets, and friendship rings. They had false hairpieces and pinned up their hair with jewelled hairpins, or wore it down in ringlets. Parasols and fans were made of peacock feathers, wood or linen.

Boys wore a white knee-length tunic with a crimson border. Men wore all-white tunics. Girls' tunics had a belt at the waist; outdoors, a second tunic that reached to the feet was worn. Children wore a bulla, a locket on a chain, cord, or strap, given to them at birth to ward off evil. Girls wore this until their wedding eve; boys wore theirs until they became citizens.

Education

At home the father taught reading, writing, law, history, and physical training. Girls were taught by their mothers to spin, weave, and sew. In about 200 BC, boys aged 6 or 7 (and some girls) were sent to school to study scrolls and books, write on boards covered with wax, and use pebbles to solve mathematics. School began before sunrise, so a boy had his own candle to see by. At 12 or 13, upper-class boys went to grammar school and, at 16, some studied at rhetoric school.

Marriage and homelife

A groom had to be at least 14, and the bride at least 12 but they were often older. As today, an engagement ring was worn on the third finger of the left hand (the Romans believed a nerve here ran directly to the heart). A woman brought what dowry her family or she could supply; these slaves, clothing, jewels and furniture became the property of her husband.

Successful tradesmen often lived over the store in relatively spacious rooms but poorer classes had cramped quarters above or behind shops. Many generations crowded into one room to live and cook, without running water – they used public latrines. The rich lived in single-storey villas and lit their homes with oil lamps (the poor went to bed as soon as it was dark). Fine brick homes had red tile roofs, with rooms around a central courtyard faced by windows and balconies. There were paintings and mosaics but little furniture. Slaves kept the furnaces burning in the bath houses, cooked, cleaned, sewed, and worked in the garden.

Entertainment and leisure

Everyone visited the baths at least once a day. There were separate sessions for men and women, hot and cold pools, steam rooms, saunas, exercise rooms, hair cutting salons, reading rooms, shops and libraries.

Toys included balls, board games, hobbyhorses, stilts, kites, model animals, and hoops with jingling pieces of metal. Boys played tic-tac-toe, knucklebones and war games with wooden swords. Girls had wax, clay or rag dolls (some with jointed legs and arms) and played board and ball games, and did weight lifting.

Travel

The rich were carried by slaves in covered litters on poles, with curtained couches. There were chariots and wheeled carts pulled by horse or ox, packhorses, and galleys to cross the seas. The Romans invented the milestone which gave the mileage to the nearest city and perhaps an intermediate place, the date and sometimes the name of whoever had paid for the road.

Historic background

509 BC
Roman Republic founded.

490 BC
Battle of Marathon.

395 - 387 BC
Corinthian War.

370 BC
1st Roman roads built.

356-323 BC
Wars of Alexander the Great.

264-146 BC
Punic Wars.

221 BC
Great Wall of China built.

215 BC
Archimedes discovers gravity.

168 BC
Rome conquers Macedonia.

144 BC
Aqueducts bring Rome water.

58-43 BC
Caesar conquers Gaul and Britain.

44 BC
Caesar assassinated.

25 AD
Han Dynasty founded.

30 AD
Christ crucified.

54 AD
Claudius murdered; Nero rules.

64 AD
Rome nearly destroyed in fire.

79 AD
Vesuvius destroys Pompeii.

80-404 AD
Colosseum used for gladiator games.

122 AD
Hadrian's Wall built.

235-284 AD
Roman civil wars.

317 AD
Tartar warriors break through Great Wall of China.

320 AD
Gupta Empire: golden age of Indian culture.

330 -335 AD
Emperor Constantine I creates new capital at Constantinople and makes Christianity legal.

Ancient Rome

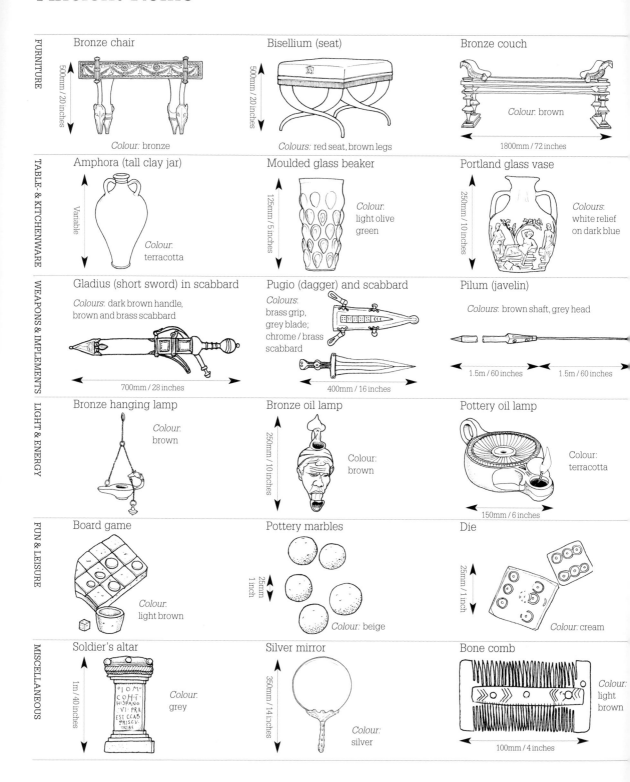

FURNITURE

Bronze chair
500mm / 20 inches
Colour: bronze

Bisellium (seat)
500mm / 20 inches
Colours: red seat, brown legs

Bronze couch
Colour: brown
1800mm / 72 inches

TABLE- & KITCHENWARE

Amphora (tall clay jar)
Variable
Colour: terracotta

Moulded glass beaker
125mm / 5 inches
Colour: light olive green

Portland glass vase
250mm / 10 inches
Colours: white relief on dark blue

WEAPONS & IMPLEMENTS

Gladius (short sword) in scabbard
Colours: dark brown handle, brown and brass scabbard
700mm / 28 inches

Pugio (dagger) and scabbard
Colours: brass grip, grey blade; chrome / brass scabbard
400mm / 16 inches

Pilum (javelin)
Colours: brown shaft, grey head
1.5m / 60 inches   1.5m / 60 inches

LIGHT & ENERGY

Bronze hanging lamp
Colour: brown

Bronze oil lamp
250mm / 10 inches
Colour: brown

Pottery oil lamp
Colour: terracotta
150mm / 6 inches

FUN & LEISURE

Board game
Colour: light brown

Pottery marbles
25mm 1 inch
Colour: beige

Die
25mm / 1 inch
Colour: cream

MISCELLANEOUS

Soldier's altar
1m / 40 inches
I O M
COH T
HISPANO
VI PRA
EST CCAB
PRISCV
TRIBV
Colour: grey

Silver mirror
350mm / 14 inches
Colour: silver

Bone comb
Colour: light brown
100mm / 4 inches

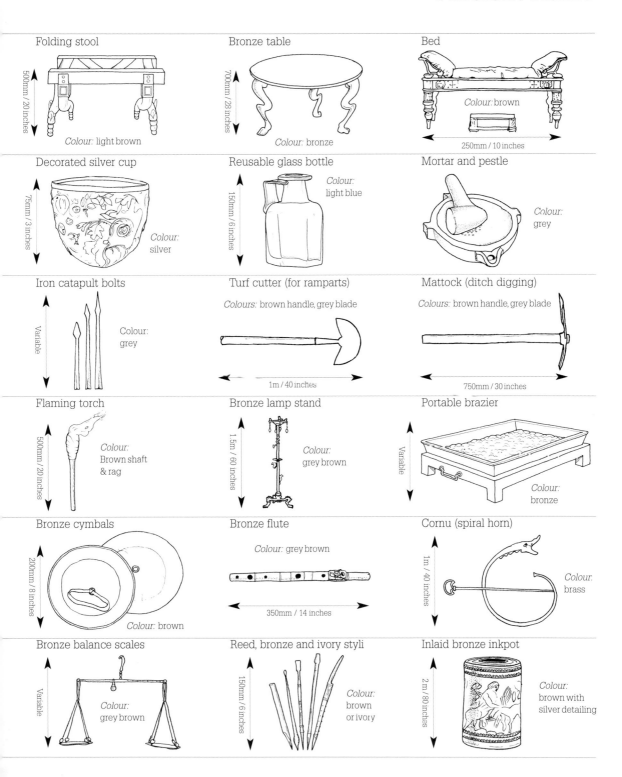

Folding stool
500mm / 20 inches
Colour: light brown

Bronze table
700mm / 28 inches
Colour: bronze

Bed
Colour: brown
250mm / 10 inches

Decorated silver cup
75mm / 3 inches
Colour: silver

Reusable glass bottle
150mm / 6 inches
Colour: light blue

Mortar and pestle
Colour: grey

Iron catapult bolts
Variable
Colour: grey

Turf cutter (for ramparts)
Colours: brown handle, grey blade
1m / 40 inches

Mattock (ditch digging)
Colours: brown handle, grey blade
750mm / 30 inches

Flaming torch
500mm / 20 inches
Colour: Brown shaft & rag

Bronze lamp stand
1.5m / 60 inches
Colour: grey brown

Portable brazier
Variable
Colour: bronze

Bronze cymbals
200mm / 8 inches
Colour: brown

Bronze flute
Colour: grey brown
350mm / 14 inches

Cornu (spiral horn)
1m / 40 inches
Colour: brass

Bronze balance scales
Variable
Colour: grey brown

Reed, bronze and ivory styli
150mm / 6 inches
Colour: brown or ivory

Inlaid bronze inkpot
2m / 80 inches
Colour: brown with silver detailing

Ancient Rome

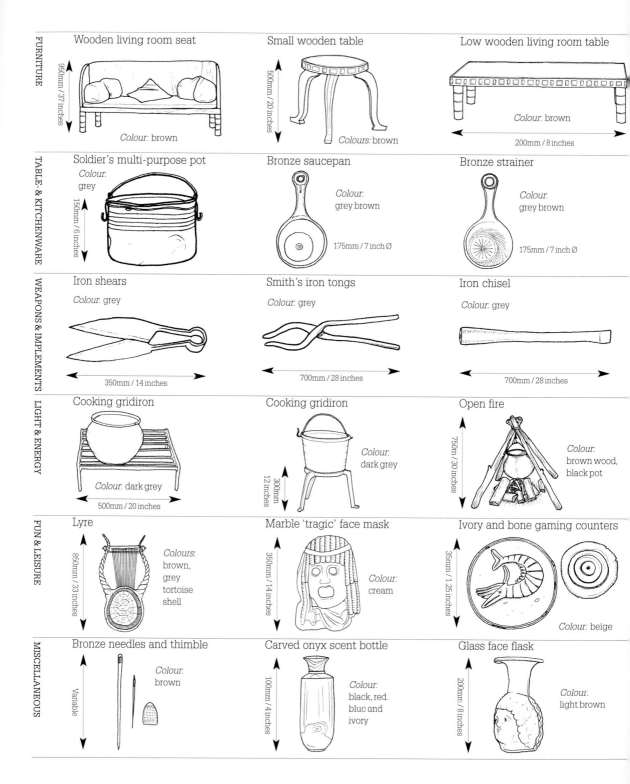

FURNITURE

Wooden living room seat
950mm / 37 inches
Colour: brown

Small wooden table
500mm / 20 inches
Colours: brown

Low wooden living room table
Colour: brown
200mm / 8 inches

TABLE- & KITCHENWARE

Soldier's multi-purpose pot
Colour: grey
150mm / 6 inches

Bronze saucepan
Colour: grey brown
175mm / 7 inch Ø

Bronze strainer
Colour: grey brown
175mm / 7 inch Ø

WEAPONS & IMPLEMENTS

Iron shears
Colour: grey
350mm / 14 inches

Smith's iron tongs
Colour: grey
700mm / 28 inches

Iron chisel
Colour: grey
700mm / 28 inches

LIGHT & ENERGY

Cooking gridiron
Colour: dark grey
500mm / 20 inches

Cooking gridiron
Colour: dark grey
300mm 12 inches

Open fire
750m / 30 inches
Colour: brown wood, black pot

FUN & LEISURE

Lyre
850mm / 33 inches
Colours: brown, grey tortoise shell

Marble 'tragic' face mask
350mm / 14 inches
Colour: cream

Ivory and bone gaming counters
35mm / 1.25 inches
Colour: beige

MISCELLANEOUS

Bronze needles and thimble
Variable
Colour: brown

Carved onyx scent bottle
100mm / 4 inches
Colour: black, red. blue and ivory

Glass face flask
200mm / 8 inches
Colour: light brown

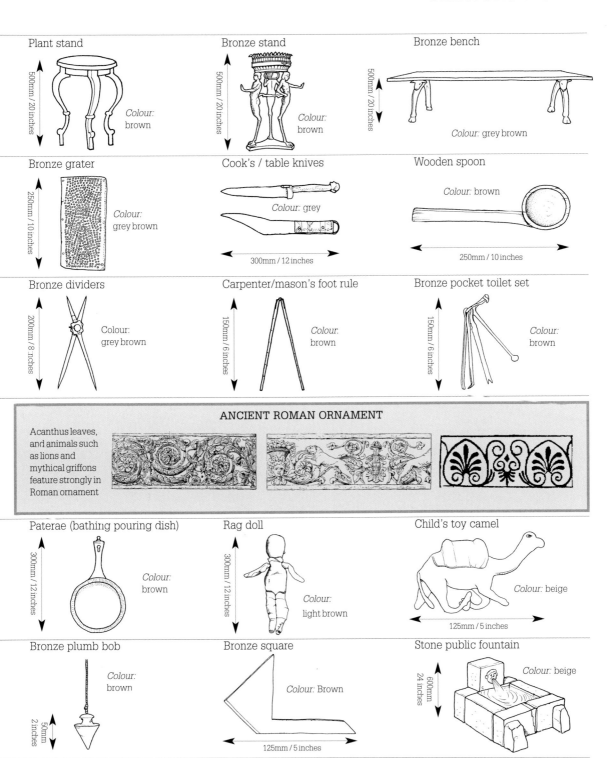

Plant stand
500mm / 20 inches
Colour: brown

Bronze stand
500mm / 20 inches
Colour: brown

Bronze bench
500mm / 20 inches
Colour: grey brown

Bronze grater
250mm / 10 inches
Colour: grey brown

Cook's / table knives
Colour: grey
300mm / 12 inches

Wooden spoon
Colour: brown
250mm / 10 inches

Bronze dividers
200mm / 8 inches
Colour: grey brown

Carpenter/mason's foot rule
150mm / 6 inches
Colour: brown

Bronze pocket toilet set
150mm / 6 inches
Colour: brown

ANCIENT ROMAN ORNAMENT

Acanthus leaves, and animals such as lions and mythical griffons feature strongly in Roman ornament

Paterae (bathing pouring dish)
300mm / 12 inches
Colour: brown

Rag doll
300mm / 12 inches
Colour: light brown

Child's toy camel
Colour: beige
125mm / 5 inches

Bronze plumb bob
Colour: brown
50mm 2 inches

Bronze square
Colour: Brown
125mm / 5 inches

Stone public fountain
Colour: beige
600mm 24 inches

27

The Dark Ages

Invaders and raiders: 500-1000 AD

With the Romans having retreated to defend their homeland, this was a period of warring tribal regions, and of invaders and raiders. In 672-735, the Venerable Bede was writing his histories, and epics such as *Beowulf*, *The Mabinogion* and Viking chronicles depict a culturally-rich society, a far cry from the supposed void suggested by early historians.

Influences on theatre

In about AD 500, following the fall of the Roman Empire, the Christian Church dominated most of the Western world – and since the Church considered drama, plays and players to be a corrupt influence, theatre development was repressed. However, roving bands of street players, jugglers, acrobats and animal trainers did manage to keep some traditions, and stock characters, alive.

In time, performances of biblical stories were allowed in churches. A stage was erected near the altar, with temporary platforms for the more distant scenes. This developed into many different stages or platforms being used for different scenes – called 'mansions'. Characters in the Easter and Nativity stories were played by priests, in productions that gradually grew more elaborate. Eventually, the performances moved from inside the church to just outside and, then into the marketplace where they developed into the popular entertainment of medieval times.

Plays set in the Dark Ages include:

Boy with a Cart – Christopher Fry

Camelot – Frederick Loewe and Alan Jay Lerner

Götterdämmerung – Richard Wagner

The Rhinegold – Richard Wagner

Siegfried – Richard Wagner

Tales of King Arthur – John Chambers

Thor, with Angels – Christopher Fry

The Valkyrie – Richard Wagner

Lifestyle

The pagan Anglo-Saxons, who invaded Britain in the 5-7th centuries, worshipped gods of nature (in springs, wells, rocks, and trees) and the weekdays, Tuesday, Wednesday, Thursday, and Friday, are named after the gods, Tiw, Odin, Thor, and Friya.

The barbarian Goths, Vandals, and Huns swept through Europe, destroying buildings and works of art. There were very few schools so education diminished and only in monasteries did the arts survive. They also managed to flourish in the eastern Roman Empire, which escaped the barbarians.

In China and India, meanwhile, great civilizations expanded.

In this time of political fragmentation, kings or chiefs and barbaric tribes dominated small enclaves. The wealthier leaders lived on estates or large farmsteads, where a large rectangular hall, decorated with wall hangings, was the scene of lavish feasts and entertainment. A king was essentially a war leader, expected to provide opportunities for plunder, land and slaves. Next in line were freemen – upper class thanes who could carry arms and speak at local assemblies, the noble class of jarls (earls) and lower class churls.

Slavery was a huge commercial enterprise. Many conquered Celtic Britons became slaves, as did unfortunates unable to pay a fine. Some children were sold into slavery for the sake of their own survival but could be ransomed later by relatives or granted freedom in an owner's will.

Land was split into tribal shires, each divided into 'hundreds', the basic units of administration and law. Reeves – or sheriffs – oversaw tax collection and judicial matters. English towns ranged in size from 5,000 people at York to 500 at St. Albans. Some towns were walled, while others were protected with earthworks.

Most utensils were crude and utilitarian but sites like Sutton Hoo reveal decorated armour and intricate jewellery. Church plate and illuminated manuscripts, including the 7th-century *Lindisfarne Gospels* and the 8th-century *Book of Kells*, exhibit great skill and creativity.

Clothes

A man's robe or tunic was gathered at the waist; he also wore hose and soft shoes. A woman's robe was full length and usually made of linen or wool. The rich had garments that were dyed and decorated with exotic borders. Brooches fixed clothing and stone amulets were worn for luck.

Weapons

War spears had a long ash shaft and an iron head; they might be thrown or jabbed. Round shields were wooden, covered with leather, and with a central iron boss. Nobles used iron swords with steel edges. Some hilts were elaborately carved, bejewelled, and inscribed with gods' names and good luck signs. The Vikings were sometimes armed with chainmail and helmets, and used short stabbing swords as well as the fierce double-headed battle axes.

Leisure and travel

Dice and chess were popular, as well as juggling balls and knives, horse racing, hunting with hounds, hawks and spears, and music – horns, lyres,

Backdrop to the Dark Ages

pan-pipes, bone whistles and the harp (played at feasts and in church). Women created fine embroidery and needlework for wall hangings and clothing. Festivals and social events provided opportunities for wrestling, tugs of war with an animal skin, storytelling, circle dances, hobby horse games and trained dogs to jump over high poles. Most travellers followed main trade routes that traced the old Roman roads and were quite busy, but quieter routes were dangerous and travellers were likely to be attacked by outlaws.

Farming and food

Horses and oxen were used for transport and heavy work; teams of oxen ploughed the narrow strips of land in large common fields. Pigs, cattle, goats, and sheep were kept while crops included peas, beans, lentils, wheat, oats, rye – and barley (used as a cereal and as the base for beer). The only sweetener, honey, was also used to make mead.

The Viking impact

By the end of the 9th century, the Danes had settled in Northumberland and East Anglia where they founded several small kingdoms in an area called Danelagen. As Viking fleets continued to raid for food and slaves, the English raised strongholds in the south to defend their territory.

The Vikings were great warriors, both on land and at sea, and colonised much of the northern world. They attacked Britain's holy places, slaughtered its monks and stole many treasures. From the end of the 700s until about 1100, they made voyages of discovery and seasonal raids, after which they returned home to farm. Their settlements, burials and

sagas reveal a fascinating culture. Trade and plunder brought wealth and the rich paid skilled craftsmen to produce beautiful artefacts.

Historic background

455
Anglo Saxons attack Britons in England.

455
Vandals sack Rome.

503 - 557
Persian-Roman Wars.

516
The historical figure of Arthur, a military leader of the Britons, battles against the Saxons at Badon, and at Camlann in 537. These will later be described in *Anales Cambriae*, c. 950.

565
Justinian the Great dies after 38 years as ruler of Byzantine Empire.

598
Pope Gregory's truce ensures Rome's independence.

604
Prince Shotoku reforms Japan.

618
T'ang Dynasty founded.

622
Mohammed flees from Mecca to Medina.

635
Persians defeated by Arabs.

637
Jerusalem surrenders to Arab forces.

642
Arabs conquer Egypt.

673 - 678
Arab siege of Constantinople fails.

700
Chinese invent gunpowder.

711-718
Conquest of Spain by Muslims.

794
The Kyoto period in Japan begins (lasts until 1185).

800
Coronation of Charlemagne.

820
Algebra invented.

843
Kingdom of Franks divides into three.

850
Mayan civilisation collapses.

851
Vikings sail up Thames to sack London.

862
Vikings found Russia.

867
Basil founds Macedonian Dynasty.

871-899
Alfred the Great, King of Wessex. He will win victory over Danes in 878.

962
Otto I crowned Holy Roman Emperor.

982
Eric the Red visits Greenland.

1000
Vikings reach America.

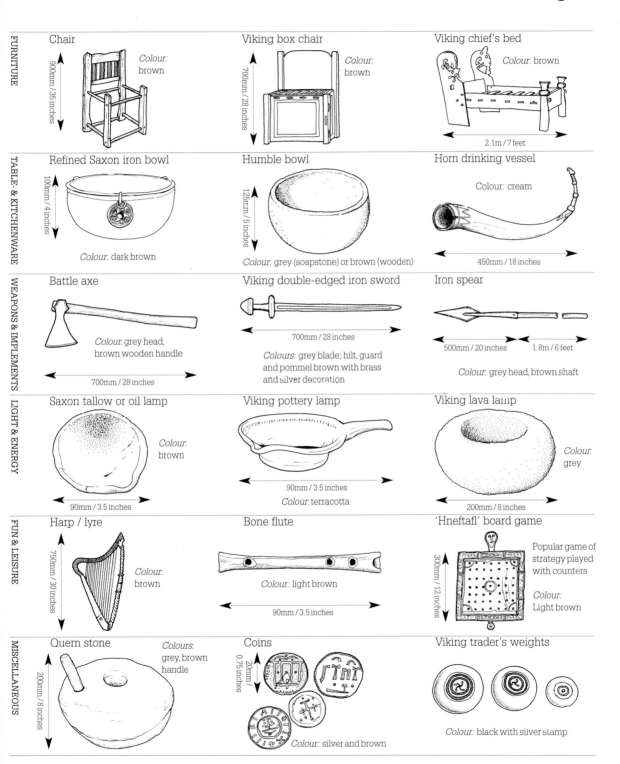

FURNITURE

Chair
Colour: brown
900mm / 35 inches

Viking box chair
Colour: brown
700mm / 28 inches

Viking chief's bed
Colour: brown
2.1m / 7 feet

TABLE- & KITCHENWARE

Refined Saxon iron bowl
100mm / 4 inches
Colour: dark brown

Humble bowl
125mm / 5 inches
Colour: grey (soapstone) or brown (wooden)

Horn drinking vessel
Colour: cream
450mm / 18 inches

WEAPONS & IMPLEMENTS

Battle axe
Colour: grey head, brown wooden handle
700mm / 28 inches

Viking double-edged iron sword
700mm / 28 inches
Colours: grey blade; hilt, guard and pommel brown with brass and silver decoration

Iron spear
500mm / 20 inches   1.8m / 6 feet
Colour: grey head, brown shaft

LIGHT & ENERGY

Saxon tallow or oil lamp
Colour: brown
90mm / 3.5 inches

Viking pottery lamp
90mm / 3.5 inches
Colour: terracotta

Viking lava lamp
Colour: grey
200mm / 8 inches

FUN & LEISURE

Harp / lyre
750mm / 30 inches
Colour: brown

Bone flute
Colour: light brown
90mm / 3.5 inches

'Hneftafl' board game
300mm / 12 inches
Popular game of strategy played with counters
Colour: Light brown

MISCELLANEOUS

Quern stone
Colours: grey, brown handle
200mm / 8 inches

Coins
20mm / 0.75 inches
Colour: silver and brown

Viking trader's weights
Colour: black with silver stamp

The Dark Ages

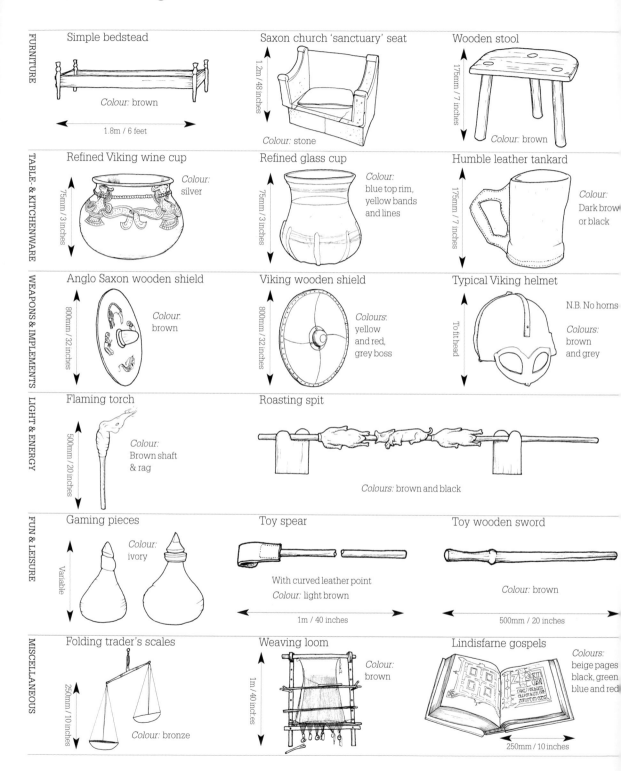

FURNITURE

Simple bedstead
Colour: brown
1.8m / 6 feet

Saxon church 'sanctuary' seat
1.2m/48 inches
Colour: stone

Wooden stool
175mm / 7 inches
Colour: brown

TABLE- & KITCHENWARE

Refined Viking wine cup
75mm / 3 inches
Colour: silver

Refined glass cup
75mm / 3 inches
Colour: blue top rim, yellow bands and lines

Humble leather tankard
175mm / 7 inches
Colour: Dark brown or black

WEAPONS & IMPLEMENTS

Anglo Saxon wooden shield
800mm / 32 inches
Colour: brown

Viking wooden shield
800mm / 32 inches
Colours: yellow and red, grey boss

Typical Viking helmet
To fit head
N.B. No horns
Colours: brown and grey

LIGHT & ENERGY

Flaming torch
500mm / 20 inches
Colour: Brown shaft & rag

Roasting spit
Colours: brown and black

FUN & LEISURE

Gaming pieces
Variable
Colour: ivory

Toy spear
With curved leather point
Colour: light brown
1m / 40 inches

Toy wooden sword
Colour: brown
500mm / 20 inches

MISCELLANEOUS

Folding trader's scales
250mm / 10 inches
Colour: bronze

Weaving loom
1m / 40 inches
Colour: brown

Lindisfarne gospels
Colours: beige pages black, green blue and red
250mm / 10 inches

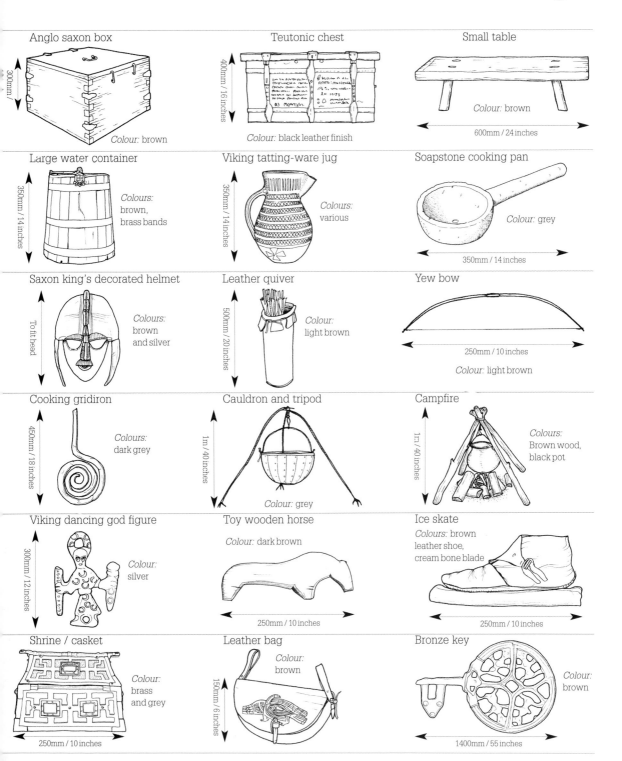

Anglo saxon box
300mm
Colour: brown

Teutonic chest
400mm / 16 inches
Colour: black leather finish

Small table
Colour: brown
600mm / 24 inches

Large water container
350mm / 14 inches
Colours: brown, brass bands

Viking tatting-ware jug
350mm / 14 inches
Colours: various

Soapstone cooking pan
Colour: grey
350mm / 14 inches

Saxon king's decorated helmet
To fit head
Colours: brown and silver

Leather quiver
500mm / 20 inches
Colour: light brown

Yew bow
250mm / 10 inches
Colour: light brown

Cooking gridiron
450mm / 18 inches
Colours: dark grey

Cauldron and tripod
1m / 40 inches
Colour: grey

Campfire
1m / 40 inches
Colours: Brown wood, black pot

Viking dancing god figure
300mm / 12 inches
Colour: silver

Toy wooden horse
Colour: dark brown
250mm / 10 inches

Ice skate
Colours: brown leather shoe, cream bone blade
250mm / 10 inches

Shrine / casket
Colour: brass and grey
250mm / 10 inches

Leather bag
Colour: brown
150mm / 6 inches

Bronze key
Colour: brown
1400mm / 55 inches

The Dark Ages

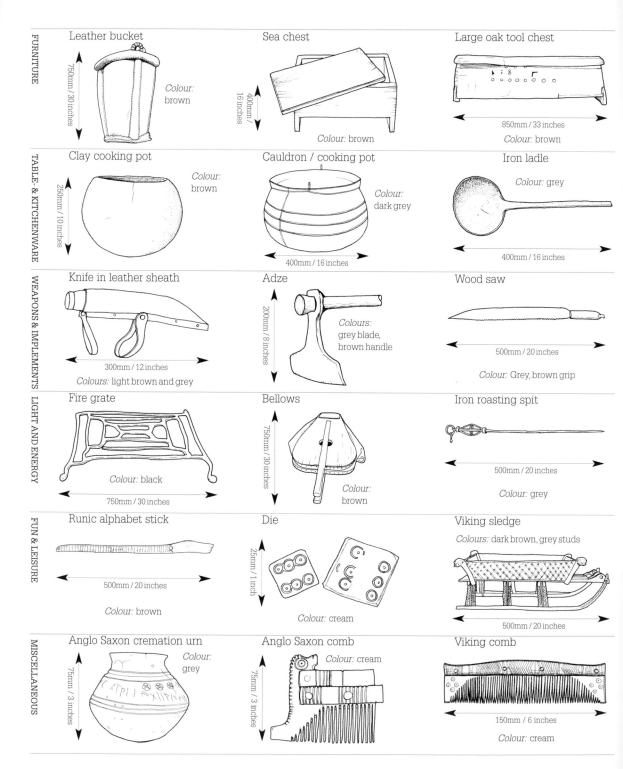

FURNITURE

Leather bucket
750mm / 30 inches
Colour: brown

Sea chest
400mm / 16 inches
Colour: brown

Large oak tool chest
850mm / 33 inches
Colour: brown

TABLE- & KITCHENWARE

Clay cooking pot
250mm / 10 inches
Colour: brown

Cauldron / cooking pot
400mm / 16 inches
Colour: dark grey

Iron ladle
Colour: grey
400mm / 16 inches

WEAPONS & IMPLEMENTS

Knife in leather sheath
300mm / 12 inches
Colours: light brown and grey

Adze
200mm / 8 inches
Colours: grey blade, brown handle

Wood saw
500mm / 20 inches
Colour: Grey, brown grip

LIGHT AND ENERGY

Fire grate
Colour: black
750mm / 30 inches

Bellows
750mm / 30 inches
Colour: brown

Iron roasting spit
500mm / 20 inches
Colour: grey

FUN & LEISURE

Runic alphabet stick
500mm / 20 inches
Colour: brown

Die
25mm / 1 inch
Colour: cream

Viking sledge
Colours: dark brown, grey studs
500mm / 20 inches

MISCELLANEOUS

Anglo Saxon cremation urn
75mm / 3 inches
Colour: grey

Anglo Saxon comb
75mm / 3 inches
Colour: cream

Viking comb
150mm / 6 inches
Colour: cream

The Middle Ages

The Gothic Period: 1000-1500

The period covers the medieval world from the Norman Conquest to the dawn of the Tudors, inspiring plays with all the romance of knights, castles and Robin Hood – also, sombre events such as the Black Death and the fierce warfare that permeated this age.

Backdrop to the Middle Ages

Influences on theatre

For a long time playacting had been regarded as ungodly by the Church so only plays with a religious theme were allowed. It is ironic that the Church, which had closed theatres, would now become the mainspring of keeping drama alive.

Ancient ritual and superstition still prevailed, so the Church linked religious holidays with pagan festivals and began to use drama to show seasonal Biblical stories.

At first the roles were played by priests in the sanctuary of the church. Eventually, performances grew more elaborate and moved outside to the church steps and then the marketplace. This lead to a much wider spread of theatre – although religious themes still dominated. Audiences were generally standing.

Travelling players, minstrels, masked bands and mummers depicted Christian ideals, and legends such as St George killing the dragon. Scripts became more complex, mixing serious religious subjects with boisterous farce.

Fixed stages began to use elaborate machinery with pulleys and ropes for special effects like moving clouds. Actors disappeared through trapdoors, while fire and smoke created the Mouth of Hell.

While fixed stages were common in Europe, movable stages were used in England and Spain. Different scenes or stories were housed on carts and wheeled around to various venues or groups of spectators.

By the 1200s, travelling entertainers wandered all over Europe, carrying everything with them on loaded wagons. There were also wandering minstrels – singers, comedians, or acrobats. Some of these performed with puppets or mime; others might recite poetry.

Itinerant actors were often regarded as vagabonds but plays were also staged by members of the local guilds at a time of celebration or festival. When artisan guilds took charge of the performances the local industry could be given some praise and promotion!

There were three types of plays written for medieval performances:
- Cycles (or mystery plays) dramatized biblical material in a series of short scenes.
- Miracle plays depicted scenes from the lives of saints and martyrs.
- Morality plays explored spiritual issues to show the conflict between Vice and Virtue.

These flourished in the mid-15th century and eventually opened the door for secular Renaissance drama which was further encouraged by the growth of towns and more stable governments in Europe.

Titles set in the Middle Ages :

Abelard and Heloise – Ronald Millar

Becket or the Honour of God – Jean Anouilh

Camelot – A J Lerner and F Loewe

Canterbury Tales – Chaucer; modernized by Phil Woods

Curtmantle – Christopher Fry

First part of King Henry IV – William Shakespeare

First part of King Henry VI – William Shakespeare

Francis – Julian Mitchell

King Henry – Shakespeare

King John – Shakespeare

King Richard II – Shakespeare

King Richard III – Shakespeare

Lady's not for Burning – Christopher Fry

Lark – Jean Anouilh, translated by Christopher Fry

The Lion in Winter – James Goldman

Richard of Bordeaux – Gordon Daviot

Robin Hood – three versions:
Larry Blamire
David Wood, Dave and Toni Arthur
David Neilsen

Second part of King Henry IV – William Shakespeare

Second part of King Henry VI – William Shakespeare

Two planks and a passion – Anthony Minghella

Styles, and trends

Many of the grander households moved around from one lord's castle to another. Furniture was reassembled and pegged and wedged. With them also travelled the more precious musical instruments, and silver and gold plate in chests placed in the baggage train or slung under a wagon.

Whether in manor house or castle, the Great Hall was furnished with trestle tables, wooden armchairs, benches and stools. Early furniture was simple and practical, easy to store away and regarded as disposable in the event of attack. Clothing and silverware were the more prized possessions.

English furniture was of oak or other local timber. It was generally painted (not polished) and patterned with simple geometric shapes made with a chisel and gouge. Some items had turned features on the legs, back supports or rails.

The Great Halls were lit by candles, sometimes on a hanging metal ring or a wooden candlebeam that could be raised or lowered. Here, food was served on trenchers. There were no forks – silver, pewter or (more typically) horn spoons were used. Guests often bring their own knives. Scented water was placed on the table in basins and ewers so that diners could rinse any grease from their fingers.

Drinks were served in earthenware or leather jugs, leather and horn mugs, and later, pewter vessels.

In the solar of grander households there were chests with cushions, as well as tapestries, settles, and curtained beds.

Historical Background

1066
Battle of Hastings, England. Tower of London built by William the Conquerer.

1095-1270
The Crusades.

1187
Muslims conquer Jerusalem.

1199
Richard the Lionheart dies.

1200
Inca dynasty founded.

1206
Genghis Khan founds Mongol Empire.

1215
Magna Carta in England.

1217
French-English wars.

1265-1321
Dante poet (Italy).

1265
English House of Commons.

1271-75
Marco visits China and court of Kublai Khan, whose empire is largest world has ever known.

1298
Scots rebel against English. Chinese develop prototype canon.

1314-17
Great European famine, the worst to strike Europe.

1326
Ottoman Empire founded.

1331
First firearms in Italy.

1337-1453
Hundred Years War.

1346
Cannons first used as field weapons.

1347-53
The Black Death.

1364
Ming Dynasty founded.

1381
Peasants Revolt in England.

1400-1410
Owain Glyndwr revolt in Wales.

1400
Death of Chaucer.

1429
Joan of Arc frees Orleans (will be burned 1431)

1438-1553
Inca dynasty in Peru

1450
Printing press invented.

1452-1519
Leonardo da Vinci.

1453
Fall of Constantinople to Turks ends Byzantine Empire.

1455–1485
Wars of the Roses.

1475-1564
Michaelangelo.

1480
Spanish Inquisition.

1485
Welsh Tudor dynasty in England begins.

1492
Columbus sets sail to discover New World

The Middle Ages

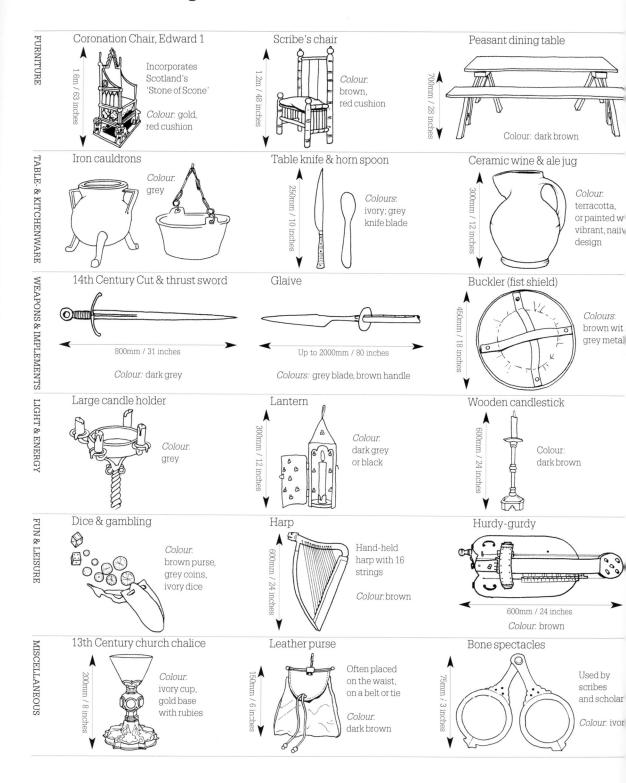

FURNITURE

Coronation Chair, Edward 1

1.6m / 63 inches

Incorporates
Scotland's
'Stone of Scone'

Colour. gold,
red cushion

Scribe's chair

1.2m / 48 inches

Colour.
brown,
red cushion

Peasant dining table

700mm / 28 inches

Colour: dark brown

TABLE- & KITCHENWARE

Iron cauldrons

Colour.
grey

Table knife & horn spoon

250mm / 10 inches

Colours.
ivory; grey
knife blade

Ceramic wine & ale jug

300mm / 12 inches

Colour.
terracotta,
or painted w
vibrant, naïv
design

WEAPONS & IMPLEMENTS

14th Century Cut & thrust sword

800mm / 31 inches

Colour: dark grey

Glaive

Up to 2000mm / 80 inches

Colours: grey blade, brown handle

Buckler (fist shield)

450mm / 18 inches

Colours.
brown wit
grey metal

LIGHT & ENERGY

Large candle holder

Colour.
grey

Lantern

300mm / 12 inches

Colour.
dark grey
or black

Wooden candlestick

600mm / 24 inches

Colour:
dark brown

FUN & LEISURE

Dice & gambling

Colour.
brown purse,
grey coins,
ivory dice

Harp

600mm / 24 inches

Hand-held
harp with 16
strings

Colour. brown

Hurdy-gurdy

600mm / 24 inches

Colour. brown

MISCELLANEOUS

13th Century church chalice

200mm / 8 inches

Colour.
ivory cup,
gold base
with rubies

Leather purse

150mm / 6 inches

Often placed
on the waist,
on a belt or tie

Colour.
dark brown

Bone spectacles

75mm / 3 inches

Used by
scribes
and scholar

Colour. ivor

The Middle Ages

15th-century lord's bed

Colours: dark brown frame, off-white sheet and pillow, grey blanket, burgundy drapes

2m / 80 inches

Rocking cradle

600mm / 24 inches

Colour: dark brown

Dole cupboard

1200mm / 48 inches

Colour: dark brown

Leather tankard

175mm / 7 inches

Colour: dark brown or black

Horn mug

150mm / 6 inches

Colours: ivory with specks and lines of grey

Ale keg

1300mm / 51 inches

Colour: dark brown

14th-century cranaquin

Colours: brown and grey

1300mm / 51 inches

Sickle

Colours: dark grey blade, brown grip

Dagger

300mm / 12 inches

Colour: grey

Wall torch

500mm / 20 inches

Colour: grey

Hand-held flaming torch

500mm / 20 inches

Colour: brown shaft and rag

Hearth in middle of room

Colours: black fire dogs and skewer forks

Bagpipes

1m / 40 inches

Colour: ivory pipes, brown bag

Lute

Colour: light brown

500mm / 20 inches

Shawm

Up to 2000mm / 80 inches

Colour: ivory

Leather flask

125mm / 5 inches

Colour: brown

Slop pail / chamber pot

600mm / 24 inches

Colour: terracotta

Writing quills & inkwells

200mm / 8 inches

Colour: ivory with specks and lines of grey

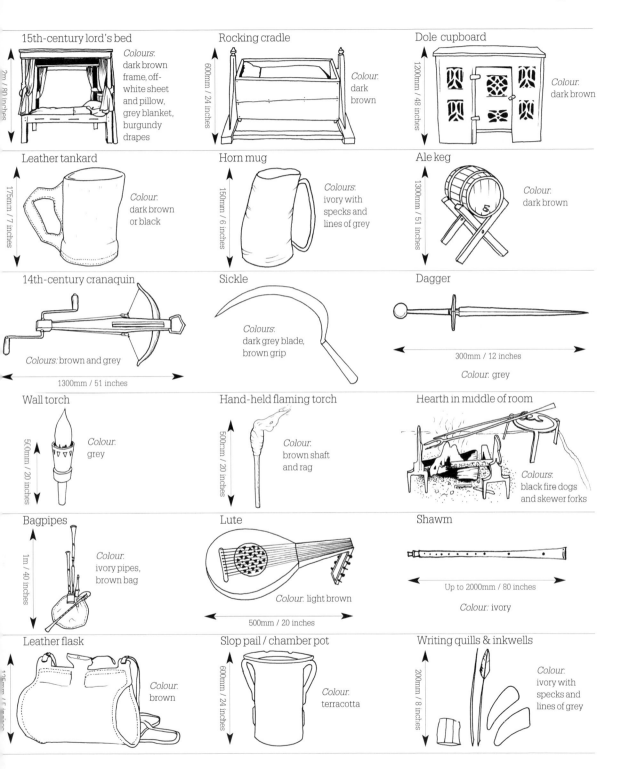

1500 - 1599

The age of Shakespeare

This was the age of Shakespeare and Tudor rule in Britain – when the Americas were explored and the first Italian opera was performed. The Renaissance saw dramatic advances in science, art and world exploration through Copernicus, Galileo, Michelangelo, Da Vinci, Magellan and Drake.

Influences on theatre

As theatre separated from religion, commedia dell'arte became hugely popular, with its knockabout humour and ribald jokes. It was performed by travelling groups who used a simple platform, painted backcloth and trap doors. Gradually productions became more lavish and permanent theatres would soon be built with raked stages to enhance scenic perspective effects (hence the terms 'upstage' and 'downstage' still used today). Meanwhile, Italy saw the first real opera, Peri's *Dafne* in 1597.

The Italians used lenses, silk filters and liquids in front of candles to colour the stage. Auditoriums were darkened to make lit stages appear brighter. Classic Roman plays were revived and the proscenium stage emerged. In England, enclosed inn courtyards had thrust stages. the audience were on three sides interacting with the performers. London's *Globe* had a circular auditorium with galleries around a thrust stage. The underside of its protruding roof was painted with moons, stars, and planets.

Shakespeare's comedies included songs, while sound effects added to the drama of tragedies and historical plays: battle and storm noises being made by percussion instruments. Lightning and heavenly bodies flew across on wires. Crude powder and paint make-up arrived; performances were mostly in natural light so the make-up did not need to be heavy.

Troupes of owner-actors, journeymen and hirelings acted simple plots and familiar stories, safe choices in the political and religious turmoil. Meanwhile, there was fear of plague being carried by itinerant actors, of apprentices being idle, of civil unrest

if theatre patrons drank too much and women of ill-repute plying their trade near public gatherings. So civil authorities often banned players and refused their entry into a town without an official licence.

Shakespeare earned income as playwright, actor and investor/share-holder in acting companies. In 1576, James Burbage built London's first public theater, known simply as *The Theatre*. London's *Globe* (completed 1599) became a showcase for Shakespeare's works and Burbage's company. Costumes defined royalty, nobility, soldiers and servants. Soon other, private, theatres opened. These were roofed with less seating capacity than the outdoor theaters.

Plays set in 1500-99 include:

Bottom's Dream – Alan Poole

The Clink – Stephen Jeffreys

Henry VIII – William Shakespeare

Luther – John Osborne

A Man for All Seasons – Robert Bolt

Mary Stuart – Friedrich Schiller

Rosencrantz and Guildenstern are Dead – Tom Stoppard

Royal Hunt of the Sun – Peter Shaffer

Vivat! Vivat! Regina! – Robert Bolt

. . . plus numerous Shakespeare plays

Lifestyle

A simple breakfast was eaten early in the morning. Pancakes were a Sunday morning treat with jam and powdered sugar. Hot caudle, thickened with eggs, was drunk at breakfast and bedtime. Dinner was the main meal from 11 am to 1 pm. Supper was from 5 to 8 pm.

The poor ate cheese with dark rye and barley bread. Middle classes ate wholemeal while the wealthy ate expensive white bread. Manchets (round browner loaves) were served with butter – except at Lent.

Midday meals for the poor included sausage, cabbage bread, pea or bean flour broth, pasties, pies, cheese and a bowl of curds. Servants had beef or fowl, good bread, pudding, salted herring, cheese, dried cod and ale. Middle and lower classes ate potages and stews. Meat was pot boiled to make it tender.

Nobility, merchants and gentlemen spent two to three hours over the main midday meal – miniature pastries, roast or boiled meat, spiced boar, broth with bacon, chicken or veal in spiced sauce, fritters and young rabbit; venison and game birds at country manors – turkey, capon, game, larks and snipes. Fish included eels, salmon, sole, turbot, whiting, lobster, crayfish, shrimps, and oysters (with brown bread and vinegar). The meal ended with cheese and desserts – strawberries, almonds, apples, plums, pears, cherries, fruit tarts and jellies; plus spiced wine to help digestion.

Even noble families grew their own fruit and vegetables. Artichokes were eaten raw, asparagus was boiled, sweet potato was roasted in ashes, sopped in wine or boiled with prunes. Peasants kept chickens, pigs, and perhaps a cow – slaughtered in November when meat and fish was smoked, dried, or salted.

Backdrop to 1500-1599

Water carried health risks; milk and flat beer was drunk. The rich drank sweet, heavy wines. Wine was kept cool in a copper tub full of water. When a guest handed back an empty goblet, it was rinsed in a wooden tub and then refilled.

People still ate with their fingers but most carried their own dagger-type knives and spoons. Forks were rare until the 1700s but some claim Henry VIII introduced these. Upper classes had their own dishes, plates, and drinking cups. Lower classes shared plates or ate on trenchers of thick unleavened bread. In time, square, wooden plates with a central, circular depression, replaced trenchers.

Well-to-do households used a cloth on the table. Elizabethans loved fine linens. A pepper box and silver chafing dishes might grace the table.

Clothing and appearance

By law, silk, satin and velvet were only allowed to be worn by the wealthy while cloth of gold and the colour purple were reserved for royalty. Spanish and French styles were popular; clothes became richer and more fitted. Everyone wore jewelery and hats. Men had colourful tights and flat-heeled shoes while women wore overshoes outside to raise their gowns above the dirt. The poor wore green and brown homespun, woollen clothing with knitted hose and hobnail shoes. In the field, they wore tunics and breeches. For four months, new babies were immobilized in swaddling bands. Young children wore simple shifts or gowns until the age of six when they were dressed as miniature adults.

Baths were thought unhealthy – although Queen Elizabeth I defied this by bathing as often as four times a year. Noblemen and women carried pomanders, hollow spheres holding a waxed perfume ball – attached to a woman's girdle or dangling from a man's chain. People cleaned their teeth with white wine and vinegar boiled with honey. Fashionable noblewomen sometimes blackened their front teeth while surgeon-dentists removed rotten ones.

Furnishings

Heavy and sparse furniture grew more elaborate, and sideboards became a fashionable way to display plate. Stools or chests were used rather than chairs. On the floor were loose rushes (often full of filth and fleas) or rushes plaited together into a rug. Male servants slept on palettes, taken up during the day. The family sat at the high table, and everyone else at trestle tables – moved to make room for games, dancing, and sleeping. The rich sometimes had Turkish carpets. Feather beds replaced straw mattress. Elaborate four-poster beds were highly valued and often left in wills.

Entertainment and games

Popular sports and entertainment included bowls, indoor tennis, long-bow practice, tilting, bull and bear-baiting, cockfighting, masques, the newly discovered fireworks and drinking in taverns. There were dice games, backgammon and games with tarot cards. Much money was lost in tabling dens.

Historical background

English rulers in this period:
1491-1547 King Henry VIII
1547-1553 Edward VI
1553-58 Queen Mary I
1558-1603 Elizabeth I

1501
Vespucci explores South American coast.

1517
Cortes conquers Mexico.

1524
German peasants rebel.

1527
Charles V sacks Rome.

1533
Pizarro executes Inca chief Atahualpa.

1534
England breaks with Church in Rome.

1542
1st European visitors to Japan.

1543
Copernicus claims earth circles sun.

1544-46
England and France 2-year war.

1547-84
Ivan the Terrible Czar of Russia.

1562
Beginning of slave trade.

1577-80
Drake circumnavigates globe.

1584
Raleigh tries to found Virginia.

1587
Mary Queen of Scots executed.

1588
Spanish Armada defeated.

1597-1601
Irish rebellion.

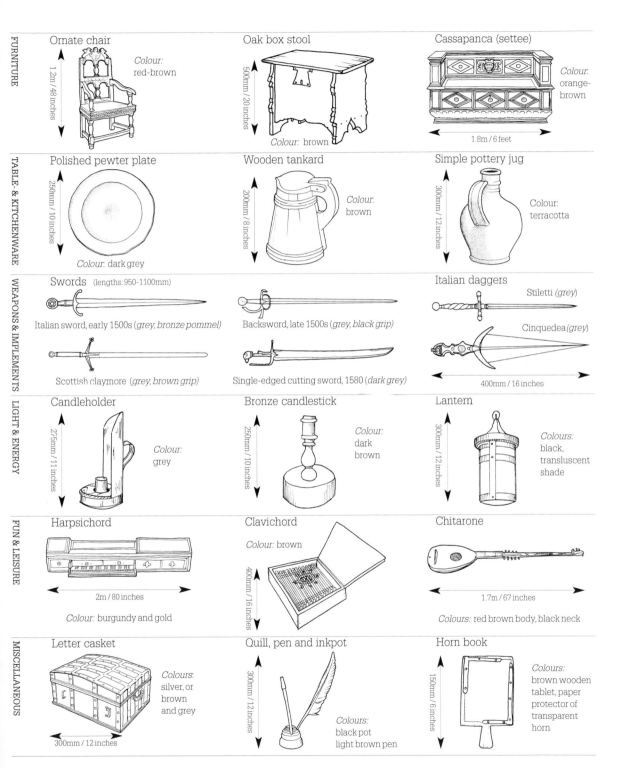

FURNITURE

Ornate chair
1.2m / 48 inches
Colour: red-brown

Oak box stool
500mm / 20 inches
Colour: brown

Cassapanca (settee)
Colour: orange-brown
1.8m / 6 feet

TABLE & KITCHENWARE

Polished pewter plate
250mm / 10 inches
Colour: dark grey

Wooden tankard
200mm / 8 inches
Colour: brown

Simple pottery jug
300mm / 12 inches
Colour: terracotta

WEAPONS & IMPLEMENTS

Swords (lengths: 950-1100mm)
Italian sword, early 1500s (grey, bronze pommel)
Scottish claymore (grey, brown grip)
Backsword, late 1500s (grey, black grip)
Single-edged cutting sword, 1580 (dark grey)

Italian daggers
Stiletti (grey)
Cinquedea (grey)
400mm / 16 inches

LIGHT & ENERGY

Candleholder
275mm / 11 inches
Colour: grey

Bronze candlestick
250mm / 10 inches
Colour: dark brown

Lantern
300mm / 12 inches
Colours: black, transluscent shade

FUN & LEISURE

Harpsichord
2m / 80 inches
Colour: burgundy and gold

Clavichord
Colour: brown
400mm / 16 inches

Chitarone
1.7m / 67 inches
Colours: red brown body, black neck

MISCELLANEOUS

Letter casket
Colours: silver, or brown and grey
300mm / 12 inches

Quill, pen and inkpot
300mm / 12 inches
Colours: black pot light brown pen

Horn book
150mm / 6 inches
Colours: brown wooden tablet, paper protector of transparent horn

1500-1599

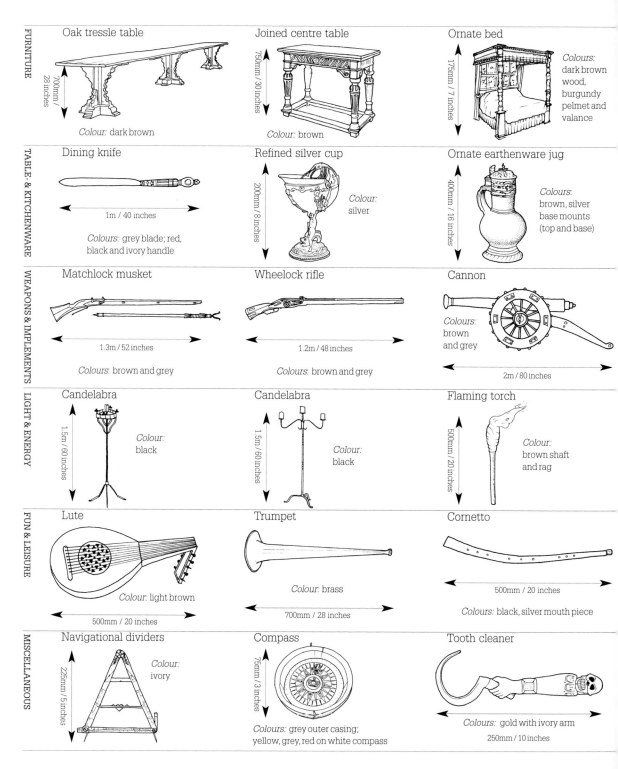

FURNITURE

Oak tressle table
700mm / 28 inches
Colour: dark brown

Joined centre table
750mm / 30 inches
Colour: brown

Ornate bed
175mm / 7 inches
Colours: dark brown wood, burgundy pelmet and valance

TABLE- & KITCHENWARE

Dining knife
1m / 40 inches
Colours: grey blade; red, black and ivory handle

Refined silver cup
200mm / 8 inches
Colour: silver

Ornate earthenware jug
400mm / 16 inches
Colours: brown, silver base mounts (top and base)

WEAPONS & IMPLEMENTS

Matchlock musket
1.3m / 52 inches
Colours: brown and grey

Wheelock rifle
1.2m / 48 inches
Colours: brown and grey

Cannon
Colours: brown and grey
2m / 80 inches

LIGHT & ENERGY

Candelabra
1.5m / 60 inches
Colour: black

Candelabra
1.5m / 60 inches
Colour: black

Flaming torch
500mm / 20 inches
Colour: brown shaft and rag

FUN & LEISURE

Lute
Colour: light brown
500mm / 20 inches

Trumpet
Colour: brass
700mm / 28 inches

Cornetto
500mm / 20 inches
Colours: black, silver mouth piece

MISCELLANEOUS

Navigational dividers
225mm / 5 inches
Colour: ivory

Compass
75mm / 3 inches
Colours: grey outer casing; yellow, grey, red on white compass

Tooth cleaner
Colours: gold with ivory arm
250mm / 10 inches

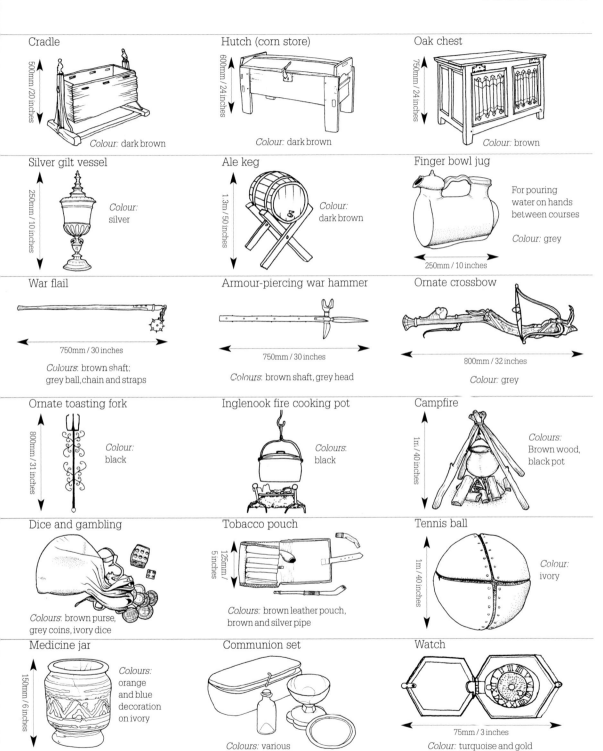

Cradle

500mm / 20 inches

Colour: dark brown

Hutch (corn store)

600mm / 24 inches

Colour: dark brown

Oak chest

750mm / 24 inches

Colour: brown

Silver gilt vessel

250mm / 10 inches

Colour: silver

Ale keg

1.3m / 50 inches

Colour: dark brown

Finger bowl jug

For pouring water on hands between courses

Colour: grey

250mm / 10 inches

War flail

750mm / 30 inches

Colours: brown shaft; grey ball, chain and straps

Armour-piercing war hammer

750mm / 30 inches

Colours: brown shaft, grey head

Ornate crossbow

800mm / 32 inches

Colour: grey

Ornate toasting fork

800mm / 31 inches

Colour: black

Inglenook fire cooking pot

Colours: black

Campfire

1m / 40 inches

Colours: Brown wood, black pot

Dice and gambling

Colours: brown purse, grey coins, ivory dice

Tobacco pouch

125mm / 5 inches

Colours: brown leather pouch, brown and silver pipe

Tennis ball

1m / 40 inches

Colour: ivory

Medicine jar

150mm / 6 inches

Colours: orange and blue decoration on ivory

Communion set

Colours: various

Watch

75mm / 3 inches

Colour: turquoise and gold

1500-1599

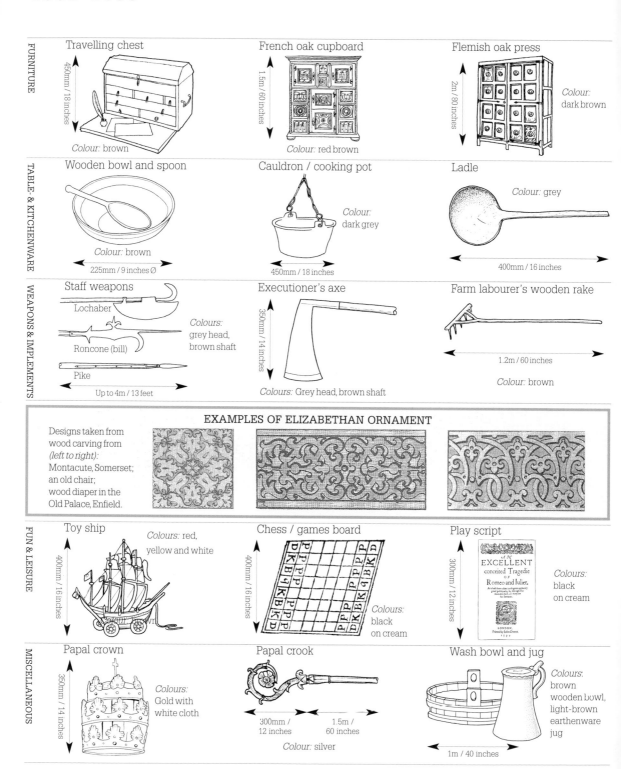

FURNITURE

Travelling chest
450mm / 18 inches
Colour: brown

French oak cupboard
1.5m / 60 inches
Colour: red brown

Flemish oak press
2m / 80 inches
Colour: dark brown

TABLE- & KITCHENWARE

Wooden bowl and spoon
Colour: brown
225mm / 9 inches Ø

Cauldron / cooking pot
Colour: dark grey
450mm / 18 inches

Ladle
Colour: grey
400mm / 16 inches

WEAPONS & IMPLEMENTS

Staff weapons
Lochaber
Roncone (bill)
Pike
Colours: grey head, brown shaft
Up to 4m / 13 feet

Executioner's axe
350mm / 14 inches
Colours: Grey head, brown shaft

Farm labourer's wooden rake
1.2m / 60 inches
Colour: brown

EXAMPLES OF ELIZABETHAN ORNAMENT

Designs taken from wood carving from *(left to right):* Montacute, Somerset; an old chair; wood diaper in the Old Palace, Enfield.

FUN & LEISURE

Toy ship
400mm / 16 inches
Colours: red, yellow and white

Chess / games board
400mm / 16 inches
Colours: black on cream

Play script
300mm / 12 inches

AN EXCELLENT
conceited Tragedie
OF
Romeo and Iuliet.

LONDON.

Colours: black on cream

MISCELLANEOUS

Papal crown
350mm / 14 inches
Colours: Gold with white cloth

Papal crook
300mm / 12 inches   1.5m / 60 inches
Colour: silver

Wash bowl and jug
Colours: brown wooden bowl, light-brown earthenware jug
1m / 40 inches

1600 - 1699

Puritanism versus opulence

This century of extremes witnessed both
Puritan severity and Cavalier extravagance.
It saw the opulence of Louis XIV's French
court, the Pilgrim Fathers sailing to America,
the English Civil War that culminated in the
beheading of Charles I, the ravages of plague
in Europe and the Great Fire of London.

Backdrop to 1600-1699

Theatre development

Wheeled carts were still used for street theatre, with pageants by travelling actors or local craftsmen. depicting religious spectacles such as Noah's Ark. Players, musicians, storytellers and conjurers visited taverns, inns and fairs. Theatres began to be roofed. Under James I, all aspects of theatre became subject to royal approval and licences. Meanwhile, the *Globe* in London burned down when cannon debris set light to its thatch.

In the 1650s, the future King Louis the XIV of France appeared in lavish ballets and masques. English actors and royalists in exile from Cromwell were influenced by French and Italian theatre as productions became ever more spectacular and expensive, depicting storms, waterfalls and avalanches. Molière founded the *Comédie Française* as Racine spearheaded tragic plays. For the first time, wings were used. The Italians used a synchronized wing system as machines moved scenery and performers. Magical effects included rolling ocean waves.

When Puritanism arrived, English drama halted. In 1642, theatres closed. After the Restoration in 1660, the city fathers still disapproved of theatre, especially as women were allowed on the stage for the first time, taking female roles instead of boys. They sought more flattering make-up and used a whitening paste made from fat and white lead with white chalk for powder. Burnt cork was applied as eyeliner and to darken eyebrows. Carmine was used on lips and cheeks. French comedy actors used flour to whiten their faces.

Stages grew larger and grander. Inigo Jones designed Whitehall's new royal palace as an elegant backdrop for ornate masques. Theatres were elaborately decorated and lit by chandeliers, oil lamps and candles. Performances still took place in daylight, but lighting created dramatic effects. Below the stage level, oil wick footlights floated on water to reduce the fire risk – hence the term 'floats'. Now lavish sets created the illusion of space and distance. Inigo Jones bewitched audiences with perspective illusions framed within an ornamental arch – the proscenium arch had arrived and became the standard, dominating Europe's theatre design and separating audience from cast.

In 1674, lights were dimmed for the first time in *The Tempest*. The area behind the proscenium was used for scenery changes, but the forestage was still the principal acting area. Wings, borders, and shutters arrived in England while machinery above and below stage moved scenery quickly. Shakespeare's plays were now considered out of date.

Plays set in 1600s include:

The Alchemist and *Bartholomew Fair* – Ben Jonson

The Country Wife – William Wycherley

The Crucible – Arthur Miller

Cyrano de Bergerac – Edmund Rostrand, trs by Christopher Fry

Devils – John Whiting

The Duchess of Malfi – John Webster

The Libertine – Stephen Jeffreys

Lorna Doone – adapted from R D Blackmore by Jill Hyem

The Misanthrope – Moliere

Roses of Eyam – Don Taylor

The Three Musketeers – adapted from Dumas by Willis Hall

Tis Pity she's a Whore – John Ford

Lifestyle: entertainment

The aristocracy hunted deer, boar, game birds, and foxes. Card gambling, indoor tennis, croquet, bowling, chess, horse racing, and backgammon were popular – as were singing, playing the guitar, piano, harpsichord or recorder. Fabulous costumes were worn at balls and masques. The middle classes enjoyed music, science and politics. At clubs, tobacco, coffee and hot chocolate from the New World were discovered. Newspapers were launched in London in 1622 and soon most towns had their own broadsheets.

Farmers, craftsmen and labourers worked up to 16 hours a day, 6 days a week. Only on Sundays and religious holidays was there leisure time for theatre, alehouse or blood sports (cock fighting, bear or bull baiting, bull fighting), all these forbidden under Cromwell's Protecorate when going to Church dominated.

Family life

Parents arranged marriages and dowries; divorce or separation was rare. Aristocrats often married in their early teens but ordinary folk married in their early twenties. The rich might maintain illegitimate children to work in their households. Poorer illegitimate infants had to be raised by the Parish unless the father could be charged with the child's custody. The mother might be fined or flogged and run out of the Parish.

A man could whip his wife, provided his switch was no thicker than his thumb. Families were large but there was a high infant mortality rate. Boys and girls dressed alike until aged 6, when a boy wore breeches. Children of poorer folk worked as soon as they were able. Working-class boys might be apprenticed to a trade, with a steep fee to the master. Wealthy boys were sent to a grammar school or had private tuition. Girls were taught by their mothers.

Homes and furniiture

Folding tables, chests of drawers, Oriental chests, carpets, porcelain, and tea sets arrived. More seats were upholstered. English potters made tin-glaze earthenware. In rich households, dishes were china, glass or precious metal, and utensils silver. In war and Puritan times, heavy taxation meant an austere lifestyle – made up for by lavish indulgence in Restoration times.

Food and dining

The rich disdained vegetables. They ate beef, mutton, venison, poultry, fish and occasional salads – with white bread and wine, followed by cheese, fruit and pastries. The midday meal was the main affair with cold leftovers served in the evening. Stews, soups and sauces were served in communal bowls. There were no serving spoons and serving dishes soon gathered bits of food from the diners' bowls dipping in and out. The tablecloth served to wipe fingers, knives and utensils; at the end of the meal diners used toothpicks and group finger bowls. Guests sat according to rank. Gentlemen wore their hats at the table except when they saluted each dish. Nobody drank the unsafe water – wine, beer, ale and porter served instead.

Poorer classes ate unleavened black bread, boiled grain, soups, cheese and vegetables including cabbage, beans and onions. They could rarely afford meat but did have milk and eggs. Food was served on bread, wood or pewter trenchers and eaten with wood or bone utensils.

Crime and weapons

Duelling was a socially acceptable. European armies, uniforms and standard weapons were introduced as heavy armour disappeared and muskets became lighter. Meanwhile, most towns had a watch or their own group to catch villains. At night, the poorly lit streets were dangerous and wise people ventured out only in groups with a lantern-bearer. The death sentence was common, as was whipping, the pillory, branding, or having ears, nose or hands cut off.

Science and medicine

Many new tools and instruments included the microscope, telescope, pendulum clock, vacuum pump and barometer. Calculus and logarithms arrived. Alchemists experimented – while the Great Plague in Europe was being spread by rats at a time when hygiene was little understood.

Historical background

British monarchs in this period:
James I 1603-25
Charles I 1625-49
Cromwell/Protectorate 1649-60
Charles II 1660-1685
James II 1685-1688
William (and Mary) 1689-1702

1600
East India Company chartered.

1605
Gunpowder plot.

1610
Galileo uses telescope.

1611
Authorized version of Bible.

1613
Russian Romanov dynasty founded.

1618-48
Thirty Years War in Europe.

1620
Landing of *Mayflower* pilgrims.

1632-49
Taj Mahal built.

1638
Galileo explains gravity.

1642-46
English Civil War.

1643-1715
Reign of French Sun-King, Louis XIV.

1644
End of Ming dynasty.

1649
Charles I of England beheaded.

1656
Pendulum clock invented.

1665
Newton announces Law of Gravity.

1665
Great Plague of London.

1666
Great Fire of London.

1692
Witch trials in Salem.

1698
Czar Peter the Great visits England.

1600-1699

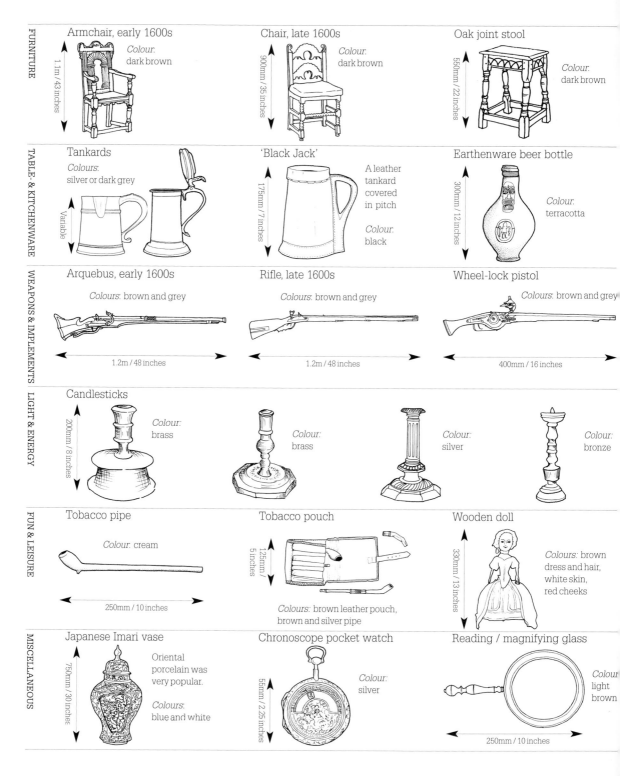

FURNITURE

Armchair, early 1600s
Colour: dark brown
1.1m / 43 inches

Chair, late 1600s
Colour: dark brown
900mm / 35 inches

Oak joint stool
Colour: dark brown
550mm / 22 inches

TABLE- & KITCHENWARE

Tankards
Colours: silver or dark grey
Variable

'Black Jack'
A leather tankard covered in pitch
Colour: black
175mm / 7 inches

Earthenware beer bottle
Colour: terracotta
300mm / 12 inches

WEAPONS & IMPLEMENTS

Arquebus, early 1600s
Colours: brown and grey
1.2m / 48 inches

Rifle, late 1600s
Colours: brown and grey
1.2m / 48 inches

Wheel-lock pistol
Colours: brown and grey
400mm / 16 inches

LIGHT & ENERGY

Candlesticks
Colour: brass
200mm / 8 inches

Colour: brass

Colour: silver

Colour: bronze

FUN & LEISURE

Tobacco pipe
Colour: cream
250mm / 10 inches

Tobacco pouch
125mm / 5 inches
Colours: brown leather pouch, brown and silver pipe

Wooden doll
Colours: brown dress and hair, white skin, red cheeks
330mm / 13 inches

MISCELLANEOUS

Japanese Imari vase
Oriental porcelain was very popular.
Colours: blue and white
750mm / 30 inches

Chronoscope pocket watch
Colour: silver
55mm / 2.25 inches

Reading / magnifying glass
Colour: light brown
250mm / 10 inches

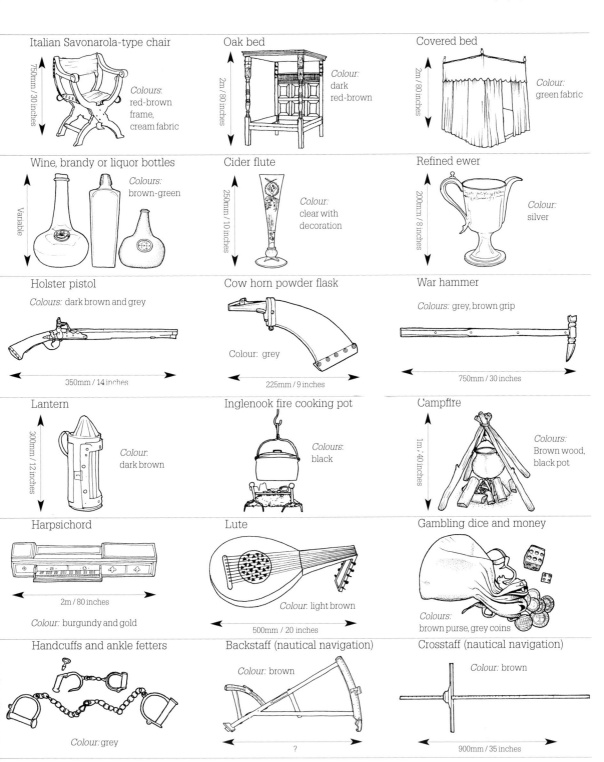

Italian Savonarola-type chair

750mm / 30 inches

Colours: red-brown frame, cream fabric

Oak bed

2m / 80 inches

Colour: dark red-brown

Covered bed

2m / 80 inches

Colour: green fabric

Wine, brandy or liquor bottles

Variable

Colours: brown-green

Cider flute

250mm / 10 inches

Colour: clear with decoration

Refined ewer

200mm / 8 inches

Colour: silver

Holster pistol

Colours: dark brown and grey

350mm / 14 inches

Cow horn powder flask

Colour: grey

225mm / 9 inches

War hammer

Colours: grey, brown grip

750mm / 30 inches

Lantern

300mm / 12 inches

Colour: dark brown

Inglenook fire cooking pot

Colours: black

Campfire

1m / 40 inches

Colours: Brown wood, black pot

Harpsichord

2m / 80 inches

Colour: burgundy and gold

Lute

Colour: light brown

500mm / 20 inches

Gambling dice and money

Colours: brown purse, grey coins

Handcuffs and ankle fetters

Colour: grey

Backstaff (nautical navigation)

Colour: brown

?

Crosstaff (nautical navigation)

Colour: brown

900mm / 35 inches

1600-1699

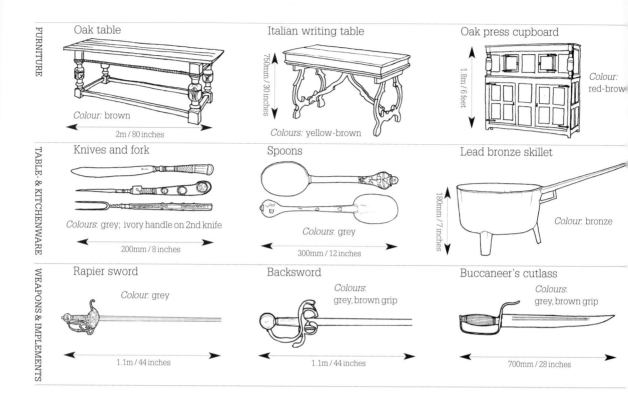

FURNITURE

Oak table
Colour: brown
2m / 80 inches

Italian writing table
750mm / 30 inches
Colours: yellow-brown

Oak press cupboard
1.8m / 6 feet
Colour: red-brow

TABLE- & KITCHENWARE

Knives and fork
Colours: grey; ivory handle on 2nd knife
200mm / 8 inches

Spoons
Colours: grey
300mm / 12 inches

Lead bronze skillet
180mm / 7 inches
Colour: bronze

WEAPONS & IMPLEMENTS

Rapier sword
Colour: grey
1.1m / 44 inches

Backsword
Colours: grey, brown grip
1.1m / 44 inches

Buccaneer's cutlass
Colours: grey, brown grip
700mm / 28 inches

Typical dining table with assortment of tableware

Kitchenware and cooking apparatus in a provincial manor house

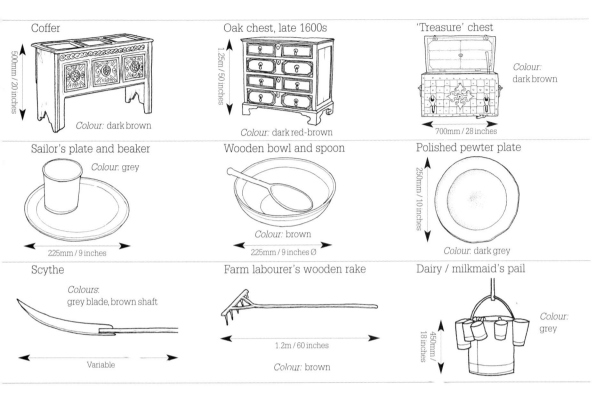

Coffer

500mm / 20 inches

Colour: dark brown

Oak chest, late 1600s

1.25m / 50 inches

Colour: dark red-brown

'Treasure' chest

Colour: dark brown

700mm / 28 inches

Sailor's plate and beaker

Colour: grey

225mm / 9 inches

Wooden bowl and spoon

Colour: brown

225mm / 9 inches Ø

Polished pewter plate

250mm / 10 inches

Colour: dark grey

Scythe

Colours: grey blade, brown shaft

Variable

Farm labourer's wooden rake

1.2m / 60 inches

Colour: brown

Dairy / milkmaid's pail

Colour: grey

450mm / 18 inches

A closed stool in a privy closet

Young child's wooden rocking horse

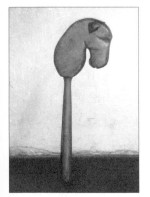

Child's (heavy) wooden toy horse

Furniture in a lady's bed chamber

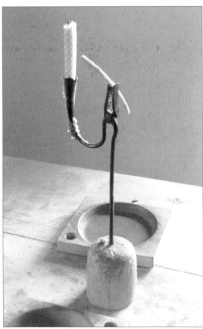

Candleholder

1700 - 1799

The age of revolutions

At the beginning of the century the Agricultural Revolution marked a more scientific approach to farming. In the later decades, there was great power redistribution with the French Revolution and American War of Independence.

Theatre development

Theatre-going became increasingly popular. More fashionable theatres were built, offering greater comfort with permanent roofs. In 1700, there were 3 theatres in Paris; by 1750, there were 20 and soon every large town had its own. Auditoriums were now divided into tiers of pit, boxes, and galleries. Seats in boxes were popular for the élite, offering seclusion for private parties.

Professional companies, led by actors such as David Garrick (1717-79) chose the plays. A typical theatre evening lasted 3 hours and included orchestral music, a prologue, a full-length play and an afterpiece (pantomime, farce, or comic opera). Between acts were variety turns – magic acts, singing, dancing, acrobatics, and animal tricks.

There was a resurgence of Puritanism after the Glorious Revolution of 1688. Playwrights wrote sentimental comedy, satires that mocked upper-class manners and tragedies featuring great heroes. However, in 1737, the government imposed strict censorship laws that halted dramatic development for some 150 years. In Italy, early operas emerged with sung dialogue.

Baroque costumes were rich and exotic, especially in masques with fabulous creatures, gods, mermaids and monsters. Silk screens, and coloured glass chimneys on oil lamps, lit the stage in rich scarlet and blue. Transparent backcloths allowed magical figures to be glimpsed behind; ballet companies used gauze; panoramas and dioramas appeared. Moving perspective sets had detailed scenic backdrops and wings that changed to create different scenes. In time, this became even more detailed and pronounced, with rows of cut-outs, one behind the other, lit by candlelight.

In the 1760s in Sweden, wings and shutters were mounted on carriages on rails below the level of the stage. Later, in England, a similar system arrived, with grooves above and below the wings, and the stage opened in several places to allow scenery to slide in and out and actors to be transported into position on bridges, manipulated by intricate stage machinery. Backcloths and borders on rollers were flown above the stage – while pyrotechnics, dramatic fog and fire effects became increasingly popular.

Plays set in 1700s include:

Amadeus – Peter Shaffer

The Beaux' Stratagem – George Farquhar

The Beggar's Opera – John Gay

Les Liaisons Dangereuses – Christopher Hampton

Lock up your Daughters – adapted by Bernard Miles and Lionel Bart from Fielding's *Rape upon Rape*

The London Merchant – George Lillo

Madness of George III – Alan Bennett

The Recruiting Officer – George Farquhar

The Rivals – Richard Brinsley Sheridan

The Scarlet Pimpernel – adapted from Baroness Orczy by Beverley Cross

The School for Scandal – Richard Brinsley Sheridan

She Stoops to Conquer – Oliver Goldsmith

A Tale of Two Cities Musical adapted from Dickens by Ross, Mullaner, Parker and Carter; also a play by Matthew Francis

Tom Jones – adapted from Henry Fielding by Joan Macalpine

The Way of the World – William Congreve

Lifestyle

The rich grew richer and the poor faced greater hardship; many peasant farmers were driven from the land as the agricultural revolution introduced land enclosure, plus crop rotation, new machinery and animal breeds. 85% of Europe's population were rural peasants or serfs. French aristocrats claimed hunting rights, dues, fees, and tithes – all deeply resented. Many landlords controlled law and justice – and revolts were easily crushed. New industries and social revolution destroyed the old order at the end of the century

About 2-3% of Europe's population had privileges that included judgment by their peers, immunity from the worst punishments, and exemption from many taxes. Aristocrats could carry a sword and had special pews in church. Many served as military officers.

Food

Peasants ate dark bread of roughly ground wheat and rye flour, soups and gruel, and vegetables – especially peas and beans, eaten fresh in summer or dried to use in soups and stews in winter. Water, wine, and beer were drunk. Potatoes and American corn were now part of

Backdrop to 1700-1799

the diet. Aristocrats ate enormous quantities of meat and fish, plus cheeses, nuts, and desserts.

Furniture and other pieces

Bold Baroque and Chinese styles influenced furniture and silver. After 1740, graceful Rococo details appeared on mirror frames, candle holders, and furniture. Mahogany was the main wood. Tables had piecrust rims and ball-and-claw feet. Heavy, richly carved pieces included marble-topped tables on gilded pedestals with birds, animals or female figures. Paintings in gilded frames included family protraits.

A typical early Georgian drawing room had carved mahogany chairs, a sofa with curved back and scroll arms, chairs with walnut legs and brass-studded covers, a tilt-top tripod table with piecrust rim, petit point firescreen, needlework rug, porcelain teabowls and pot, a cane-handled silver kettle on a stand, tea service and tea caddies with locks.

Adam style dominated from 1760-85. Furniture was slender and clean-lined; delicate inlaid and painted motifs replaced carving; glass was engraved, coloured and gilded. Derby and Worcester porcelain, Wedgwood creamware and jasperware, Sheffield plate silver, and transfer-printed pottery were popular. Classical busts simulated marble. Leather-upholstered chairs had brass-headed nails. Snuffboxes, candlesticks and inkstands graced leather-topped pedestal desks. Libraries had globes on stands, and billiard tables.

Homes and estates

Louis XIV's court encouraged other European monarchs to build fine palaces and with the aristocracy, live a grand lifestyle. In England, many landowners remained on their country estates and did not participate in court society; their large houses dominated the surrounding countryside where landed gentry invested much time, energy, and money in their rural estates. They had houses in London, in which they stayed when fulfilling Parliamentary duties, but their true homes were in the country.

Travel

The Grand Tour allowed the young rich to complete their education by making a tour of Europe's major cities – Paris, Florence, Venice, and Rome. The excavation of Roman Herculaneum and Pompeii from 1748 made these sites popular. The English aristocracy, in particular, saw travel as a vital element of education. In one year alone, 40,000 English were exploring Europe, although simply crossing the Channel then could be hazardous. At sea, there was the danger of pirates, while on land, inns were a favourite haunt of thieves.

Health and medicine

If harvests were bad, hunger and famine struck the poor while all were susceptible to diseases like influenza, smallpox, typhoid and yellow fever. Beds were often full of bed bugs, and rats and fleas still spread infection. However, hygiene was better understood after Frank's statistics on public health were published (1767) and in 1796, Jenner introduced a vaccine against smallpox. Anatomy was now studied and students sometimes resorted to paying body-snatchers to keep up the supply of cadavers. Surgery and obstetrics received more serious scientific attention, as did dentistry. False teeth were being made in Germany in 1756.

Historic background

British monarchs in this period:

William III	1694-1702
Anne	1702-1714
George I	1714-1727
George II	1727-1760
George III	1760-1820

1700s
Agricultural Revolution in England.

1701-13
War of Spanish Succession.

1706
Act of Union: England and Scotland.

1739-41
War between England and Spain.

1741
Handel composes *The Messiah*.

1756-63
Seven Years War.

1765
Watt builds steam engine.

1768-79
Captain Cook's voyages to Pacific.

1775-1781
American War of Independence.

1789
Mutiny on the *Bounty*.

1789-1795
French Revolution. Louis XVI guillotined in 1793.

1796-1815
Napoleonic wars.

1798
Britain and Russia fight France.

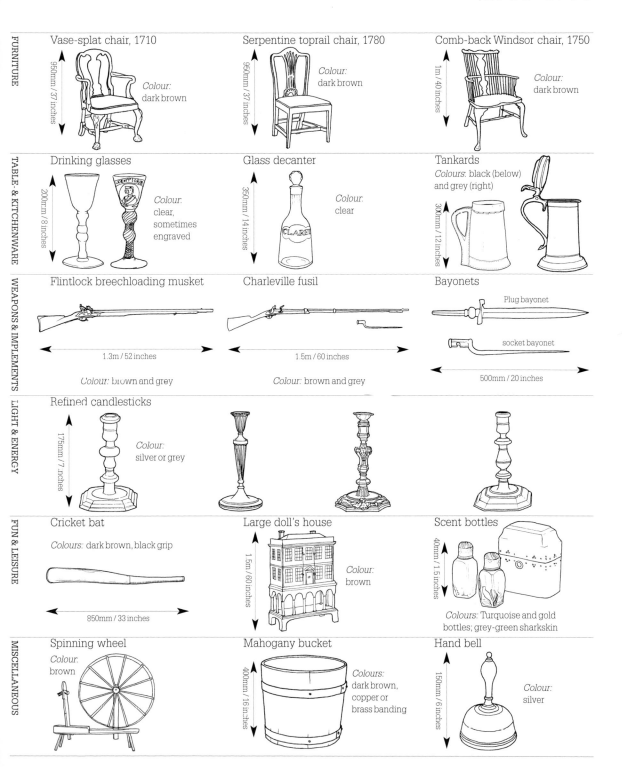

FURNITURE

Vase-splat chair, 1710
950mm / 37 inches
Colour: dark brown

Serpentine toprail chair, 1780
950mm / 37 inches
Colour: dark brown

Comb-back Windsor chair, 1750
1m / 40 inches
Colour: dark brown

TABLE & KITCHENWARE

Drinking glasses
200mm / 8 inches
Colour: clear, sometimes engraved

Glass decanter
350mm / 14 inches
Colour: clear
CLARET

Tankards
Colours: black (below) and grey (right)
300mm / 12 inches

WEAPONS & IMPLEMENTS

Flintlock breechloading musket
1.3m / 52 inches
Colour: brown and grey

Charleville fusil
1.5m / 60 inches
Colour: brown and grey

Bayonets
Plug bayonet
socket bayonet
500mm / 20 inches

LIGHT & ENERGY

Refined candlesticks
175mm / 7 inches
Colour: silver or grey

FUN & LEISURE

Cricket bat
Colours: dark brown, black grip
850mm / 33 inches

Large doll's house
1.5m / 60 inches
Colour: brown

Scent bottles
40mm / 1.5 inches
Colours: Turquoise and gold bottles; grey-green sharkskin

MISCELLANEOUS

Spinning wheel
Colour: brown

Mahogany bucket
400mm / 16 inches
Colours: dark brown, copper or brass banding

Hand bell
150mm / 6 inches
Colour: silver

1700-1799

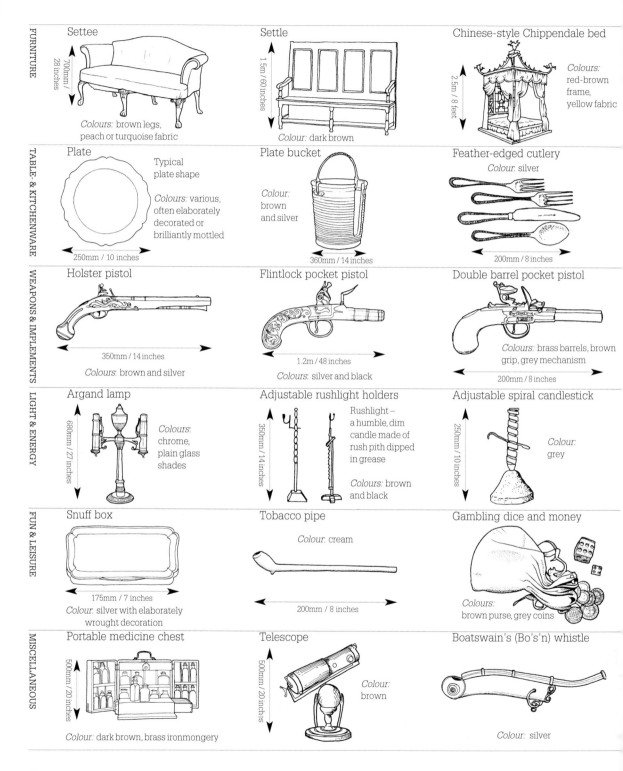

FURNITURE

Settee
700mm / 28 inches
Colours: brown legs, peach or turquoise fabric

Settle
1.5m / 60 inches
Colour: dark brown

Chinese-style Chippendale bed
2.5m / 8 feet
Colours: red-brown frame, yellow fabric

TABLE- & KITCHENWARE

Plate
Typical plate shape
Colours: various, often elaborately decorated or brilliantly mottled
250mm / 10 inches

Plate bucket
Colour: brown and silver
360mm / 14 inches

Feather-edged cutlery
Colour: silver
200mm / 8 inches

WEAPONS & IMPLEMENTS

Holster pistol
350mm / 14 inches
Colours: brown and silver

Flintlock pocket pistol
1.2m / 48 inches
Colours: silver and black

Double barrel pocket pistol
Colours: brass barrels, brown grip, grey mechanism
200mm / 8 inches

LIGHT & ENERGY

Argand lamp
680mm / 27 inches
Colours: chrome, plain glass shades

Adjustable rushlight holders
350mm / 14 inches
Rushlight – a humble, dim candle made of rush pith dipped in grease
Colours: brown and black

Adjustable spiral candlestick
250mm / 10 inches
Colour: grey

FUN & LEISURE

Snuff box
175mm / 7 inches
Colour: silver with elaborately wrought decoration

Tobacco pipe
Colour: cream
200mm / 8 inches

Gambling dice and money
Colours: brown purse, grey coins

MISCELLANEOUS

Portable medicine chest
500mm / 20 inches
Colour: dark brown, brass ironmongery

Telescope
500mm / 20 inches
Colour: brown

Boatswain's (Bo's'n) whistle
Colour: silver

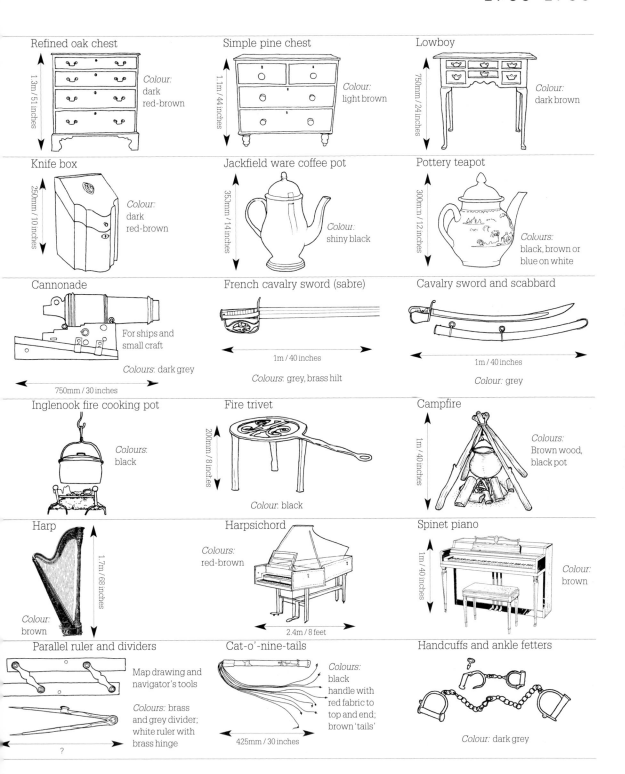

Refined oak chest
1.3m / 51 inches

Colour: dark red-brown

Simple pine chest
1.1m / 44 inches

Colour: light brown

Lowboy
750mm / 24 inches

Colour: dark brown

Knife box
250mm / 10 inches

Colour: dark red-brown

Jackfield ware coffee pot
350mm / 14 inches

Colour: shiny black

Pottery teapot
300mm / 12 inches

Colours: black, brown or blue on white

Cannonade
For ships and small craft

Colours: dark grey

750mm / 30 inches

French cavalry sword (sabre)
1m / 40 inches

Colours: grey, brass hilt

Cavalry sword and scabbard
1m / 40 inches

Colour: grey

Inglenook fire cooking pot
Colours: black

Fire trivet
200mm / 8 inches

Colour: black

Campfire
1m / 40 inches

Colours: Brown wood, black pot

Harp
1.7m / 68 inches

Colour: brown

Harpsichord
Colours: red-brown

2.4m / 8 feet

Spinet piano
1m / 40 inches

Colour: brown

Parallel ruler and dividers
Map drawing and navigator's tools

Colours: brass and grey divider; white ruler with brass hinge

?

Cat-o'-nine-tails
Colours: black handle with red fabric to top and end; brown 'tails'

425mm / 30 inches

Handcuffs and ankle fetters
Colour: dark grey

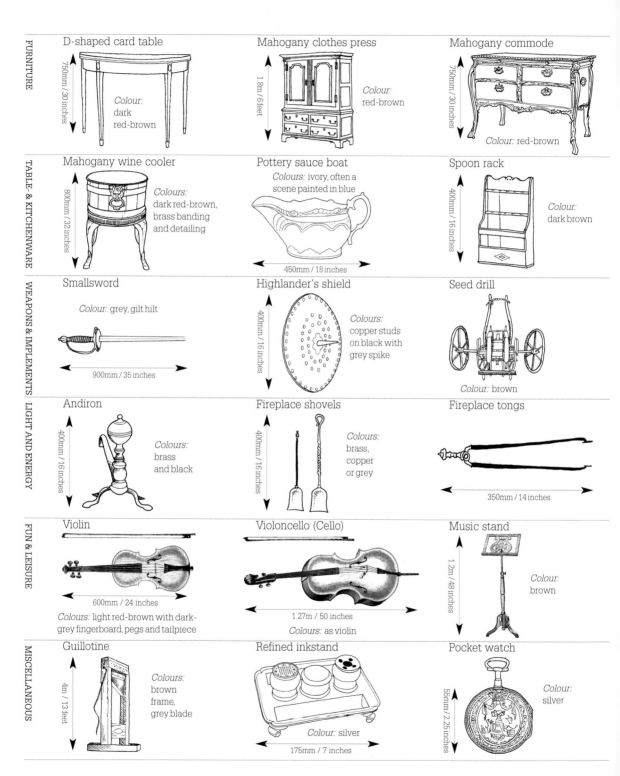

FURNITURE

D-shaped card table
750mm / 30 inches
Colour: dark red-brown

Mahogany clothes press
1.8m / 6 feet
Colour: red-brown

Mahogany commode
750mm / 30 inches
Colour: red-brown

TABLE- & KITCHENWARE

Mahogany wine cooler
800mm / 32 inches
Colours: dark red-brown, brass banding and detailing

Pottery sauce boat
Colours: ivory, often a scene painted in blue
450mm / 18 inches

Spoon rack
400mm / 16 inches
Colour: dark brown

WEAPONS & IMPLEMENTS

Smallsword
Colour: grey, gilt hilt
900mm / 35 inches

Highlander's shield
400mm / 16 inches
Colours: copper studs on black with grey spike

Seed drill
Colour: brown

LIGHT AND ENERGY

Andiron
400mm / 16 inches
Colours: brass and black

Fireplace shovels
400mm / 16 inches
Colours: brass, copper or grey

Fireplace tongs
350mm / 14 inches

FUN & LEISURE

Violin
600mm / 24 inches
Colours: light red-brown with dark-grey fingerboard, pegs and tailpiece

Violoncello (Cello)
1.27m / 50 inches
Colours: as violin

Music stand
1.2m / 48 inches
Colour: brown

MISCELLANEOUS

Guillotine
4m / 13 feet
Colours: brown frame, grey blade

Refined inkstand
Colour: silver
175mm / 7 inches

Pocket watch
55mm / 2.25 inches
Colour: silver

1800-1839

Heroes and heroines

These three decades saw Napoleon's rise and his attempts to dominate Europe, resisted on sea and land by Nelson and Wellington. This period is vividly depicted in Jane Austen's novels. The Industrial Revolution saw the growth of factories and towns and the development of the steam locomotive.

Backdrop to 1800-1839

Theatre development

In the large proscenium playhouses of London and Paris, melodrama, farce, and comedy were popular. Despite the Napoleonic Wars, demand for theatre grew along with expanding urban populations. The Magic Lantern became popular and its slide projection technique was used as a theatre device at Drury Lane in 1820, to create patterns and colours on the stage. There were now more touring companies. As railways expanded, especially in the US, so did the number of travelling productions, undermining resident theatres in outlying areas. Stars began to be promoted to help 'sell' plays.

The Romantic movement rose in Germany with a vast array of emotional drama that soon dominated European theatre – led by Schiller, and by Goethe who wrote *Faust* (1808 and 1832). Playwright, de Pixérécourt, paved the way for French Romanticism, leading to Victor Hugo's *Hernani* (1830). Italy saw the rise of the great operas of the 19th century and many of their dramatists wrote operatic libretti.

Spectacular disaster or large-scale effects were popular – such as sinking ships, submarines, or airships taking off. Mechanical sound effect machines simulated weather, transport and disaster noises. In 1822, the *Opera* in Paris created real waterfalls and fountains on stage.

In 1816, gas light was first used on stage in the USA and soon reached Covent Garden and Drury Lane in London. All areas of the stage could now be lit and seen with equal clarity; the main characters no longer had to dominate the downstage area – they could move to the back of the stage and still be seen. The arrival of gas also meant that a central control could raise and dim lights, allowing fading and cross-fading. Gauze transformations could be exploited properly and fire effects, setting suns and starlit skies were possible. In 1816, limelight also arrived, first used as a follow spot operated from the wings but its great intensity meant that it was soon implemented for sun and moon beams.

Plays set in 1800-1839 include:

Frankenstein – adapted from Mary Shelley by Tim Kelly

Les Miserables – adapted from Victor Hugo by Alain Boublil and Claude-Michel Schönberg

Mansfield Park – adapted from Jane Austen by Willis Hall

Murder of Maria Marten – Melodrama by Brian J Burton

Northanger Abbey – adapted from Jane Austen by Matthew Francis

Peer Gynt – Henrik Ibsen

Pickwick Papers – adapted from Charles Dickens by Lynn Brittney

Pride and Predjudice – adapted from Jane Austen by Helen Jerome

Lifestyle: Homelife

Few working people owned their own homes; they rented space in town houses, terraced rows, farms and cottages – or they lived in as servants. Wood or coal was hauled indoors for the stove and fires. Homes were still lit by candles. Water was collected from pumps – a precious commodity but often carrying disease; cholera was pandemic in Europe and the USA. Bathing involved dragging a large tin tub into the kitchen, to be filled with water heated on the stove or fireplace; then all the members of the family would take it in turn to bathe.

The women of the household spent hours preserving and storing fruits and vegetables as well as smoking and drying meat. Children helped with the chores. Boys were expected to do the dirty, heavy tasks such as cleaning ash from the wood stove, stoking the coal furnace, or pumping water outdoors. Girls made beds, aired linen, and cared for the younger children. Meanwhile, for many, heavy labour in factories and mines meant a gruelling life, with children working up to 16 hours a day.

Newspapers rarely carried illustrations until the late 1830s, but public events and figures could be seen in prints, and satirical cartoons.

Wealthy lifestyle

The wealthy moved from town, to spa, to seaside resort and back to their country houses. Households would have 6 or more servants (with at least 1 living in), a gentleman-in-waiting and housekeeper.

If entertaining, a vast breakfast was served at 10 or 11 am, and then an informal light luncheon. By 6.30-7.00pm, everyone dressed for dinner and gathered in the drawing room before processing into the dining room where at least one servant served every guest.

Typical dishes would be soup, fish, chicken fricasée, cutlets, veal, hare, a great variety of vegetables, tart, melon, pineapple, grapes, peaches, nectarines with wine. Often servants left the desserts on a side table, so guests could serve themselves and talk privately. A side table would be ready with glasses, wines, plates, ice and port, Madeira and little cakes.

The dining table had ornately cut glass, heavy silverware, richly decorated porcelain – but plain white plates for the earlier courses. Standard dinner and dessert services were now being made with 12, 24 or 36 place settings. Diners would have a glass rinser set before them, in which to swish a used glass before the next wine arrived. Cellarets held bottles of red wine and lead-lined wine coolers filled with ice held white wine; most country estates had an ice house to store ice cut during winter. At the end of the meal the ladies retired to the withdrawing room, leaving the gentlemen free to gossip.

Regency furniture and pieces

Furniture in Neoclassical, Rococo and Gothic styles, often in mahogany, was solid, robust and decorated. Woods were dark, patterned, gilded or painted. Legs were splayed or swelled out at the centre and then tapered down again. Round tables had pedestals with scrolls or carved paws. Chaise longues, ottomans and sofas became increasingly popular.

After 1815, richer, dark rosewood, mahogany, maple veneers and inlays arrived. Knobs were glass, china or wood. Furniture often now stood in the middle of a room. New pieces included nests of tables, ladies' work tables, card tables and small bookcases. Sectional tables clamped together to extend dining space.

Grandiose tablepieces, vases and bone china were produced by Worcester, Minton and Derby – decorated with flowers, animals, country scenes, dragons and coats of arms. Cutlery and silver became heavier and ornate, in swirling Rococo and upright Gothic styles. Glassware was deep cut or fluted. There were cascading cut-glass chandeliers, ornate candelabra, sporting pictures and scenes by Turner, large mirrors, black marble, glass domes covering birds on branches, and robust houseplants.

General decoration included Classical maidens, elaborate borders, swags of flowers and foliage, and Egyptian motifs. Fringes, tassels and braids abounded. Sofas, easy chairs and ottomans were fully sprung and padded, with buttons and good, thick upholstery. Rounded backs on sofas and easy chairs curved into arms. Balloon-back chairs with elegant curved woodwork had straight legs. Prie-dieus had low seats, high backs and bright Berlin woolwork.

Servants' rooms were fitted with cheap furniture – caned bedroom chairs, painted pine chests of drawers, and cast-iron bedsteads.

Clothes

Ladies wore tight corsets to achieve tiny waists; this hampered breathing so they often swooned. Voluminous ankle-length dresses covered some nine petticoats. Puffed leg-of-lamb were the fashion until the 1840s. Gentlemen wore light-coloured, narrowly cut trousers with dark frock-coats, full-skirted to near knee length, left unbuttoned at the waist and fastened high on the chest. A narrow cravat was tied in a wide bow.

Historic background

British monarchs in this period:
George III 1760-1820
George IV 1820-1830
William IV 1830-1837
Victoria 1837-1901

1800
Act of Union ends Irish Parliament.

1803
Great Britain declares war against France and Napoleon.

1804-15
Napoleon Emperor of France.

1805
Battle of Trafalgar: British keep naval superiority for over 100 years.

1807
Slave trade abolished in England.

1808
Beethoven's *Fifth Symphony*.

1808-14
Peninsular War.

1812-14
War of American independence.

1812
Battle of Borodino: Napoleon enters Moscow but is forced to retreat.

1815
Battle of Waterloo.
German Confederation established.

1821
Greek War of Independence.

1829
Stephenson's *Rocket* wins prize.

1832
1st Reform Act: British middle classes gain vote.

1835
Boers Great Trek north in South Africa.

1839
First photograph by Daguerre.

1800-1839

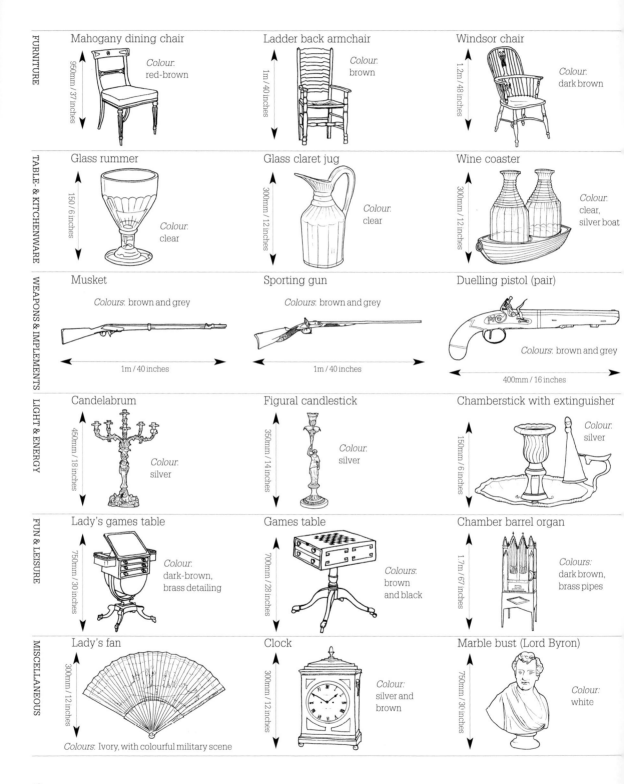

FURNITURE

Mahogany dining chair
950mm / 37 inches
Colour. red-brown

Ladder back armchair
1m / 40 inches
Colour. brown

Windsor chair
1.2m / 48 inches
Colour. dark brown

TABLE- & KITCHENWARE

Glass rummer
150 / 6 inches
Colour. clear

Glass claret jug
300mm / 12 inches
Colour. clear

Wine coaster
300mm / 12 inches
Colour. clear, silver boat

WEAPONS & IMPLEMENTS

Musket
Colours. brown and grey
1m / 40 inches

Sporting gun
Colours. brown and grey
1m / 40 inches

Duelling pistol (pair)
Colours. brown and grey
400mm / 16 inches

LIGHT & ENERGY

Candelabrum
450mm / 18 inches
Colour. silver

Figural candlestick
350mm / 14 inches
Colour. silver

Chamberstick with extinguisher
150mm / 6 inches
Colour. silver

FUN & LEISURE

Lady's games table
750mm / 30 inches
Colour. dark-brown, brass detailing

Games table
700mm / 28 inches
Colours. brown and black

Chamber barrel organ
1.7m / 67 inches
Colours: dark brown, brass pipes

MISCELLANEOUS

Lady's fan
300mm / 12 inches
Colours. Ivory, with colourful military scene

Clock
300mm / 12 inches
Colour: silver and brown

Marble bust (Lord Byron)
750mm / 30 inches
Colour. white

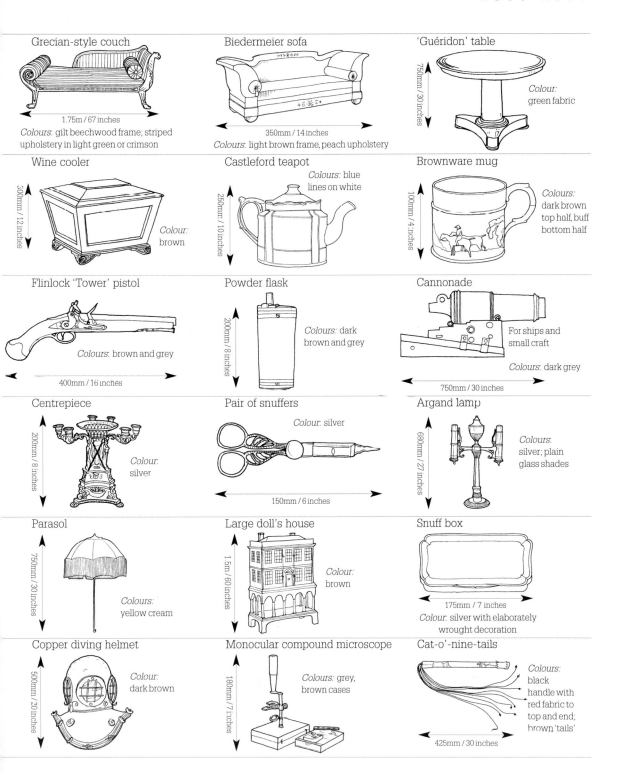

Grecian-style couch

1.75m / 67 inches

Colours: gilt beechwood frame; striped upholstery in light green or crimson

Biedermeier sofa

350mm / 14 inches

Colours: light brown frame, peach upholstery

'Guéridon' table

750mm / 30 inches

Colour: green fabric

Wine cooler

300mm / 12 inches

Colour: brown

Castleford teapot

250mm / 10 inches

Colours: blue lines on white

Brownware mug

100mm / 4 inches

Colours: dark brown top half, buff bottom half

Flinlock 'Tower' pistol

Colours: brown and grey

400mm / 16 inches

Powder flask

200mm / 8 inches

Colours: dark brown and grey

Cannonade

For ships and small craft

Colours: dark grey

750mm / 30 inches

Centrepiece

200mm / 8 inches

Colour: silver

Pair of snuffers

Colour: silver

150mm / 6 inches

Argand lamp

680mm / 27 inches

Colours: silver; plain glass shades

Parasol

750mm / 30 inches

Colours: yellow cream

Large doll's house

1.5m / 60 inches

Colour: brown

Snuff box

175mm / 7 inches

Colour: silver with elaborately wrought decoration

Copper diving helmet

500mm / 20 inches

Colour: dark brown

Monocular compound microscope

180mm / 7 inches

Colours: grey, brown cases

Cat-o'-nine-tails

Colours: black handle with red fabric to top and end; brown 'tails'

425mm / 30 inches

1800-1839

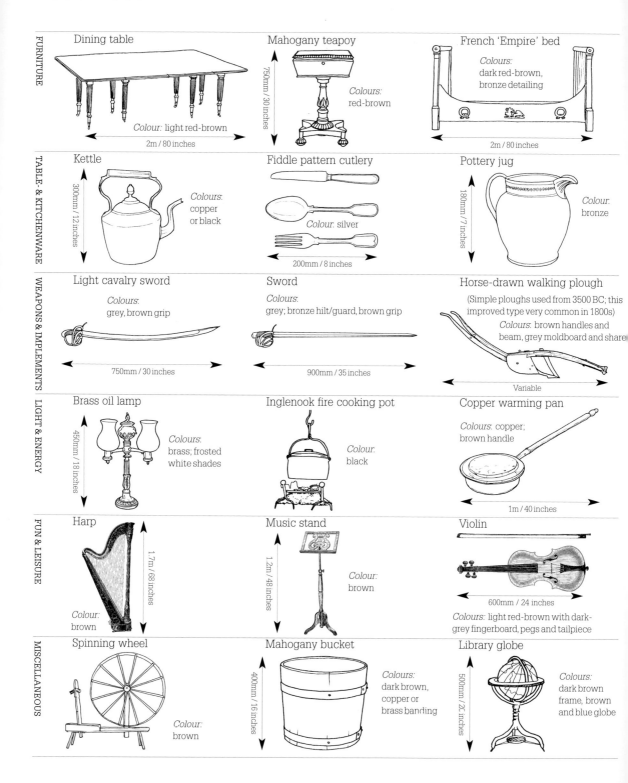

FURNITURE

Dining table

Colour: light red-brown

2m / 80 inches

Mahogany teapoy

750mm / 30 inches

Colours:
red-brown

French 'Empire' bed

Colours:
dark red-brown,
bronze detailing

2m / 80 inches

TABLE- & KITCHENWARE

Kettle

300mm / 12 inches

Colours:
copper
or black

Fiddle pattern cutlery

Colour: silver

200mm / 8 inches

Pottery jug

180mm / 7 inches

Colour:
bronze

WEAPONS & IMPLEMENTS

Light cavalry sword

Colours:
grey, brown grip

750mm / 30 inches

Sword

Colours:
grey; bronze hilt/guard, brown grip

900mm / 35 inches

Horse-drawn walking plough

(Simple ploughs used from 3500 BC; this
improved type very common in 1800s)
Colours: brown handles and
beam, grey moldboard and share

Variable

LIGHT & ENERGY

Brass oil lamp

450mm / 18 inches

Colours:
brass; frosted
white shades

Inglenook fire cooking pot

Colour:
black

Copper warming pan

Colours: copper;
brown handle

1m / 40 inches

FUN & LEISURE

Harp

1.7m / 68 inches

Colour:
brown

Music stand

1.2m / 48 inches

Colour:
brown

Violin

600mm / 24 inches

Colours: light red-brown with dark-
grey fingerboard, pegs and tailpiece

MISCELLANEOUS

Spinning wheel

Colour:
brown

Mahogany bucket

400mm / 16 inches

Colours:
dark brown,
copper or
brass banding

Library globe

500mm / 20 inches

Colours:
dark brown
frame, brown
and blue globe

1840-1869

Imperialism and industry

Queen Victoria's reign brought stability and increasing British domination. This period witnessed the American Civil War, the Indian Mutiny, industrial growth – spearheaded by the growth in railways and canals – and great poverty and squalor, with appalling conditions in factories, mills and mines.

Backdrop to 1840-1869

Theatre development

In 19th-century Europe, there was a much stronger focus on historical accuracy and creating the illusion of real life. From the 1850s, greater naturalism brought about changes in acting, scenery and costumes.

This was a period of great development in lighting and effects. In 1860, the combination of a hood and lens with a carbon arc created the first proper spotlight. In 1843, actresses at the *Comédie Française* in Paris complained that the new gaslight was too harsh. To counteract this, the performers needed better make-up. Supply met the demand and, for the first time, stage make-up was produced commercially.

Mirror flats were introduced to reflect all the available light back onto the stage. Meanwhile scenic effects continued to develop. In 1854, the hydraulic lift was first used in the *National Opera House* in Budapest. In the 1860s, the *Lyceum* in London introduced a prototype cyclorama. With its sky and backdrop effects, this was soon to be a professional theatre 'standard'. Huge dioramas suggesting a vast landscape circled round to create the impression of movement in whatever was in front. Actors, or any scenic device, could be static in front – or move in the opposite direction to the background, to create the impression of even faster movement.

Circuses became more as we think of them today, expanding to include animal acts and clowns, as well as acrobats. Originally performed in huge circus rings in front of conventional theatre stages, the circus changed to become travelling theatre in the 19th century, spreading in line with the growth of the railways – an easier means to move from one place to another.

Plays set in 1840-1869

Adam Bede – adapted from George Eliot by Geoffrey Beevers

Barnum – musical by Cy Coleman, Michael Stewart and Mark Bramble

Camille – Pam Gems

A Christmas Carol – several plays and musicals adapted from Charles Dickens

East Lynne or *Never called me Mother* – melodrama adapted from Mrs Henry Wood by Brian J Burton

The Heiress – adapted from Henry James by Ruth and Augustus Goetz

Jane Eyre – adapted from Charlotte Brontë by Willis Hall

Jekyll and Hyde – adapted from R L Stevenson by L H Caddy

Lady Audley's Secret – melodrama by Brian J Burton

A Month in the Country – two versions adapted from Turgenev by Brian Friel, or Emlyn Williams

My Cousin Rachel – adapted from Daphne du Maurier by Diana Morgan

Robert and Elizabeth – musical by Miller and Grainer, adapted from The *Barretts of Wimpole Street* by R Besier

Sweeney Todd the Barber – various adaptations from G D Pitt include plays by Brian J Burton and Austin Rosser and a musical by Sondheim

Tale of Two Cities – various adaptations from Charles Dickens include versions by Mark Fitzgibbons and Matthew Francis

Treasure Island – adapted from R L Stevenson by Bernard Miles, Peter Coe and Josephine Wilson

Trelawny of the 'Wells' – Arthur W Pinero

Woman in White – adapted from Wilkie Collins by Constance Cox

Lifestyle

This was a time of great social unrest. In 1848, there were revolutions or uprisings in France, Italy, Hungary, Austria and Ireland, while Chartists protested in England. 1853-56 saw the Crimean War, 1857-58, the Indian Mutiny and 1861-65, the US Civil War.

In Britain, canals and railways threaded through the nation, and a family visit to the seaside became fashionable.

Meanwhile, early Victorian society remained moral and pious, looking back at Regency excesses with some distaste. The middle classes, with Queen Victoria as a role model, concentrated on family life, with large numbers of children.

In middle class homes, the lady of the house in the 1840s carried out formal duties in the drawing room. During the morning this was the setting for brief visits, and in the afternoon, it was where the hostess presided over tea, cakes and conversation.

Before dinner in the evening, guests gathered in the drawing room and at the end of the meal, the ladies returned there, leaving the men to linger over port and cigars.

Ladies spent their time cultivating accomplishments like painting, music, making wax flowers and fruit, creating pictures from feathers or shells, painting vases, decorative poker work, embroidering covers for footstools and workboxes, stitching patchwork cushion covers or crocheting antimacassars.

Well-to-do families now sometimes had a bathroom but others still washed and bathed in the bedroom, using basins and hip-baths filled with jugs of water brought by a servant.

Walls were decorated with women's handiwork. From needlepoint to embroidery, hangings featured mottoes or floral designs stitched with desirable virtues. The sentimental Victorian woman wove the hair of family members into framed pictures and jewellery.

Crinolines were worn from 1840 to about 1865. The sewing machine arrived and with it, mass production of clothes.

Isabella Beeton's *Book of Household Management*, published in 1861, was an immediate success, selling 60,000 copies in under a year. The most successful European home-care book ever published, it is constantly up-dated and continues to sell worldwide today.

Poverty

For the less well privileged, this was a time of great poverty and squalor, with appalling conditions in factories, mills, mines, and potteries. Many suffered dreadful injuries in machines, developed lung illnesses or were paralysed from working such long hours, breathing in dust and noxious fumes. So did chimney sweep boys, who often developed cancers from the soot. Meanwhile, the injustices of the 1838 Poor Law incarcerated many, old and young, in the parish workhouse, providing only gruel and bread to eat and often separating family members from each other. Attitudes were slowly changing, however. In 1868, it became illegal to employ children under eight in agricultural gangs.

Photography

From 1851, new processes allowed amateurs to experiment with photography. Now people could create cheap portraits of themselves – as one-off prints or printed into sets and then cut into visiting cards or sent to friends. Portraits of families and friends were collected in albums – with images of the royal family, poets and politicians, sensational subjects such as disasters, or trick photographs of ghosts.

Medicine

Florence Nightingale spearheaded changes in nursing in the late 1850s after her experiences in the Crimean War. Anaesthetics arrived and eased both theatre surgery and childbirth – especially after Queen Victoria used chloroform during the birth of Prince Leopold, in 1853.

Meanwhile, when Joseph Lister spearheaded the use of antiseptics, deaths from surgery dropped from over 40% to less than 1%; and John Snow ended a cholera epidemic by proving its association with a contaminated water source.

Historic background

British monarch in this period:
Queen Victoria 1837-1901

1840
Samuel Morse devises Morse Code.

1848
Revolution in Paris.
Karl Marx publishes his *Communist Manifesto*.

1849
Gold Rush: 80,000 '49ers' head for California.

1851
Great Exhibition in Crystal Palace, London.

1854-56
Crimean War.

1855
Livingstone discovers Victoria Falls.

1859
Darwin publishes *Origin of the Species*.

1859
First internal combustion engine.

1860
Garibaldi takes southern Italy and stengthens Italian unity.

1861-65
American Civil War.

1863
Lincoln abolishes slavery in US.

1865
President Lincoln assassinated.

1866
Blue Danube Waltz by Strauss.

1868
Revolution in Spain.

1869
Suez Canal opens.

1840-1869

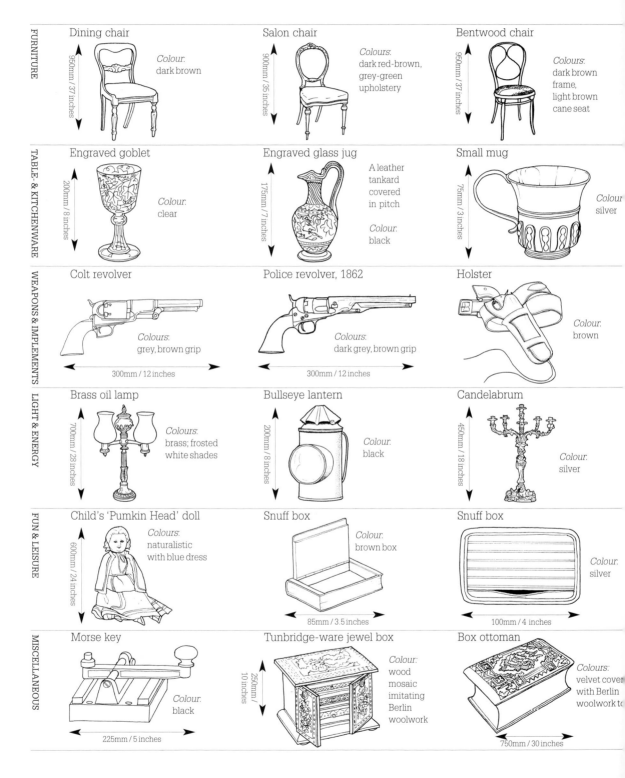

FURNITURE

Dining chair
950mm / 37 inches
Colour. dark brown

Salon chair
900mm / 35 inches
Colours. dark red-brown, grey-green upholstery

Bentwood chair
950mm / 37 inches
Colours. dark brown frame, light brown cane seat

TABLE- & KITCHENWARE

Engraved goblet
200mm / 8 inches
Colour. clear

Engraved glass jug
175mm / 7 inches
A leather tankard covered in pitch
Colour. black

Small mug
75mm / 3 inches
Colour silver

WEAPONS & IMPLEMENTS

Colt revolver
Colours. grey, brown grip
300mm / 12 inches

Police revolver, 1862
Colours. dark grey, brown grip
300mm / 12 inches

Holster
Colour. brown

LIGHT & ENERGY

Brass oil lamp
700mm / 28 inches
Colours. brass; frosted white shades

Bullseye lantern
200mm / 8 inches
Colour. black

Candelabrum
450mm / 18 inches
Colour. silver

FUN & LEISURE

Child's 'Pumkin Head' doll
600mm / 24 inches
Colours. naturalistic with blue dress

Snuff box
Colour. brown box
85mm / 3.5 inches

Snuff box
Colour. silver
100mm / 4 inches

MISCELLANEOUS

Morse key
Colour. black
225mm / 5 inches

Tunbridge-ware jewel box
250mm / 10 inches
Colour: wood mosaic imitating Berlin woolwork

Box ottoman
Colours: velvet cover with Berlin woolwork t
750mm / 30 inches

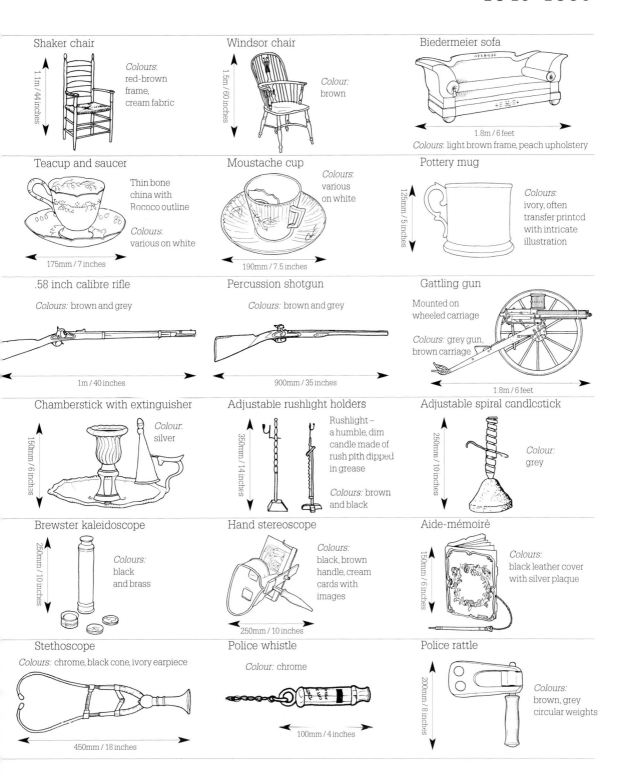

Shaker chair

1.1m / 44 inches

Colours:
red-brown
frame,
cream fabric

Windsor chair

1.5m / 60 inches

Colour:
brown

Biedermeier sofa

1.8m / 6 feet

Colours: light brown frame, peach upholstery

Teacup and saucer

Thin bone
china with
Rococo outline

Colours:
various on white

175mm / 7 inches

Moustache cup

Colours:
various
on white

190mm / 7.5 inches

Pottery mug

125mm / 5 inches

Colours:
ivory, often
transfer printed
with intricate
illustration

.58 inch calibre rifle

Colours: brown and grey

1m / 40 inches

Percussion shotgun

Colours: brown and grey

900mm / 35 inches

Gattling gun

Mounted on
wheeled carriage

Colours: grey gun,
brown carriage

1.8m / 6 feet

Chamberstick with extinguisher

Colour:
silver

150mm / 6 inches

Adjustable rushlight holders

350mm / 14 inches

Rushlight –
a humble, dim
candle made of
rush pith dipped
in grease

Colours: brown
and black

Adjustable spiral candlestick

250mm / 10 inches

Colour:
grey

Brewster kaleidoscope

250mm / 10 inches

Colours:
black
and brass

Hand stereoscope

Colours:
black, brown
handle, cream
cards with
images

250mm / 10 inches

Aide-mémoirè

150mm / 6 inches

Colours:
black leather cover
with silver plaque

Stethoscope

Colours: chrome, black cone, ivory earpiece

450mm / 18 inches

Police whistle

Colour: chrome

100mm / 4 inches

Police rattle

200mm / 8 inches

Colours:
brown, grey
circular weights

1840-1869

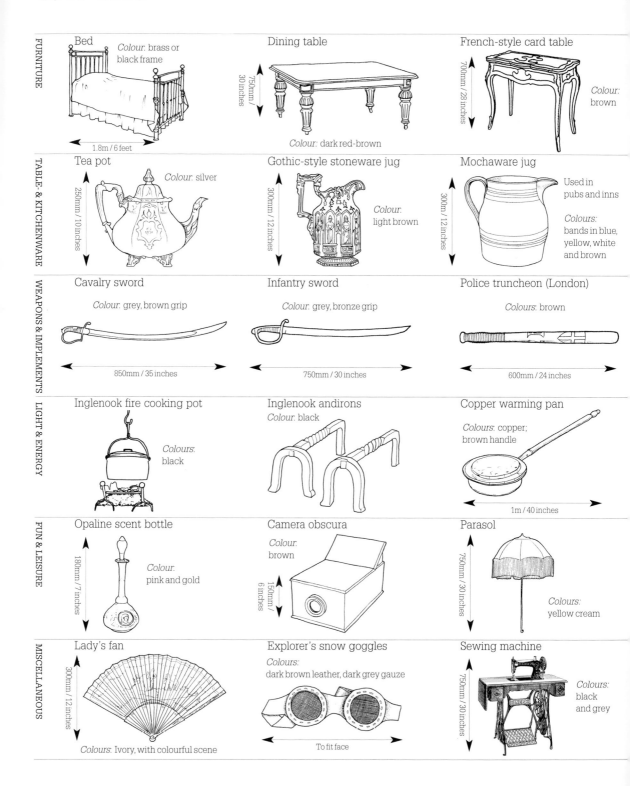

FURNITURE

Bed
Colour: brass or black frame
1.8m / 6 feet

Dining table
750mm / 30 inches
Colour: dark red-brown

French-style card table
700mm / 28 inches
Colour: brown

TABLE- & KITCHENWARE

Tea pot
250mm / 10 inches
Colour: silver

Gothic-style stoneware jug
300mm / 12 inches
Colour: light brown

Mochaware jug
300m / 12 inches
Used in pubs and inns
Colours: bands in blue, yellow, white and brown

WEAPONS & IMPLEMENTS

Cavalry sword
Colour: grey, brown grip
850mm / 35 inches

Infantry sword
Colour: grey, bronze grip
750mm / 30 inches

Police truncheon (London)
Colours: brown
600mm / 24 inches

LIGHT & ENERGY

Inglenook fire cooking pot
Colours: black

Inglenook andirons
Colour: black

Copper warming pan
Colours: copper; brown handle
1m / 40 inches

FUN & LEISURE

Opaline scent bottle
180mm / 7 inches
Colour: pink and gold

Camera obscura
Colour: brown
150mm / 6 inches

Parasol
750mm / 30 inches
Colours: yellow cream

MISCELLANEOUS

Lady's fan
300mm / 12 inches
Colours: Ivory, with colourful scene

Explorer's snow goggles
Colours: dark brown leather, dark grey gauze
To fit face

Sewing machine
750mm / 30 inches
Colours: black and grey

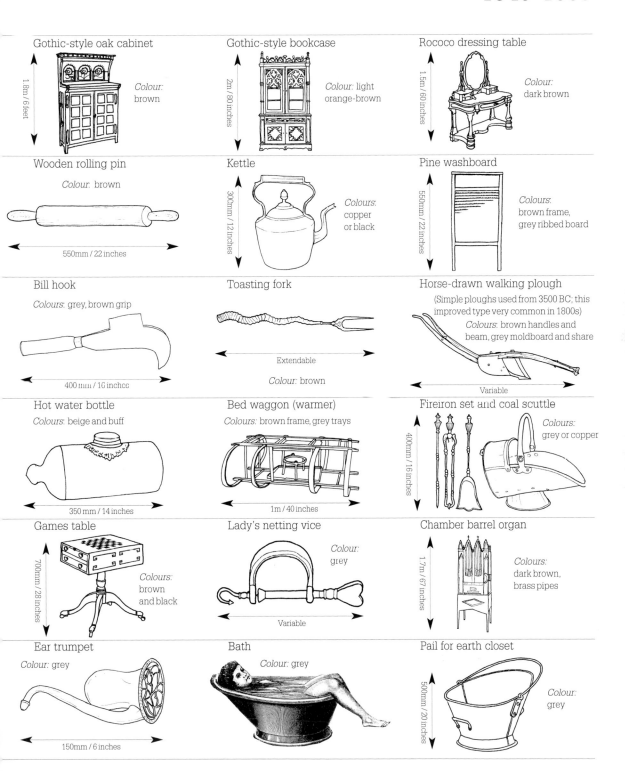

Gothic-style oak cabinet

1.8m / 6 feet

Colour: brown

Gothic-style bookcase

2m / 80 inches

Colour: light orange-brown

Rococo dressing table

1.5m / 60 inches

Colour: dark brown

Wooden rolling pin

Colour: brown

550mm / 22 inches

Kettle

300mm / 12 inches

Colours: copper or black

Pine washboard

550mm / 22 inches

Colours: brown frame, grey ribbed board

Bill hook

Colours: grey, brown grip

400 mm / 16 inches

Toasting fork

Extendable

Colour: brown

Horse-drawn walking plough

(Simple ploughs used from 3500 BC; this improved type very common in 1800s)

Colours: brown handles and beam, grey moldboard and share

Variable

Hot water bottle

Colours: beige and buff

350 mm / 14 inches

Bed waggon (warmer)

Colours: brown frame, grey trays

1m / 40 inches

Fireiron set and coal scuttle

400mm / 16 inches

Colours: grey or copper

Games table

700mm / 28 inches

Colours: brown and black

Lady's netting vice

Colour: grey

Variable

Chamber barrel organ

1.7m / 67 inches

Colours: dark brown, brass pipes

Ear trumpet

Colour: grey

150mm / 6 inches

Bath

Colour: grey

Pail for earth closet

500mm / 20 inches

Colour: grey

1870 - 1899

The thrust for change

New technological advances such as electric
light, the gramophone and telephone
changed lifestyles - as did indoor sanitation
and the arrival of the motor car. Meanwhile,
art sought new expression through
Impressionism and Art Nouveau and women
began to seek more active roles, riding
bicycles and training for the professions.

Theatre development

Extravagant Grand Opera, Gilbert and Sullivan light operettas, plus a great variety of drama – from Chekhov to melodrama and Christmas pantomimes – now offered audiences enormous choice. However, melodramas vanished as quickly as they had arrived when cinema suddenly delivered even more life-like, sensational material. Many theatres that had once hosted melodrama became cinemas.

In 1878, Sir Henry Irving developed many lighting innovations and controls, including masking to prevent light spill and consistent darkness in the auditorium. In 1879, a US theatre was the first to install electric lighting. In 1881, electricity was used throughout a performance at London's *Savoy*. In 1883, in Gilbert and Sullivan's *Iolanthe* – the fairies wore illuminated stars in their hair. The light was produced by means of a cell storing electricity – hence the term 'fairy lights'. Lycopodium and magnesium powder created flashes. However, this led to several serious fires and so steam was often used instead. By the end of the century, a large theatre might use up to 30 limelights in a production.

By 1890, Henrik Ibsen was promoting more naturalistic acting. While many productions sought realism, there was an 'anti-realistic' reaction by avant-garde theatre. Many believed that naturalism could only ever be superficial and that a greater truth lay in revitalizing theatre. Traditionalists felt that theatre had lost touch with its origins and should concentrate on being good entertainment.

Composer, Richard Wagner, proposed that the playwright's job was to portray an ideal world, to depict the inner core of characters rather than superficial aspects and to unify all the dramatic elements. Wagner also reformed theatre architecture with his *Festival Theatre* (1876) – boxes, balconies and auditorium were replaced by sloping, fan-shaped seating, giving an equal view of the stage to all spectators. In the 1880s, the Symbolist movement in France adopted Wagner's ideas. This lead to plays by Maeterlinck, Claudel, Chekhov, Ibsen, Strindberg, Eugene O'Neill, Tennessee Williams and Pinter. Abstract settings and lighting created atmosphere.

In 1896, a production of *Ubu Roi* in Paris caused a great stir with its puppet-like characters and avant-garde approach. This paved the way for Zola in France, Ibsen and Strindberg in Scandinavia, Chekhov in Russia, Hauptmann in Germany, Galsworthy and Shaw in England – and directors such as Stanislavsky at the Moscow Art Theater. By 1900, realism dominated playwriting and theatrical production in the West.

Plays set in 1870-1899

Charley's Aunt – Brandon Thomas

Can Can – musical by Cole Porter and Abe Burrows

The Cherry Orchard – Chekhov

Count Dracula – based on Bram Stoker by Ted Tiller

Gaslight – Patrick Hamilton

The Government Inspector – N Gogol

The Great Waltz – musical by Chodorov, Korngold, Wright, Forrest

Hedda Gaber – adapted from Henrik Ibsen by John Osborne

The Hound of the Baskervilles – adapted from Sir Arthur Conan Doyle by Tim Kelly

The Importance of Being Earnest – Oscar Wilde

Jack the Ripper – R Pember and D de Marne

Lark Rise – from Flora Thomson by Keith Dewhurst

The Magistrate – A W Pinero

The Matchgirls – musical by Bill Owen and Tony Russell

Oliver Twist – adapted from Charles Dickens by Jeremy Brock

The Picture of Dorian Grey – adapted from Oscar Wilde by John Osborne

The Seagull – Anton Chekhov

The Strange Case of Dr Jekyll and Mr Hyde – based on R L Stevenson by D Edgar

Tess of the d'Ubervilles – adapted from Thomas Hardy by Michael Fry

The Turn of the Screw – adapted from Henry James by Ken Whitmore

The Wind of Heaven – Emlyn Williams

Lifestyle: homes and water

Homes had gas lighting, kerosene lamps and some had electric lighting from 1890s. Piped water reached town houses in the 1870s, and bathrooms became 'a must'. At first, dressing rooms or minor bedrooms were converted but in new housing, purpose-built bathrooms arrived – with washbasin and roll top, cast-iron bath. However, poorer homes

Backdrop to 1870-1899

and rural houses still had an outside earth closet; in cities, toilets might be shared by over a hundred people. The poor rented their homes and were liable to be evicted onto the streets if they fell behind with the payments. In 1878, William Booth founded the Salvation Army, providing shelter for the needy. By 1875, town councils were responsible for street cleaning and the supply of clean water.

Food and health

Heinz had introduced canning to preserve foods during the American Civil War and now many foods could be preserved and exported. By 1874, steam-driven ships travelled faster. Grain, sugar, tea, coffee and cocoa reduced in price. From 1880, refrigerated trains brought cheaper provisions from abroad and improved rail links delivered fresh food. As foreign foods flooded in, British farmers specialised to produce cheaper goods and implemented new techniques and machinery. Farm workers were paid less or laid off and went to work in factories and mines, or emigrated.

Coal-fired stoves and new kitchen equipment made cooking easier Poorer families who had no stove took food to be cooked in bakers' ovens . Some foods had dangerous additives: lead was used to colour cheese, acid was added to wine, and chalk to flour. For the rich, French chefs and dining out was popular. For the poor, pies, baked potatoes, and soup were sold on the city streets.

Inventions, art and design

Now it was possible to telephone London from Paris, to travel by electric underground railway, to produce letters on a typewriter, to listen to the phonograph, and talk on the telephone. Electric light bulbs arrived in 1878 and street lighting appeared in London. By the turn of the century, diesel engines and X-rays had arrived. Mangles and primitive washing machines were used for laundry and families took photographs with a Kodak camera. As photography seized the role of realism, so art sought new expression through artists such as Cezanne, Manet, Renoir, Monet and Whistler. Impressionism changed the world of art just as inventions changed the world of science.

Led by William Morris, the Arts and Crafts movement (c. 1860-1910) used the medieval system of trades and guilds to sell goods, mainly bought by the wealthy middle classes. Art Nouveau (c. 1880-1910) drew inspiration from the natural world, with curvy lines or the more austere linear look of Charles Rennie Mackintosh. Ornaments, clocks, frames, and jewellery boxes were silver, pewter and glass.

Women's roles and fashion

The bustle dominated fashion from the 1870s. Heavy corsets, petticoats, and frills were replaced by shirtwaist blouses and long skirts. Now women could play tennis or ride a bicycle. Women began to demand greater opportunities and in 1870, Elizabeth Garrett Anderson became the first female doctor. By 1882, women could keep inherited wealth; it no longer went straight to their husbands.

Education and employment

In 1870 under the Education Act, all children under 10 had to go to school and new schools were built in areas that had none. Reading, writing (on slates) and arithmetic were taught in large classes. Under-9s could not be employed from 1874. Richer children might be taught by a governess. Their toys included French china dolls, clockwork trains, jigsaw puzzles and the first pop-up books.

Historic background

Queen Victoria 1837-1901
(Empress of India from 1877)

1870
Papal power ends; Italy unified.

1871
Germany proclaims Second Reich.

1875
Stanley explores River Congo.

1876
Bell demonstrates telephone.
Custer and 256 troops killed at Battle of Little Big Horn.

1877
Germ theory of disease.
Phonograph invented by Edison.

1879
Electric Light invented by Edison.
Zulu War.

1885
Louis Pasteur injects against rabies.

1887
Motor car engine and gramophone.

1888
Eastman patents hand-held camera.
Jack the Ripper terrorises London.

1890
Eiffel Tower built.

1898
Spanish American War.

1899-1902
Boer War in Africa.

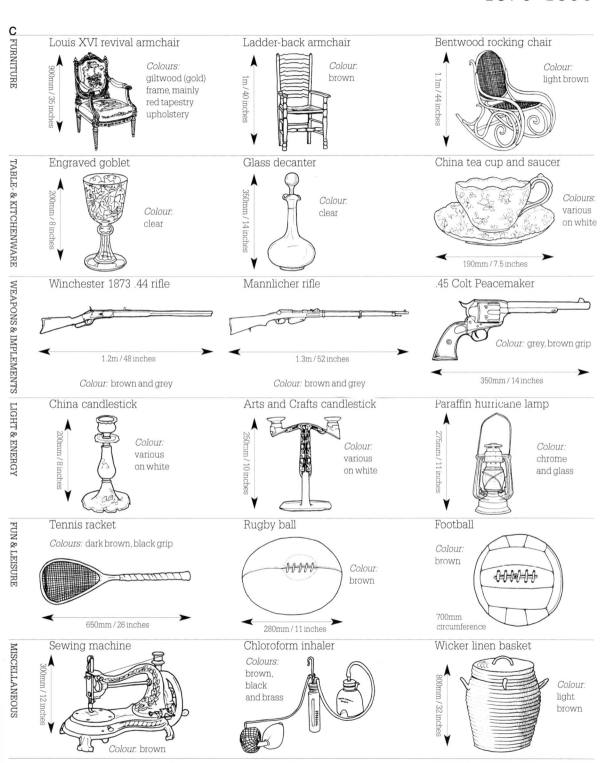

C

FURNITURE

Louis XVI revival armchair

900mm / 35 inches

Colours: giltwood (gold) frame, mainly red tapestry upholstery

Ladder-back armchair

1m / 40 inches

Colour: brown

Bentwood rocking chair

1.1m / 44 inches

Colour: light brown

TABLE- & KITCHENWARE

Engraved goblet

200mm / 8 inches

Colour: clear

Glass decanter

350mm / 14 inches

Colour: clear

China tea cup and saucer

190mm / 7.5 inches

Colours: various on white

WEAPONS & IMPLEMENTS

Winchester 1873 .44 rifle

1.2m / 48 inches

Colour: brown and grey

Mannlicher rifle

1.3m / 52 inches

Colour: brown and grey

.45 Colt Peacemaker

350mm / 14 inches

Colour: grey, brown grip

LIGHT & ENERGY

China candlestick

200mm / 8 inches

Colour: various on white

Arts and Crafts candlestick

250mm / 10 inches

Colour: various on white

Paraffin hurricane lamp

275mm / 11 inches

Colour: chrome and glass

FUN & LEISURE

Tennis racket

Colours: dark brown, black grip

650mm / 26 inches

Rugby ball

280mm / 11 inches

Colour: brown

Football

Colour: brown

700mm circumference

MISCELLANEOUS

Sewing machine

300mm / 12 inches

Colour: brown

Chloroform inhaler

Colours: brown, black and brass

Wicker linen basket

800mm / 32 inches

Colour: light brown

1870-1899

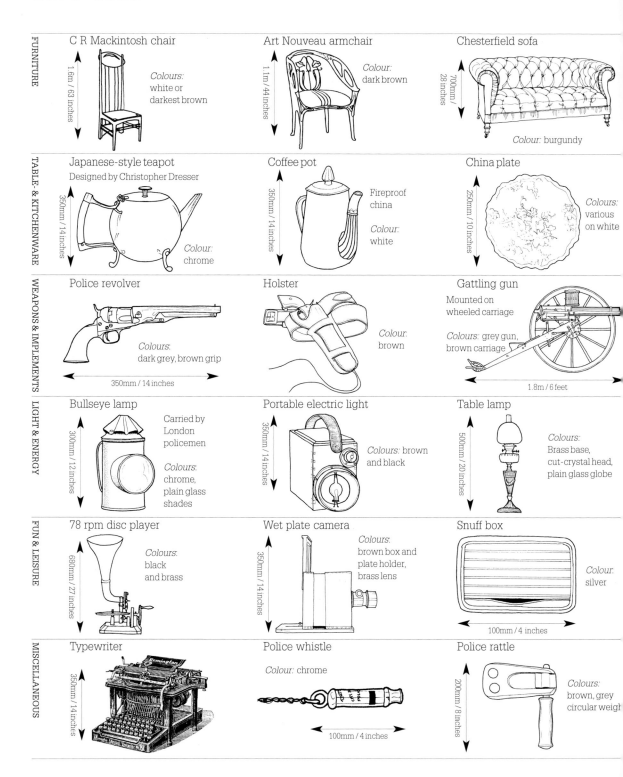

FURNITURE

C R Mackintosh chair
1.6m / 63 inches
Colours: white or darkest brown

Art Nouveau armchair
1.1m / 44 inches
Colour: dark brown

Chesterfield sofa
700mm / 28 inches
Colour: burgundy

TABLE & KITCHENWARE

Japanese-style teapot
Designed by Christopher Dresser
350mm / 14 inches
Colour: chrome

Coffee pot
350mm / 14 inches
Fireproof china
Colour: white

China plate
250mm / 10 inches
Colours: various on white

WEAPONS & IMPLEMENTS

Police revolver
Colours: dark grey, brown grip
350mm / 14 inches

Holster
Colour: brown

Gattling gun
Mounted on wheeled carriage
Colours: grey gun, brown carriage
1.8m / 6 feet

LIGHT & ENERGY

Bullseye lamp
300mm / 12 inches
Carried by London policemen
Colours: chrome, plain glass shades

Portable electric light
350mm / 14 inches
Colours: brown and black

Table lamp
500mm / 20 inches
Colours: Brass base, cut-crystal head, plain glass globe

FUN & LEISURE

78 rpm disc player
680mm / 27 inches
Colours: black and brass

Wet plate camera
350mm / 14 inches
Colours: brown box and plate holder, brass lens

Snuff box
Colour: silver
100mm / 4 inches

MISCELLANEOUS

Typewriter
350mm / 14 inches

Police whistle
Colour: chrome
100mm / 4 inches

Police rattle
200mm / 8 inches
Colours: brown, grey circular weight

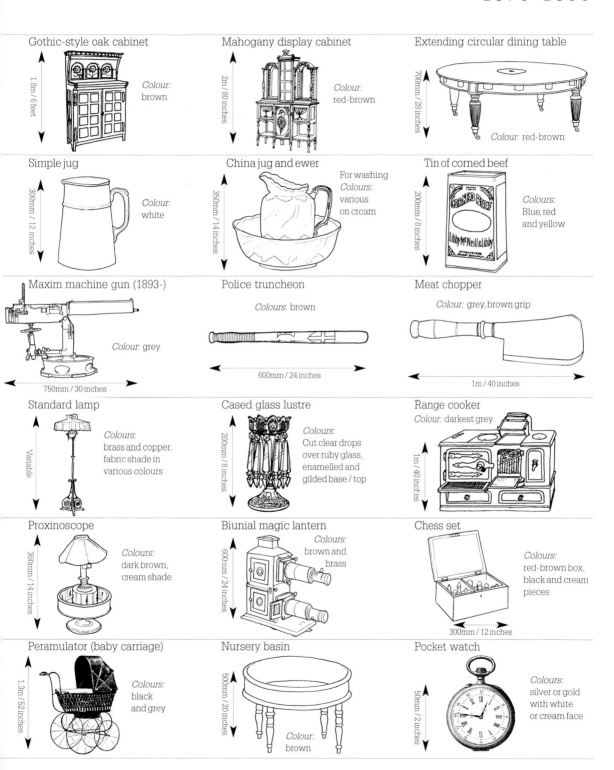

Gothic-style oak cabinet
1.8m / 6 feet
Colour: brown

Mahogany display cabinet
2m / 80 inches
Colour: red-brown

Extending circular dining table
700mm / 28 inches
Colour: red-brown

Simple jug
300mm / 12 inches
Colour: white

China jug and ewer
350mm / 14 inches
For washing
Colours: various on cream

Tin of corned beef
200mm / 8 inches
Colours: Blue, red and yellow

CORNED BEEF
Libby McNeill & Libby

Maxim machine gun (1893-)
Colour: grey
750mm / 30 inches

Police truncheon
Colours: brown
600mm / 24 inches

Meat chopper
Colour: grey, brown grip
1m / 40 inches

Standard lamp
Variable
Colours: brass and copper. fabric shade in various colours

Cased glass lustre
200mm / 8 inches
Colours: Cut clear drops over ruby glass, enamelled and gilded base / top

Range cooker
Colour: darkest grey
1m / 40 inches

Proxinoscope
360mm / 14 inches
Colours: dark brown, cream shade

Biunial magic lantern
600mm / 24 inches
Colours: brown and brass

Chess set
Colours: red-brown box, black and cream pieces
300mm / 12 inches

Peramulator (baby carriage)
1.3m / 52 inches
Colours: black and grey

Nursery basin
500mm / 20 inches
Colour: brown

Pocket watch
50mm / 2 inches
Colours: silver or gold with white or cream face

1870-1899

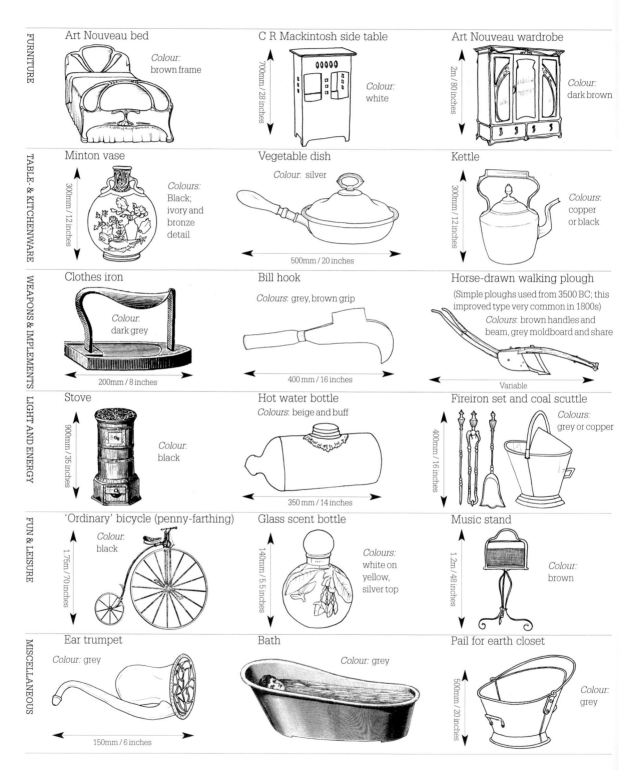

FURNITURE

Art Nouveau bed
Colour: brown frame

C R Mackintosh side table
700mm / 28 inches
Colour: white

Art Nouveau wardrobe
2m / 80 inches
Colour: dark brown

TABLE- & KITCHENWARE

Minton vase
300mm / 12 inches
Colours: Black; ivory and bronze detail

Vegetable dish
Colour: silver
500mm / 20 inches

Kettle
300mm / 12 inches
Colours: copper or black

WEAPONS & IMPLEMENTS

Clothes iron
Colour: dark grey
200mm / 8 inches

Bill hook
Colours: grey, brown grip
400 mm / 16 inches

Horse-drawn walking plough
(Simple ploughs used from 3500 BC; this improved type very common in 1800s)
Colours: brown handles and beam, grey moldboard and share
Variable

LIGHT AND ENERGY

Stove
900mm / 35 inches
Colour: black

Hot water bottle
Colours: beige and buff
350 mm / 14 inches

Fireiron set and coal scuttle
400mm / 16 inches
Colours: grey or copper

FUN & LEISURE

'Ordinary' bicycle (penny-farthing)
Colour: black
1.75m / 70 inches

Glass scent bottle
140mm / 5.5 inches
Colours: white on yellow, silver top

Music stand
1.2m / 48 inches
Colour: brown

MISCELLANEOUS

Ear trumpet
Colour: grey
150mm / 6 inches

Bath
Colour: grey

Pail for earth closet
500mm / 20 inches
Colour: grey

1900-1919

The world marches to war

Affordable motor cars, powered flight and women's emancipation arrived. Most people lived in towns and worked in factories, mines, shops or offices. In Britain, a new king revitalized the social whirl. Political risings in Russia, Ireland and China, plus the First World War, soon took a heavy toll of lives and ideals.

Backdrop to 1900-1919

Drama and theatre

Faster communications encouraged international touring companies and the exchange of ideas, artists, and productions, with plays often published in several languages. Symbolism, and the theatre of the absurd, were explored but Realism remained popular. The Expressionist movement grew, especially in Germany, exploring the human psyche, to create a nightmare world. Music Hall and Vaudeville were popular entertainment. Hydraulic lowering and lifting devices arrived in 1913 and could lower entire stage sections. Electric lighting (with 1,000-watt lamps) was available in Europe by 1913, and spotlights soon replaced footlights. In 1916, Linnebach projected large-scale slides onto the stage.

Plays set in 1900-1919

A Flea in her Ear – George Feydeau

An Inspector Calls – J B Priestley

Gigi – musical adapted from Colette by Lerner and Loewe

Hotel Paradiso – G Feydeau and M Desvallieres

Journey's End – R C Sheriff

La Ronde – Arthur Schnitzler

The Mother – Bertolt Brecht

My Fair Lady – musical adapted from Bernard Shaw by Lerner and Loewe

The Plough and the Stars – O'Casey

Ross – Terence Rattigan

State of Revolution – Robert Bolt

Summer and Smoke – Tennessee Williams

The Admirable Crichton – J M Barrie

Travesties – Tom Stoppard

When We Are Married – J B Priestley

The Winslow Boy – Terence Rattigan

Furniture and furnishings

Art Nouveau styles continued. Furniture might also be in Baroque, Rococo or Empire styles, or with medieval lines in dark woods. Arts and Crafts furniture was lighter and simple. The rich enjoyed Sheraton furniture. Elegant and delicate pieces were made in pale hardwoods; wicker, cane and bamboo arrived and inlays added decoration. Furniture was sometimes painted in soft colours or with highlights in gilt. Well-stuffed armchairs, wing chairs and sofas had chintz or damask covers. Embroidery and needlepoint cushions had floral motifs or Art Nouveau designs.

Electric lamps in grander homes had fabric lampshades in soft colours with frills and tassels, Tiffany lamps or reclining female bronze figures. Meanwhile, the Orient inspired blue and white china, palm leaf fans, screens, and oriental rugs.

There were gramophones with conical shells, tiered, silver cake stands, silver photograph frames, tapestry fire screens, framed samplers, textiles, runners for the table and books illustrated by Aubrey Beardsley. Copper and pewter items often had a hammered finish. Pictures and embroidery depicted stylised flowers. Ecclesiastical styles, Bible allegories or Celtic motifs were used. Simple flower arrangements or a potted house palm were typical. Stained glass was very popular, because of its medieval feel.

Women's role and marriage

Suffragettes spearheaded votes for women from 1903, which eventually became law in 1918. Divorce was rare. If a man committed adultery, this was not grounds for divorce – unless he deserted his wife; if a woman did so, divorce was immediate. A divorced woman often lost both money and children. None the less, among the upper classes, adultery was commonplace. Edward VII had many mistresses and was unlikely to attend a social event unless one had been invited. At weekend parties, a bell was often rung at 6am so that gentlemen could return to their own bedrooms before the maids came round to make the fires.

Below stairs, however, male and female servants were kept apart with bedrooms at opposite ends of the house, the women in the attic, the men in the basement. A romance usually led to instant dismissal. Yet almost half of all illegitimate children born in 1911 were born to women in service, who would often end up at the workhouse, or in prostitution.

Sport and leisure

Newspapers, beer and cigarettes became increasingly popular, as did silent movies, rugby and football, and travel by motor car, bus and rail – often to the seaside. The rich enjoyed hunting – foxes were even imported from Europe to meet demand – plus shooting and fishing, followed by banquets, music and parlour games. Horse-racing, formerly a sport of the masses, became fashionable for the wealthy, who now owned racehorses. Gentlemen might place bets of more than £10,000 (500 times a footman's annual wage) but some 80% of working-class men also bet regularly and gambled generally.

Dinner parties

Serving eight-course dinners, a footman wore thin-soled shoes and moved silently as he deposited plates, glasses and cutlery. At a dinner party for 20, 50 pieces of silver, china and crystal might be used by each guest – all counted in and out of the silver safe at every meal. If anything was lost, the servants were locked out of the house while their rooms were searched.

French luxuries such as truffles, oysters, patisseries, fine chocolates and champagne were served after large quantities of meat and offal. Rich families employed male chefs – French chefs became especially sought after and could earn 10 times a butler's wage. After a meal, ladies withdrew for coffee in the drawing room. The men had port, brandy and cigars before joining them.

Fashion

Alexandra, both as Princess and Queen, led fashion with her fine clothes, high-piled hair and multi-stranded pearl chokers. The ideal female form was buxom with an exaggerated 'S' shape. New corsets allowed for easier breathing but the craze for small waists persisted. The bust bodice, the precurser of the bra, was in use by 1905. After 1907, the wasp waist became less acute and corsets straighter, creating a long, slim silhouette. By 1912, corsets increased in length to almost reach the knees. A lady's personal maid pulled the lacing tight, reducing the waistline from, say, 26 to 20 inches. Some dressmakers considered a 16-inch waist ideal! This corsetting was a status symbol since a woman could scarcely move in it; so it was only worn by ladies of leisure.

Helped by her maid, a lady might change her clothes and adjust her hair six times a day. To achieve the fashionable full hairstyle, the hair was wound around balls of padding. These elaborate styles provided a platform for elegant picture hats, with feathers and trimmings, anchored by hat pins with jewelled or enamelled ends. Hats could cost up to 50 guineas (£3,000 at today's prices).

Maids wore print dresses for the mornings, black dress and white cap and apron for afternoons, and her own clothes for church. She had one bath a week in a tin bath, filled by carrying up jugs of hot water, and then carrying down jugs of dirty water. If staff met the family unexpectedly, they had to stand still and avert their gaze, while the family ignored them. Breakages were deducted from wages; female staff were forbidden to smoke or have followers; fraternising with the opposite sex meant dismissal.

War and politics

The First World War had a huge impact, with 10 million lives lost and 20 million injured. There was general political upheaval with the Easter Rising in Ireland and the Russian Revolution. Meanwhile, old age pensions arrived in Britain.

Historic background

British monarchs in this period:
Queen Victoria 1837-1901
Edward VII 1901-1910
George V 1910-1936

1900
1st Zeppelin developed.

1901
Social Revolutionary Party founded in Russia.

1903
Wright Brothers aeroplane flies.

1905
Sinn Fein founded.

1908-27
Ford's Model T car.

1909
First newsreel shown by C Pathe.
Peary reaches North Pole.

1911
Revolution in Central China

1911-12
Amundsen, and later, Scott reach South Pole.

1912
War in Balkans.

1914
Archduke Ferdinand assassinated.

1914-18
First World War.

1915
Lusitania sunk by a German submarine.
1st transcontinental telephone conversation.

1916/19
Einstein's *Theory of Relativity*.

1917
US declares war on Germany.
October Revolution in Russia.

1918
Tsar Nicholas II and family murdered.

1900-1919

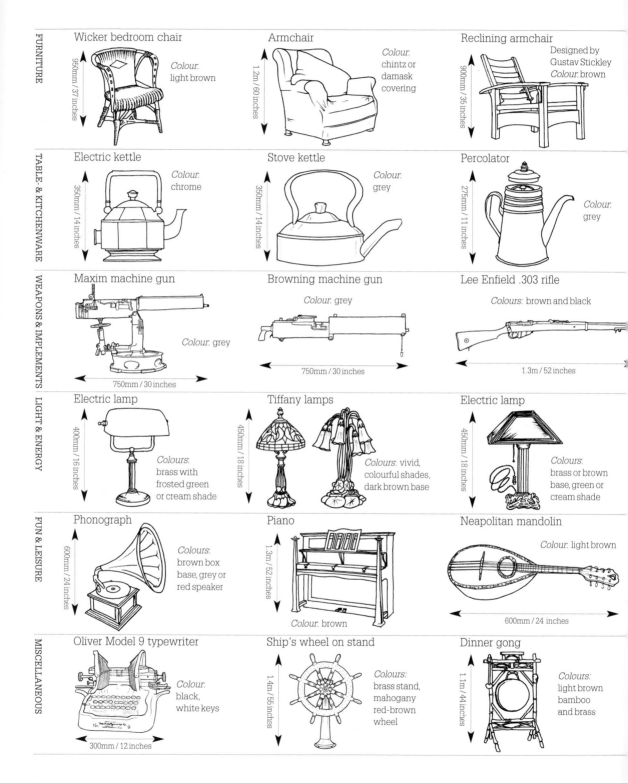

FURNITURE

Wicker bedroom chair
950mm / 37 inches
Colour. light brown

Armchair
1.2m / 60 inches
Colour. chintz or damask covering

Reclining armchair
Designed by Gustav Stickley
Colour. brown
900mm / 35 inches

TABLE- & KITCHENWARE

Electric kettle
350mm / 14 inches
Colour. chrome

Stove kettle
350mm / 14 inches
Colour. grey

Percolator
275mm / 11 inches
Colour. grey

WEAPONS & IMPLEMENTS

Maxim machine gun
Colour. grey
750mm / 30 inches

Browning machine gun
Colour. grey
750mm / 30 inches

Lee Enfield .303 rifle
Colours: brown and black
1.3m / 52 inches

LIGHT & ENERGY

Electric lamp
400mm / 16 inches
Colours. brass with frosted green or cream shade

Tiffany lamps
450mm / 18 inches
Colours. vivid, colourful shades, dark brown base

Electric lamp
450mm / 18 inches
Colours. brass or brown base, green or cream shade

FUN & LEISURE

Phonograph
600mm / 24 inches
Colours. brown box base, grey or red speaker

Piano
1.3m / 52 inches
Colour. brown

Neapolitan mandolin
Colour. light brown
600mm / 24 inches

MISCELLANEOUS

Oliver Model 9 typewriter
Colour. black, white keys
300mm / 12 inches

Ship's wheel on stand
1.4m / 55 inches
Colours: brass stand, mahogany red-brown wheel

Dinner gong
1.1m / 44 inches
Colours: light brown bamboo and brass

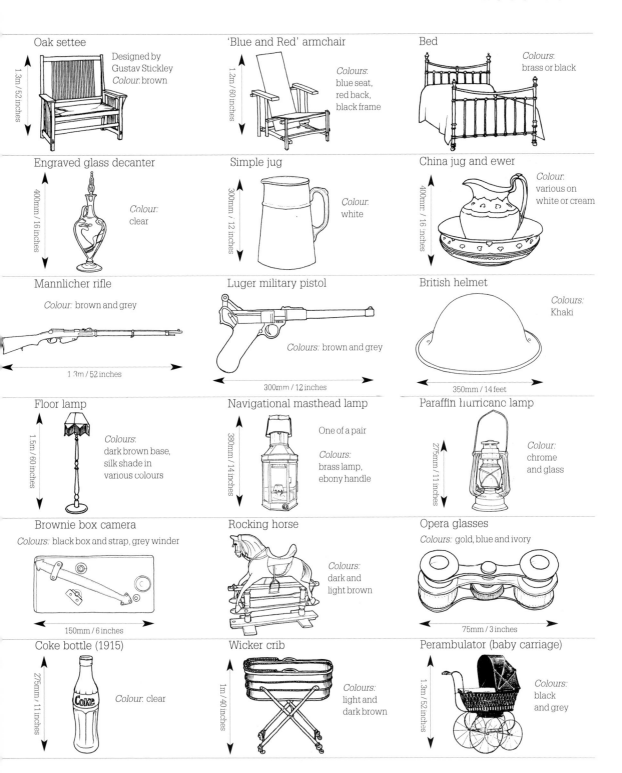

Oak settee

Designed by
Gustav Stickley
Colour: brown

1.3m / 52 inches

'Blue and Red' armchair

Colours:
blue seat,
red back,
black frame

1.2m / 60 inches

Bed

Colours:
brass or black

Engraved glass decanter

400mm / 16 inches

Colour:
clear

Simple jug

300mm / 12 inches

Colour:
white

China jug and ewer

400mm / 16 inches

Colour:
various on
white or cream

Mannlicher rifle

Colour: brown and grey

1.3m / 52 inches

Luger military pistol

Colours: brown and grey

300mm / 12 inches

British helmet

Colours:
Khaki

350mm / 14 feet

Floor lamp

1.5m / 60 inches

Colours:
dark brown base,
silk shade in
various colours

Navigational masthead lamp

One of a pair

Colours:
brass lamp,
ebony handle

380mm / 14 inches

Paraffin hurricane lamp

275mm / 11 inches

Colour:
chrome
and glass

Brownie box camera

Colours: black box and strap, grey winder

150mm / 6 inches

Rocking horse

Colours:
dark and
light brown

Opera glasses

Colours: gold, blue and ivory

75mm / 3 inches

Coke bottle (1915)

275mm / 11 inches

Colour: clear

Wicker crib

1m / 40 inches

Colours:
light and
dark brown

Perambulator (baby carriage)

1.3m / 52 inches

Colours:
black
and grey

1900-1919

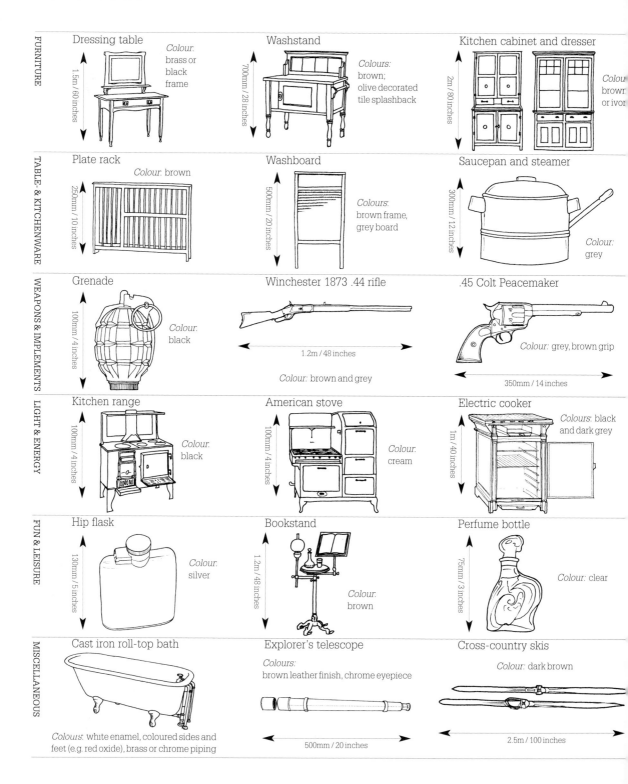

FURNITURE

Dressing table
Colour: brass or black frame
1.5m / 60 inches

Washstand
Colours: brown; olive decorated tile splashback
700mm / 28 inches

Kitchen cabinet and dresser
Colour: brown or ivory
2m / 80 inches

TABLE- & KITCHENWARE

Plate rack
Colour: brown
250mm / 10 inches

Washboard
Colours: brown frame, grey board
500mm / 20 inches

Saucepan and steamer
Colour: grey
300mm / 12 inches

WEAPONS & IMPLEMENTS

Grenade
Colour: black
100mm / 4 inches

Winchester 1873 .44 rifle
1.2m / 48 inches
Colour: brown and grey

.45 Colt Peacemaker
Colour: grey, brown grip
350mm / 14 inches

LIGHT & ENERGY

Kitchen range
Colour: black
100mm / 4 inches

American stove
Colour: cream
100mm / 4 inches

Electric cooker
Colours: black and dark grey
1m / 40 inches

FUN & LEISURE

Hip flask
Colour: silver
130mm / 5 inches

Bookstand
Colour: brown
1.2m / 48 inches

Perfume bottle
Colour: clear
75mm / 3 inches

MISCELLANEOUS

Cast iron roll-top bath
Colours: white enamel, coloured sides and feet (e.g. red oxide), brass or chrome piping

Explorer's telescope
Colours: brown leather finish, chrome eyepiece
500mm / 20 inches

Cross-country skis
Colour: dark brown
2.5m / 100 inches

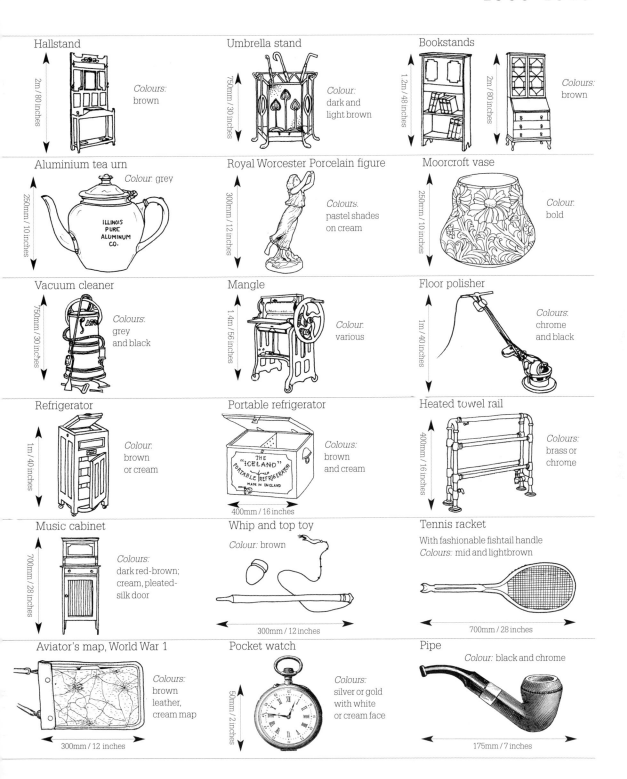

Hallstand
2m / 80 inches
Colours: brown

Umbrella stand
750mm / 30 inches
Colour: dark and light brown

Bookstands
1.2m / 48 inches
2m / 80 inches
Colours: brown

Aluminium tea urn
250mm / 10 inches
Colour: grey
ILLINOIS PURE ALUMINUM CO.

Royal Worcester Porcelain figure
300mm / 12 inches
Colours: pastel shades on cream

Moorcroft vase
250mm / 10 inches
Colour: bold

Vacuum cleaner
750mm / 30 inches
Colours: grey and black

Mangle
1.4m / 56 inches
Colour: various

Floor polisher
1m / 40 inches
Colours: chrome and black

Refrigerator
1m / 40 inches
Colour: brown or cream

Portable refrigerator
THE "ICELAND" PORTABLE REFRIGERATOR MADE IN ENGLAND
Colours: brown and cream
400mm / 16 inches

Heated towel rail
400mm / 16 inches
Colours: brass or chrome

Music cabinet
700mm / 28 inches
Colours: dark red-brown; cream, pleated-silk door

Whip and top toy
Colour: brown
300mm / 12 inches

Tennis racket
With fashionable fishtail handle
Colours: mid and lightbrown
700mm / 28 inches

Aviator's map, World War 1
Colours: brown leather, cream map
300mm / 12 inches

Pocket watch
50mm / 2 inches
Colours: silver or gold with white or cream face

Pipe
Colour: black and chrome
175mm / 7 inches

1920-1939

The Jazz age

This period covers the Great Depression, prohibition in the USA, the Charleston dance, the abdication of Edward VIII in England, the discovery of Tutankhamun's tomb and the outbreak of World War Two.

Influences on theatre

This period began with the Charleston and all the razzmatazz of the Roaring Twenties but it also saw Prohibition, the Wall Street stock market crash, the Great Depression and the rise of Hitler and the Nazis in Europe, ultimately leading to yet another world war. Theatre, cinema and the adulation of glamorous movie stars offered an escape from an increasingly fraught world
.

Director Theodore Komisarjevski arrived in Britain from Russia in 1919 and introduced a new realism and sensitivity into productions over the next decades.

The first 'club theatres' opened in Britain, including *The Gate* in 1925. In the 1930s, director Tyrone Guthrie emphasised how attention to detail in all theatrical effects heightened dramatic impact.

Showboat appeared on Broadway in 1927 and became a classic musical production. Meanwhile the Fred Astaire movies furthered the dance craze, together with Busby Berkeley's dance formation effects.

However, the impact of the movie theatre and the wireless at home lessened the numbers of theatre-going public and on Broadway, for example, the numbers of productions diminished. Travelling theatre companies all but disappeared.

Noel Coward was writing throughout these two decades with plays such as *Private Lives*, set in a luxurious hotel in the South of France – but also *This Happy Breed*, where the action takes place in a an ordinary working-class home from 1917-37.

Several Somerset Maugham and Agatha Christie plays (or stories adapted for theatre) are set in this period. Eugene O'Neill won worldwide fame in 1920 with *Beyond the Horizon*.

Plays set in the 20s include:

The Boyfriend - Music and lyrics by Sandy Wilson

Daisy pulls it off - Denise Deegan

The Front Page - Ben Hecht and Charles MacArthur

Hay Fever - Noel Coward

Juno and the Paycock - Sean O'Casey

Rookery Nook - Ben Travers

Thark - Ben Travers

This Happy Breed - Noel Coward

Plays set in the 30s include:

Anastasia - Marcelle Maurette

Cabaret - Kander and Ebb

Cause Célèbre - Terence Rattigan

Cold Comfort Farm - Paul Doust (adapted from Stella Gbbons' novel)

Corpse! - Gerald Moon

Crown Matrimonial - Royce Ryton

Night Must Fall - Emlyn Williams

Of Mice and Men - John Steinbeck

Prime of Miss Jean Brodie - Jay Presson Allen

Private Lives - Noel Coward

Sound of Music - Richard Rodgers and Oscar Hammerstein

This Happy Breed - Noel Coward

Styles and trends

Modernism swept away the old order with more severe styles so that glassware, lamps, furniture and so on were designed to be functional rather than frivolous.

Largely because of the harsh economic climate, this had little immediate effect on the average home in Britain but appealed to the wealthier clientele who wanted to follow the latest trends, especially in France, Germany and the USA.

Similarly, Art Deco appealed to the more affluent classes with its racy and geometric shapes, and bold progressive styles.

It was not until the two movements softened each other's edges in the 30s – and Modernist Art Deco emerged – that items were manufactured en masse and became affordable for all.

Meanwhile, the Bauhaus influence introduced tubular chrome-plated chairs and tables, and the use of Bakelite and enamel. US influences also increased in the 1930s.

Susie Cooper used bright abstract designs for her pottery and Claris Cliff introduced bold motifs that were hand painted – but still produced in huge numbers.

At home

Increased mechanization lead to many labour-saving household

Backdrop to 1920-1939

devices – vacuum cleaners, of fairly standard design, appeared in more and more homes.

Home entertainment sources increased with wireless and gramophones as well as pianos.

Scandinavian wood and lamination became widely available for furniture and furnishings.

Furniture was bulbous, highly polished and glowingly coloured. Upholstery was often in shiny fabric.

Decoration included:
- Sunray motifs
- Stepped motifs
- Wild spashes of colour
and some styles showed the influence of a growing interest in:
- Ancient Egypt
- China
- Rococo styles

There was a building boom in the 1920s and 30s. As the householder's buying power increased in the suburbs, factories created crockery, tableware, and ornaments for this new flourishing marketplace.

Portable radios and car radios arrived in the US in 1922. In Germany, encouraged by Hitler, people's cars (Volkswagens) became the most popular cars in the world. The "beetle' had arrived.

By 1933, as President milions of new jobs were creared and America Roosevelt introduced his New Deal to boost the US economy and America began to recover from famine, drought and unemployment.

Further afield, under Stalin, agricultural reform in Russia combined farms into vast units but the peasants resisted this and millions were sent to labour camps while the seizure of grain lead to famine in the eartly 30s.

Historic background

1920
Gandhi leads Indian Independence Movement.

1920-1933
Prohibition in USA.

1922
Irish Free State established.
Tutankhamun's tomb discovered.

1923
End of Ottoman Empire.

1924
First around-the-world flight.

1926
Stalin controls Soviets. Trotsky ousted – assassinated in Mexico.

1927
Transatlantic radio telephone.

1927
Television invented.
Lindbergh crosses Atlantic.

1928
Invention of electric razor.

1929
Stock market crash.

1930
Reaction to and after-effects of the 1929 Great Depression.
Revolution in Brazil.
Gandhi leads revolt in India.
Flash bulb introduced.
Airship disaster in France.

1931
Empire State Building open.
Japan and China at War.

1932
Russian famine.
Atom split.
Roosevelt President of USA.

1933
Hitler Chancellor of Germany.
Fascist and Nazi movements grow.
Dachau established after Nazis round up opponents and Jews.
Japan leaves League of Nations.
Prohibition repealed.
Boeing 247 launched.

1934
The Long March in China.

1935
Earhart is first woman to fly Pacific.

1935-36
Abyssinia War.

1936
Edward VIII abdicates throne and George VI becomes British king.
Oppression and Apartheid in South Africa.
Rome-Berlin Axis.
Revolt in Japan.

1936-39
Spanish Civil War.

1937
Sino-Japanese War resumes.
Amelia Earhart lost.

1938
Germany annexes Austria.
Munich pact signed.

1939
Outbreak of World War Two.
Passenger service across Atlantic.
Ocean
Igor Sikorsky flies helicopter.

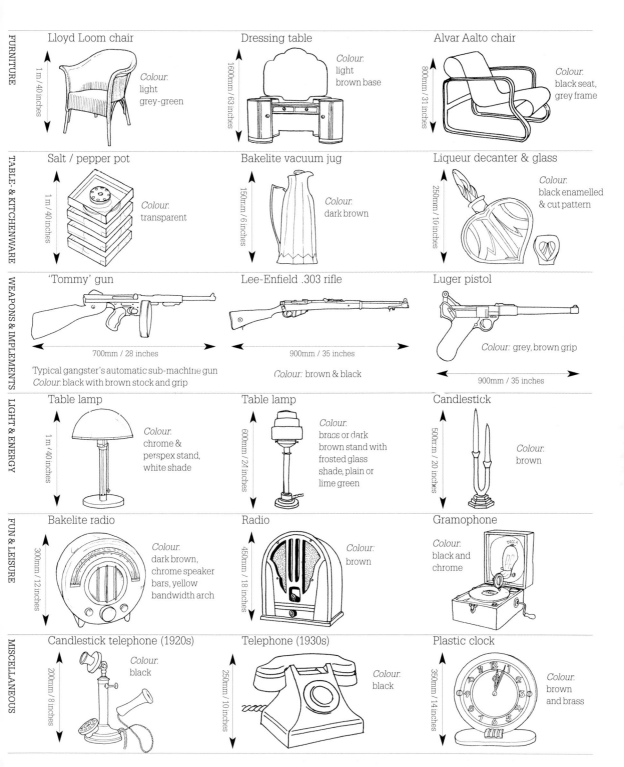

FURNITURE

Lloyd Loom chair
1 m / 40 inches
Colour: light grey-green

Dressing table
1600mm / 63 inches
Colour: light brown base

Alvar Aalto chair
800mm / 31 inches
Colour: black seat, grey frame

TABLE- & KITCHENWARE

Salt / pepper pot
1 m / 40 inches
Colour: transparent

Bakelite vacuum jug
150mm / 6 inches
Colour: dark brown

Liqueur decanter & glass
250mm / 10 inches
Colour: black enamelled & cut pattern

WEAPONS & IMPLEMENTS

'Tommy' gun
700mm / 28 inches
Typical gangster's automatic sub-machine gun
Colour: black with brown stock and grip

Lee-Enfield .303 rifle
900mm / 35 inches
Colour: brown & black

Luger pistol
Colour: grey, brown grip
900mm / 35 inches

LIGHT & ENERGY

Table lamp
1 m / 40 inches
Colour: chrome & perspex stand, white shade

Table lamp
600mm / 24 inches
Colour: brass or dark brown stand with frosted glass shade, plain or lime green

Candlestick
500mm / 20 inches
Colour: brown

FUN & LEISURE

Bakelite radio
300mm / 12 inches
Colour: dark brown, chrome speaker bars, yellow bandwidth arch

Radio
450mm / 18 inches
Colour: brown

Gramophone
Colour: black and chrome

MISCELLANEOUS

Candlestick telephone (1920s)
200mm / 8 inches
Colour: black

Telephone (1930s)
250mm / 10 inches
Colour: black

Plastic clock
350mm / 14 inches
Colour: brown and brass

1920-1939

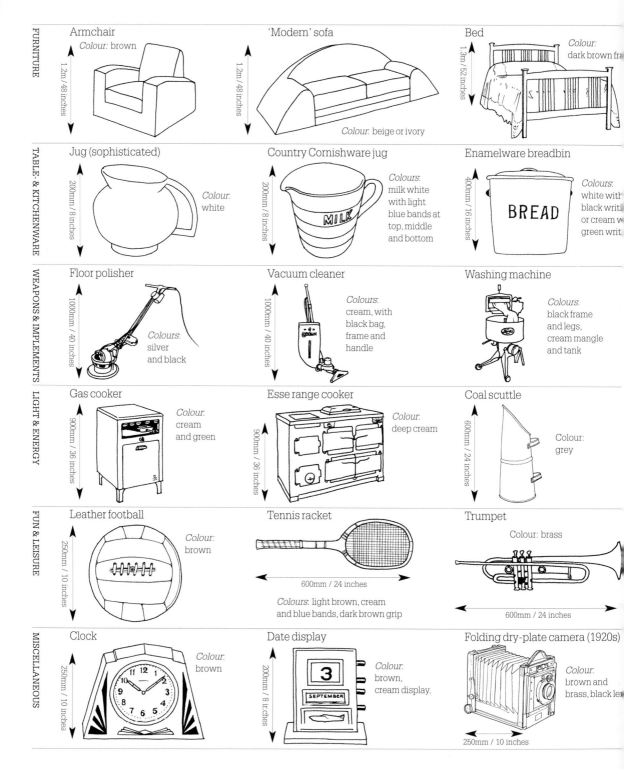

FURNITURE

Armchair
Colour: brown
1.2m / 48 inches

'Modern' sofa
1.2m / 48 inches
Colour: beige or ivory

Bed
1.3m / 52 inches
Colour: dark brown fra

TABLE- & KITCHENWARE

Jug (sophisticated)
200mm / 8 inches
Colour: white

Country Cornishware jug
200mm / 8 inches
Colours: milk white with light blue bands at top, middle and bottom
MILK

Enamelware breadbin
400mm / 16 inches
BREAD
Colours: white with black writi or cream w green writi

WEAPONS & IMPLEMENTS

Floor polisher
1000mm / 40 inches
Colours: silver and black

Vacuum cleaner
1000mm / 40 inches
Colours: cream, with black bag, frame and handle

Washing machine
Colours: black frame and legs, cream mangle and tank

LIGHT & ENERGY

Gas cooker
900mm / 36 inches
Colour: cream and green

Esse range cooker
900mm / 36 inches
Colour: deep cream

Coal scuttle
600mm / 24 inches
Colour: grey

FUN & LEISURE

Leather football
250mm / 10 inches
Colour: brown

Tennis racket
600mm / 24 inches
Colours: light brown, cream and blue bands, dark brown grip

Trumpet
Colour: brass
600mm / 24 inches

MISCELLANEOUS

Clock
250mm / 10 inches
Colour: brown

Date display
200mm / 8 inches
Colour: brown, cream display.
3
SEPTEMBER

Folding dry-plate camera (1920s)
Colour: brown and brass, black le
250mm / 10 inches

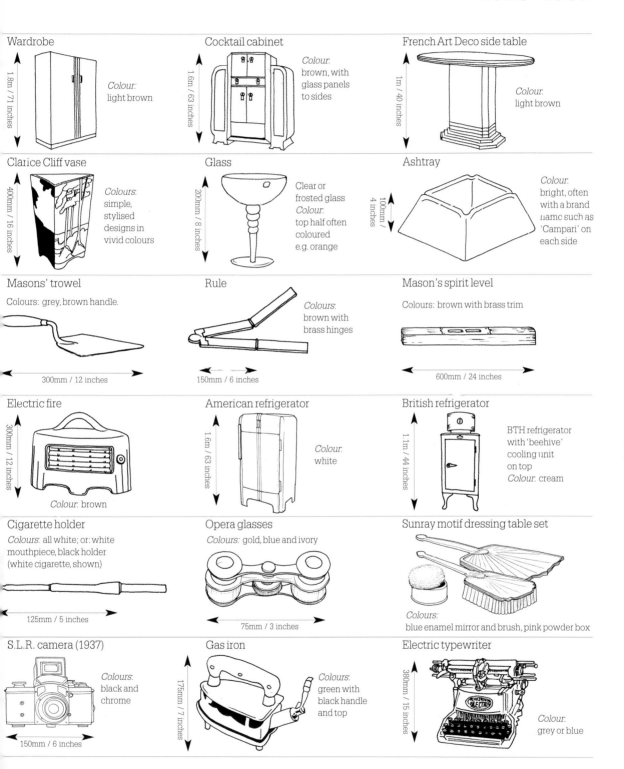

Wardrobe

1.8m / 71 inches

Colour: light brown

Cocktail cabinet

1.6m / 63 inches

Colour: brown, with glass panels to sides

French Art Deco side table

1m / 40 inches

Colour: light brown

Clarice Cliff vase

400mm / 16 inches

Colours: simple, stylised designs in vivid colours

Glass

200mm / 8 inches

Clear or frosted glass *Colour:* top half often coloured e.g. orange

Ashtray

100mm / 4 inches

Colour: bright, often with a brand name such as 'Campari' on each side

Masons' trowel

Colours: grey, brown handle.

300mm / 12 inches

Rule

Colours: brown with brass hinges

150mm / 6 inches

Mason's spirit level

Colours: brown with brass trim

600mm / 24 inches

Electric fire

300mm / 12 inches

Colour: brown

American refrigerator

1.6m / 63 inches

Colour: white

British refrigerator

1.1m / 44 inches

BTH refrigerator with 'beehive' cooling unit on top *Colour:* cream

Cigarette holder

Colours: all white; or: white mouthpiece, black holder (white cigarette, shown)

125mm / 5 inches

Opera glasses

Colours: gold, blue and ivory

75mm / 3 inches

Sunray motif dressing table set

Colours: blue enamel mirror and brush, pink powder box

S.L.R. camera (1937)

Colours: black and chrome

150mm / 6 inches

Gas iron

175mm / 7 inches

Colours: green with black handle and top

Electric typewriter

380mm / 15 inches

Colour: grey or blue

The 1940s

War, austerity and escapism

The first half of this period saw the impact of World War Two. Many plays and films have been inspired by the conflict which was finally ended by the atomic bombing of Hiroshima. The Cold War emerged to divide Europe and there was great post-war austerity here. Theatre and cinema offered a great escape from this.

Drama and theatre

Pure naturalism was not so popular after World War I, but realist drama still dominated the commercial theatre, especially in the U S. Now, however, plays sought to explore the psyche of characters, with nonrealistic scenic and dramatic devices. The plays of Arthur Miller and Tennessee Williams, for example, included cinematic-inspired devices, like dream sequences and memory flash-backs.

The magnetic tape recorder became freely available in the late 1940s as all the technical equipment grew gradually more sophisticated. Profile spots were now used in the US but not yet in the UK as the difference in voltages prevented their exportation.

The American musical was highly popular with Rodgers and Hammerstein's *Oklahoma* a stunning landmark that took dance to new heights, in 1943. Their *South Pacific* followed in 1949. Meanwhile, many British plays were still of the 'drawing-room' variety. Noel Coward remained popular and his perennial, *Blithe Spirit*, arrived in 1941.

Big bands and variety shows often went on tour with acts like the Crazy Gang and, after the war, many new stars rose from the ranks of forces entertainment.

Plays set in 1940s include:

All's Fair – Frank Vickery

And a Nightingale Sang – C P Taylor

Arsenic and Old Lace – Joseph Kesselring

Blue Remembered Hills – Dennis Potter

Brideshead Revisited – adapted from Evelyn Waugh by Roger Parsley

Broadway Bound – Neil Simon

Caucasian Chalk Circle – Bertolt Brecht

The Chiltern Hundreds – William Douglas Home

City of Angels – musical by Cy Coleman and David Zippel

The Dame of Sark – William Douglas Home

Death of a Salesman – Arthur Miller

The Diary of Anne Frank – Dramatized by F Goodrich and A Hackett

The Dresser – Ronald Harwood

Flare Path – Terence Rattigan

The Glass Menagerie – Tennessee Williams

The Happiest Days of Your Life – John Dighton

The Long and the Short and the Tall – Willis Hall

Lost in Yonkers – Neil Simon

The Morning Star – Emlyn Williams

The Night of the Iguana – Tennessee Williams

Privates on Parade – Peter Nichols

Rebecca – adapted from Daphne du Maurier by Clifford Williams

See How They Run – Philip King

South Pacific – musical by Rodgers and Hammerstein

Taking Sides – Ronald Harwood

Trespass – Emlyn Williams

Lifestyle

The war imposed rationing and restraint and a lack of new product in the UK that continued even after hostilities ended. In America however, especially in Hollywood, film star elegance and the glamour of cinema offered temporary escape from austerity, enjoyed on both sides of the Atlantic.

By 1941 women worked in munitions, tank and aircraft factories as more men joined the forces – soon followed by women in both the forces and the Land Army – manning anti-aircraft batteries, driving trains and tractors, or operating cranes

Gas masks arrived as bombs fell, and cities burned.

Homelife and furnishings

After the war, 200,000 people in Britain had to be rehoused while some stayed on in 'prefabs' – meant to be temporary but turned into permanent homes. In suburbia, many semi-detached homes had living rooms with the latest cocktail cabinet, leather-look trunks and real or mock leather sofas, free-standing matching lamps with chrome bases and dark shades, lots of cushions and a black bakelite telephone. A chandelier might grace a larger establishment or fine restaurant.

During the war, utility furniture from 1943 was basic and functional but well designed. Food was scarce and certain items remained so long after

Backdrop to the 1940s

the war, with rationing continuing and items like bananas and chocolate still a rare treat.

Modernist furniture began in the US with curved shapes that echoed natural forms. After the war, home improvement and DIY arrived, along with hire purchase 'easy terms'.

Fashion

World War Two had an effect on the fashion industry everywhere. After the Nazis occupied Paris, couture houses closed down, expensive fabrics such as silks and lace were no longer available and ordinary fabrics were rationed. Parachute silk was sometimes used to make wedding dresses! Meanwhile, there was a mass exodus of Jewish fashion workers from Nazi-dominated parts of Europe.

Women wore fur coats if they could afford them and elegant hats, often pill-box shaped, that sported flowers and feathers. American women enjoyed fuller skirts, colourful high-heeled shoes and nylon stockings. Teenagers there wore Levi jeans and sloppy Joe sweaters – girls in short cotton socks and flat-soled loafers idolised Frank Sinatra. Working women took to wearing slacks, and by summer, 1944, five times more women's trousers had been sold than in the previous year.

In Britain, silk stockings were in short supply. Women wore leg make-up and drew seams with eyebrow pencil down the back of each leg. Short skirts, flat shoes and square shouldered jackets echoed the uniforms. Working women wore trousers or dungarees with scarves or snoods to protect their hair from factory machines. Meanwhile, clothes coupons rationed new

purchases so older clothes and men's suits were revamped. Heavy blankets were turned into fashionable overcoats as old jumpers were unpicked to make new ones, or slippers and socks. Sewing patterns conformed to stringent guidelines – with limits imposed on hems and pleats. Utility clothing was introduced towards the end of 1941 by the British government, stamped or labelled with a utility mark, CC41. Pockets were restricted, shirt lengths limited and trouser turn-ups banned.

After the war, rationing continued in the UK until 1949 when Dior's New Look with full flaring skirts. Elasticized swimwear and the bikini appeared. Men wore double-breasted jackets, padded shoulders, and sheepskin-lined flying jackets.

Historic background

British monarch in this period:
George VI 1936-1952

1940
Germany invades much of Europe.
British army evacuated from Dunkirk.
Battle of Britain – British air victory prevents German invasion.

1941
Germany invades Russia.
Italy and Germany invade Egypt.
Japanese attack Pearl Harbor.
Penicillin used on humans.

1942
Americans bomb Japan.
Battle of Midway.
Allies defeat Rommel at El Alamein.
Nuclear chain reaction achieved.

1943
Germans surrender at Stalingrad.
US begins recapture of Japanese-held islands in the Pacific.
Italian government surrenders.

1944
Allies land in Normandy, German forces begin to retreat.
Allies liberate Paris and Brussels.

1945
Allies invade Germany.
Mussolini assassinated.
Hitler commits suicide.
Germany surrenders.
Soviet forces liberate Auschwitz;
First Atomic bombs on Hiroshima and Nagasaki; Japan surrenders.

1946
Peron is dictator of Argentina.
Iron Curtain descends on Europe.
Chinese Civil War resumes.
Atomic test at Bikini Atoll.
Nuremburg trials: 9 Nazi leaders hung for war crimes.
1st electronic computer
League of Nations ends.

1947
Marshall Aid for Europe introduced.
India gains independence.
Partition of Palestine agreed by UN.

1948
New state of Israel – Arab states attack it.
Polaroid camera on sale.

1949
NATO founded.
Ireland republic declared.
Germany divided into Federal Republic (east) and German Democratic Republic (west).
Soviets detonate A-bomb.
Communist victory in China.

The 1940s

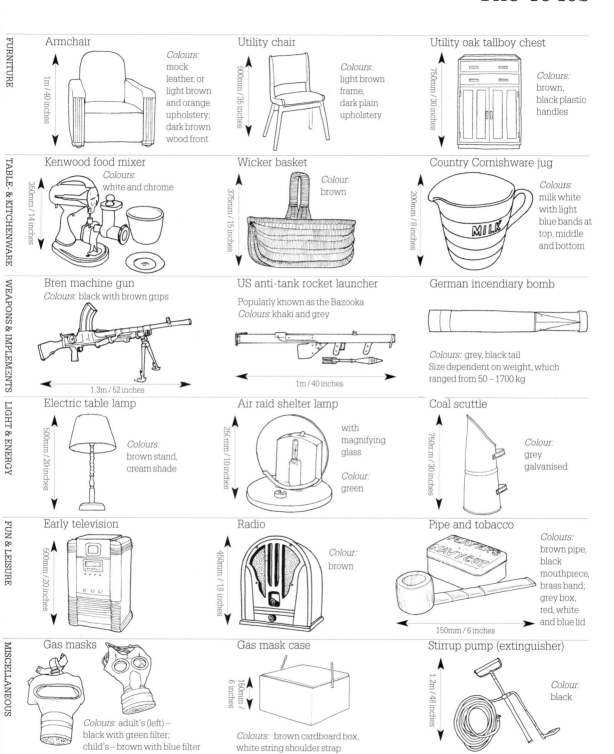

FURNITURE

Armchair
1m / 40 inches
Colours: mock leather, or light brown and orange upholstery; dark brown wood front

Utility chair
900mm / 35 inches
Colours: light brown frame, dark plain upholstery

Utility oak tallboy chest
750mm / 30 inches
Colours: brown, black plastic handles

TABLE & KITCHENWARE

Kenwood food mixer
350mm / 14 inches
Colours: white and chrome

Wicker basket
375mm / 15 inches
Colour: brown

Country Cornishware jug
200mm / 8 inches
Colours: milk white with light blue bands at top, middle and bottom

WEAPONS & IMPLEMENTS

Bren machine gun
Colours: black with brown grips
1.3m / 52 inches

US anti-tank rocket launcher
Popularly known as the Bazooka
Colours: khaki and grey
1m / 40 inches

German incendiary bomb
Colours: grey, black tail
Size dependent on weight, which ranged from 50 – 1700 kg

LIGHT & ENERGY

Electric table lamp
500mm / 20 inches
Colours: brown stand, cream shade

Air raid shelter lamp
250mm / 10 inches
with magnifying glass
Colour: green

Coal scuttle
750mm / 30 inches
Colour: grey galvanised

FUN & LEISURE

Early television
500mm / 20 inches

Radio
450mm / 18 inches
Colour: brown

Pipe and tobacco
150mm / 6 inches
Colours: brown pipe, black mouthpiece, brass band; grey box, red, white and blue lid

MISCELLANEOUS

Gas masks
Colours: adult's (left) – black with green filter; child's – brown with blue filter

Gas mask case
150mm / 6 inches
Colours: brown cardboard box, white string shoulder strap

Stirrup pump (extinguisher)
1.2m / 48 inches
Colour: black

The 1940s

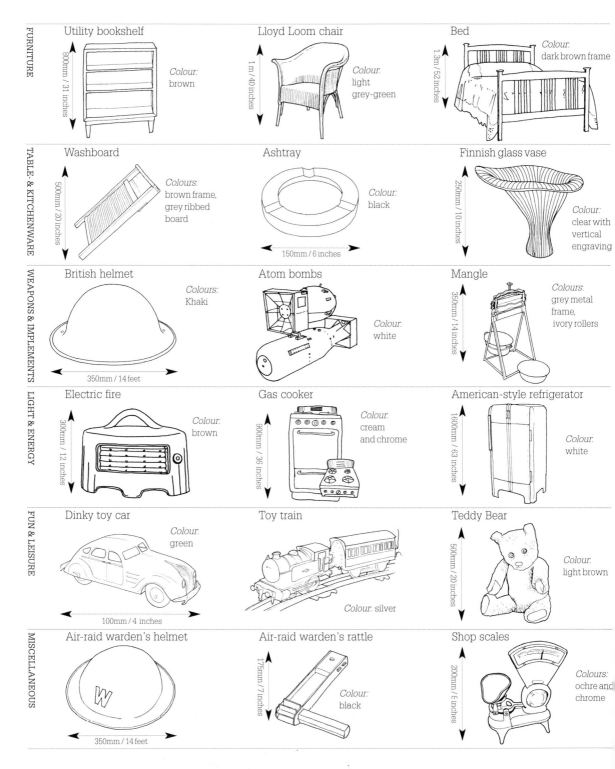

FURNITURE

Utility bookshelf
800mm / 31 inches
Colour: brown

Lloyd Loom chair
1 m / 40 inches
Colour: light grey-green

Bed
1.3m / 52 inches
Colour: dark brown frame

TABLE & KITCHENWARE

Washboard
500mm / 20 inches
Colours: brown frame, grey ribbed board

Ashtray
150mm / 6 inches
Colour: black

Finnish glass vase
250mm / 10 inches
Colour: clear with vertical engraving

WEAPONS & IMPLEMENTS

British helmet
350mm / 14 feet
Colours: Khaki

Atom bombs
Colour: white

Mangle
350mm / 14 inches
Colours: grey metal frame, ivory rollers

LIGHT & ENERGY

Electric fire
300mm / 12 inches
Colour: brown

Gas cooker
900mm / 36 inches
Colour: cream and chrome

American-style refrigerator
1600mm / 63 inches
Colour: white

FUN & LEISURE

Dinky toy car
100mm / 4 inches
Colour: green

Toy train
Colour: silver

Teddy Bear
500mm / 20 inches
Colour: light brown

MISCELLANEOUS

Air-raid warden's helmet
350mm / 14 feet
W

Air-raid warden's rattle
175mm / 7 inches
Colour: black

Shop scales
200mm / 8 inches
Colours: ochre and chrome

The 1950s

We've never had it so good

When Elizabeth II became Queen in 1952,
Britain was optimistic that a new golden age
was beginning. Here, and in the US, a youth
cult developed with rock-and-roll and
distinctive clothes – as televisions arrived in
force, the birth control pill was introduced and
the first satellites launched the space age.

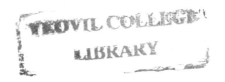

Backdrop to the 1950s

Drama and theatre

One of the most influential genres of the 20th century was absurdism; this peaked in the 1950s. Mankind was seen as being lost in a world where action became senseless, and characters archetypes.

European drama concentrated on exploring ideas, with works by Italian Luigi Pirandello, French playwrights Jean Anouilh and Jean Giraudoux, and Belgian playwright Michel de Ghelderode. Eugene O'Neill's later works used poetic dialogue that softened the hard edges of realism. In England, John Osborne's *Look Back in Anger* (1956) became a focus for the postwar, 'angry young men'.

Meanwhile, the US pioneered musical theatre as the most popular form of commercial and amateur entertainment. Broadway, in New York, became synonymous with the production of musicals, both revivals and new works; these were often lavish productions costing multi-millions of dollars.

Scenery was now often suggestive rather than realistic. Modern dimmers and lighting equipment accelerated the improvements in lighting technology while projected slides and moving film were often used to set the scene. Meanwhile, the emergence of the compact magnetic tape in the 1950s made theatrical sound systems much more versatile and easier to use.

The late 1950s saw a revolution in the quality of reproduced sound, while the emergence of rock-and-roll music spearheaded the growth of electronic sound and sophisticated mixing consoles. Televisions were arriving in many homes and did have an impact on cinema and theatre attendance, which sometimes struggled to survive, especially in local, smaller communities.

Plays set in 1950s include:

Billy Liar – K Waterhouse and W Hall

Cat Among the Pigeons – Duncan Greenwood

Collaborators – John Mortimer

The Darling Buds of May – H E Bates

The Deep Blue Sea – Terence Rattigan

Fings Aint Wot They Used T'be – musical by Frank Norman and Lionel Bart

Five Finger Exercise – Peter Shaffer

Grease – Musical by Jacobs and Casey

Once a Catholic – Mary O'Malley

Portraits – William Douglas Home

Roots – Arnold Wesker

September Tide – Daphne du Maurier

Single Spies (to 1960s) – Alan Bennett

Shadowlands – William Nicholson

Someone Waiting – Emlyn Williams

The Talented Mr Ripley – adapted from P Highsmith by P Nagy

A Taste of Honey – Shelagh Delaney

Under Milk Wood – by Dylan Thomas

West Side Story – Musical by Leonard Bernstein and Jerome Robbins

Lifestyle: homes

Reproductions of famous paintings could now be bought at a rational cost and Constable's *Haywain* and Shepherd's elephants graced many a living room.

Homes were heated by a coal fire in the main room and additional electric or gas fires for short bursts of heat elsewhere. Water heating was by a coal fire back burner, an Ascot gas heater or by immersion heater. Electricity and gas were expensive and many people had a cold wash in the morning – or boiled the kettle. Not many houses had telephones but there were many more public phone boxes than now.

The Festival of Britain in 1951 was a focal point for new trends and inspired chairs and coffee tables with a steel rod base and ball feet and smaller items like magazine racks with black rods tipped with bright plastic beads. There were abstract prints with spidery black lines or squiggles on fabrics, upholstery and Formica surfaces. There were pouffes and scattered rugs, portable record players, transistor radios and slender curving tulip chairs and tables. American designs arrived with laminated surfaces while Scandinavian furniture was just putting in an appearance with its contemporary, clean lines.

Entertainment

At the start of the decade, the radio was the main source of home entertainment with the news, weather, comedy, music, and plays provided by three main BBC radio stations. In the evening it was possible to pick up some European channels, including popular music on Radio Luxembourg.

Black-and-white television was a new luxury and although some families bought one to watch the Coronation, joined by their neighbours, televisions were not common until the commercial channel arrived in 1955. There were few daytime broadcasts except *Watch with Mother* at midday. Evening programmes usually finished at midnight. Gaps were filled by a static image or 'intermissions' – short films that included a sped-up train journey from London to Brighton, a potter's wheel and a kitten playing with wool. These were also broadcast to cover fairly frequent breakdowns in service.

This was the time of rock and roll, skiffle and beatniks. Popular music artists included Al Martino, Frankie Laine, Doris Day, Pat Boone, The Everley Brothers, Bill Haley and the Comets, Elvis Presley and Cliff Richard whose first hit was *Living Doll* in 1959. Youngsters rode scooters and listened to music on jukeboxes in milk or coffee bars.

Food

Food was plainer and fattier than we eat today because of post-war Britain shortages. Fairly heavy rich deserts included suet pudding, pies, and jam roly poly. A few people had domestic fridges but there were no freezers - so food but had to be eaten promptly or stored in cool larders; tinned meat was common – corned beef, ham and spam from America, sometimes cooked as a fritter! A typical salad – only available in summer and often from the vegetable garden or allotment plot – was lettuce, tomato and cucumber, sometimes with radishes, beetroot or spring onions plus the essential Heinz salad cream.

Transport

There were few cars. Most trains were still steam driven although a few were diesel by the mid-50s and some Southern Region trains were electric. Many people rode bicycles to school or work.

Toys

Children's toys included clockwork and electric train sets, Meccano, pedal cars, very early Lego, yoyos, small metal cars by Dinky and Corgi (often racing cars), skipping ropes, bicycles, tricycles and scooters, pedal cars, model soldiers and cowboys, model farms and animals, toy prams and walking-talking dolls. Hula-hoops became a craze.

Fashion

National Service meant than many young men were in uniform for two years. The Teddy Boy era saw bright coloured shirts, jackets with wide lapels, velvet collars, narrow ties, drainpipe trousers, fluorescent socks and 'winklepicker' pointed shoes.

Girls wore wide skirts with lots of net underskirts and tight shiny belts. The bust was big news with pointed bras to emphasise them and with Marilyn Monroe, Jayne Mansfield and Diana Dors as well-endowed icons. Stiletto shoes were worn, especially at evening dances when ball gowns and stoles were *de rigeur*.

Young lads had crew cuts and side burns; girls had pony tails or bouffant back-combed hair; women rolled their hair up into a neat French pleat or had short waved styles.

Historic background

British monarchs in this period:
George VI 1936-1952
Elizabeth II 1952-

1950
Korean War (until 1953).
Anglo-Egyptian dispute over Sudan and Suez Canal.
US Senator McCarthy heads inquiry into Communist activities.

1951
US tests H-bomb on Pacific island.
British troops occupy Suez Canal.
1st commercial digital computer.
1st color television broadcast.

1952
George VI dies; Elizabeth II is Queen.
Polio vaccine.

1953
Korean armistice.
Hilary and Tensing climb Everest.

1954
Vietnam divided.
McCarthy's Communist witch–hunt.
1st kidney transplant operation.

1956
Suez War.
1st Trans-Atlantic telephone cable.

1957
Common Market established.
Sputnik launched by Russians.

1958
First US satellite in orbit.
Invention of microchip.

1959
Castro seizes power in Cuba.
First shots of far side of moon.

The 1950s

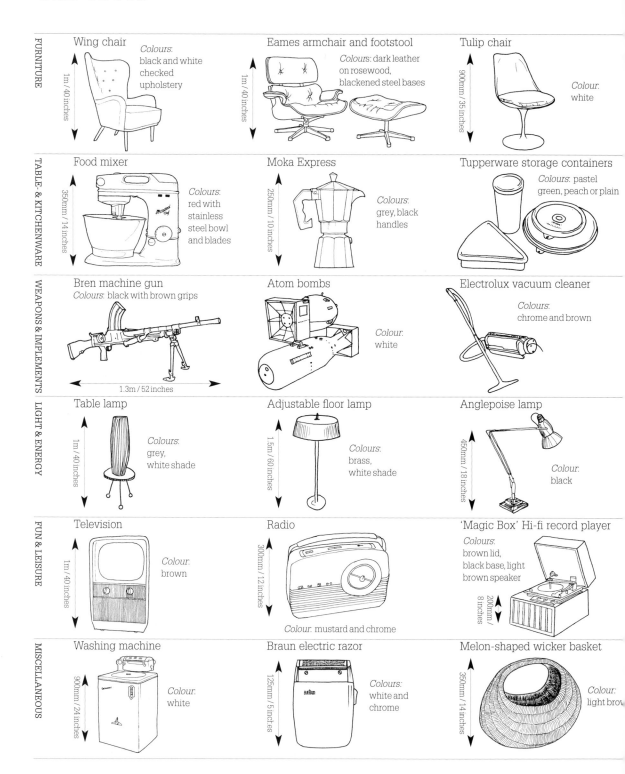

FURNITURE

Wing chair
1m / 40 inches
Colours: black and white checked upholstery

Eames armchair and footstool
1m / 40 inches
Colours: dark leather on rosewood, blackened steel bases

Tulip chair
900mm / 35 inches
Colour: white

TABLE- & KITCHENWARE

Food mixer
350mm / 14 inches
Colours: red with stainless steel bowl and blades

Moka Express
250mm / 10 inches
Colours: grey, black handles

Tupperware storage containers
Colours: pastel green, peach or plain

WEAPONS & IMPLEMENTS

Bren machine gun
Colours: black with brown grips
1.3m / 52 inches

Atom bombs
Colour: white

Electrolux vacuum cleaner
Colours: chrome and brown

LIGHT & ENERGY

Table lamp
1m / 40 inches
Colours: grey, white shade

Adjustable floor lamp
1.5m / 60 inches
Colours: brass, white shade

Anglepoise lamp
450mm / 18 inches
Colour: black

FUN & LEISURE

Television
1m / 40 inches
Colour: brown

Radio
300mm / 12 inches
Colour: mustard and chrome

'Magic Box' Hi-fi record player
Colours: brown lid, black base, light brown speaker
200mm / 8 inches

MISCELLANEOUS

Washing machine
900mm / 24 inches
Colour: white

Braun electric razor
125mm / 5 inches
Colours: white and chrome

Melon-shaped wicker basket
350mm / 14 inches
Colour: light brow

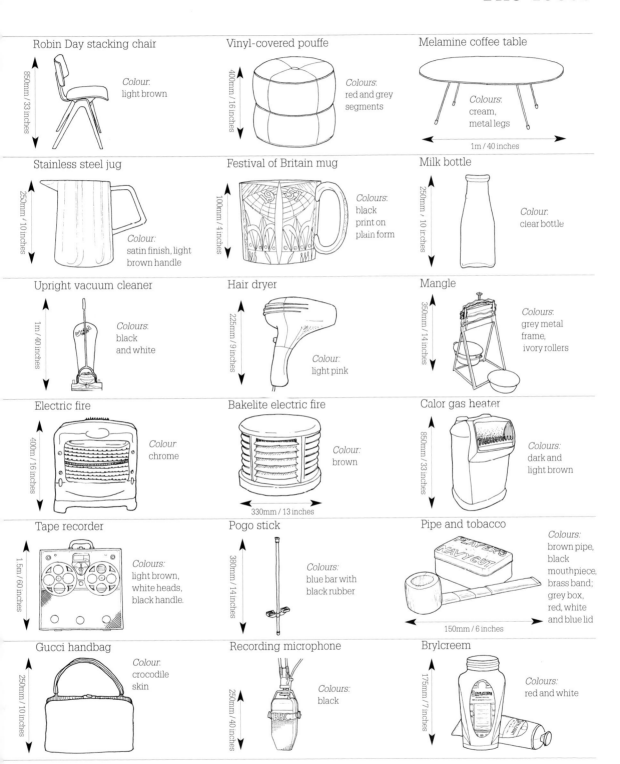

Robin Day stacking chair

850mm / 33 inches

Colour: light brown

Vinyl-covered pouffe

400mm / 16 inches

Colours: red and grey segments

Melamine coffee table

Colours: cream, metal legs

1m / 40 inches

Stainless steel jug

250mm / 10 inches

Colour: satin finish, light brown handle

Festival of Britain mug

100mm / 4 inches

Colours: black print on plain form

Milk bottle

250mm / 10 inches

Colour: clear bottle

Upright vacuum cleaner

1m / 40 inches

Colours: black and white

Hair dryer

225mm / 9 inches

Colour: light pink

Mangle

350mm / 14 inches

Colours: grey metal frame, ivory rollers

Electric fire

400m / 16 inches

Colour: chrome

Bakelite electric fire

Colour: brown

330mm / 13 inches

Calor gas heater

850mm / 33 inches

Colours: dark and light brown

Tape recorder

1.5m / 60 inches

Colours: light brown, white heads, black handle.

Pogo stick

380mm / 14 inches

Colours: blue bar with black rubber

Pipe and tobacco

Colours: brown pipe, black mouthpiece, brass band; grey box, red, white and blue lid

150mm / 6 inches

Gucci handbag

250mm / 10 inches

Colour: crocodile skin

Recording microphone

250mm / 40 inches

Colours: black

Brylcreem

175mm / 7 inches

Colours: red and white

The 1960s

The swinging decade

The swinging sixties saw greater optimism and affluence, faster motorway and air travel, and space exploration – but the Cold War continued, with nuclear war a strong threat. The era was marked by the assassination of J F Kennedy and Martin Luther King. The first successful heart transplant took medicine into a new domain.

Drama and theatre

The Ensemble Theatre movement saw plays created without an original written script. Productions by an group of actors evolved over months of explorative work. Movement and sound dominated dialogue. Peter Brook's *Theatre of Cruelty Workshop* and the *Théâtre du Soleil* (the French workers' cooperative) were two well-known ensemble theatres.

The early dramas of American playwright, Edward Albee, were classified as absurd with their illogical characters' actions. Pinter, too, wrote 'absurd' plays that can seem dark and impenetrable but Pinter believed that they were actually realistic because, in the normal world, we are exposed only to fragments of activity and dialogue, often unexplained.

The American theater saw the rise of Afro American, Latino, Asian American, feminist, and homosexual theatre groups and a surge in regional professional companies. Government subsidy of US arts from 1965 helped non-profit-making theatres, as well as orchestras, museums, and opera and dance companies. Meanwhile, many playwrights (including Sam Shepard in the US and Tom Stoppard in the UK) explored language and its use other than as an exchange of information – as a game or a barrier, or just as a sound, or as a reflection of society. Many plays mirrored society's frustration with what seemed to be, with the threat of nuclear war, a world bent on self-destruction.

Plays set in 1960s

Alfie – Bill Naughton

Blue Murder – Peter Nichols

Generations Apart – Peter Gordon

Hair – Musical by Ragni, Rado and MacDermot

The Homecoming – Pinter

Kingdom of Earth – Tennessee Williams

The Knack – Ann Jellicoe

La Turista – Sam Shepard

A Letter of Resignation – Hugh Whitemore

Quartermaine's Terms – Simon Gray

Savages – Christopher Hampton

Spring and Port Wine – Bill Naughton

Stop the World, I want to get off – Musical by L Bricusse and A Newley

What I Did in the Holidays – Philip Osment

Who's Afraid of Virginia Woolf? – Edward Albee

You're a Good Man, Charlie Brown – adapted from C M Schultz by C Gesner, M Mayer and A Lippa

Lifestyle

At home there were twin tub washing machines and spin dryers now (with fully automatic washing machines at the turn of the decade) and although refrigerators were not in every home, they were becoming more common. Meanwhile, supermarkets spread – while the laundrette meant those without the latest washing appliances at home could still make use of them. At work, manual typewriters were still used, often in 'typing pools', but electric typewriters were arriving. Secretarial colleges generated new recruits as the numbers of 'white collar' office workers rose.

Transport

Production lines and factory conveyor belts dominated manufacture of mass products, especially cars – the Mini soon became the most popular small car. Motorways arrived; construction had begun in the late 1950s but continued at a pace through this decade. At first, there were no speed restrictions and cars could travel over 100mph. This changed when the 70mph limit was introduced, as a trial, in 1965. Motorways halved journey times and ushered in many new fast cars. Scooters and motor bikes were popular and mods and rockers sought their own identities through these as well as their clothes.

Fashion and styles

Mini skirts were big news, seeming to grow shorter by the minute as tights replaced stockings and suspenders. This was the time of Andy Warhol, hippies and flower power. Psychedelic and ethnic designs were used for both clothes and home furnishings. Mary Quant was designing clothes and make-up, geared to the young market, while Vidal Sassoon pioneered short boyish hair bobs. Men now had their hair styled too. In the second half of the decade, the model looks were skinny like Twiggy and often with long, straight hair à la Jean Shrimpton – while the Beatles had a huge impact on the young cult.

Houses and furniture

New semi-detached houses were quite large and often had a garage

Backdrop to the 1960s

and generous gardens where growing vegetables and roses grew in popularity. Separate lounge and dining rooms were replaced by the through dining room/lounge and open-plan kitchens. Garages and porches often had flat roofs covered with asphalt. Thermoplastic tiles covered floors, usually carpeted in a tweedy design later, when the budget allowed. There were shelving dividers and new houses sometimes offered central heating.

PVC, smoked glass and various plastics arrived as Pop Art brought in brash colours and shapes on posters and record sleeves. Terence Conran founded Habitat in 1964, bringing good functional design at an affordable price into the home. Now there was stainless steel cutlery and self-assembly furniture, usually in bold, primary colours. Psychedelic and ethnic designs were used for both clothes and home furnishings. King-sized beds gained in popularity. At the end of the 60s, less than half of UK households had a telephone but in the USA, 80% of families had a telephone by 1966.

Urban development saw the rise of tower blocks and the demolition of many old buildings to make way for new modern shopping centres and multi-storey car parks.

Art and leisure

Pop art and new wave photography exploded onto the scene. Meanwhile the publication of D H Lawrence's *Lady Chatterley's Lover* changed censorship laws and spearheaded far more explicit material in all the media. BBC2 television arrived in 1964. Even in 1961, 75% of British households had a TV set; in 1966, many viewers watched England win the football World Cup. By the end of the sixties, TV ownership was almost universal. Many television comedies and 'sit-coms' typified daily life in suburbia, including *Hancock's Half-Hour*. Other popular programmes included *Top of the Pops, Dr Finlay's Casebook, Perry Mason, Dr Who, Morecambe and Wise* and *Z Cars*. Colour television was first broadcast in 1967 but the sets were very expensive and colour did not reach all three channels until 1969 – as television viewers watched US astronauts landing on the moon.

Pirate radio broadcast pop music until 1967, when the BBC broadcast Radio 1 for the first time. The Beatles were the greatest phenomena of the 1960s, but other pop stars included Adam Faith, Tom Jones, Shirley Bassey, Cilla Black, Lulu, Dusty Springfield, The Beach Boys, Gerry and The Pacemakers, The Rolling Stones, Jimi Hendrix, The Kinks, The Who, The Animals and Pink Floyd. At the end of the decade, open-air pop festivals became a feature.

For children, Dinky toys were still popular and Lego (launched 1955) was now widely available. Barbie Doll was on every toy supplier's list; male action style figures, like Action Man, arrived, as did Scalextric. Meanwhile, the Space Age and *Dr Who* inspired countless space toys and robots.

Money and coins

This was seen as an affluent time when the young, especially, achieved much greater earning power, with jobs readily available. Decimalisation was imminent. The Royal Mint's output of old coins from 1967 to 1970 was all dated 1967. Then, in 1968, they started to mint new 5 and 10 pence coins to replace the 1- and 2-shilling pieces in preparation for full decimalisation in 1971.

Historic background

1960
Lasers invented.

1961
Kennedy inaugurated.
Berlin Crisis: Wall built.
Yuri Gagarin is 1st man in space.

1962
1st American in space.
Cuban missile crisis.
Telstar satellite.

1963
French veto Britain joining Common Market.
First test ban agreement between US and Soviet Union.
President Kennedy assassinated.
Vaccine against measles.

1964
Beatles visit America.
Dr King receives Nobel Prize.

1965
Vietnam War escalates.
First commercial satellite.

1966
First direct dial phones.

1967
Christian Barnard performs first heart transplant.
Abortion made legal in UK (US: 1973).

1968
Martin Luther King, Jr assassinated.
Robert Kennedy killed.

1969
1st 747 Flight.
Concorde airborne.
Woodstock Music and Art Festival.
US lands first men on the moon.

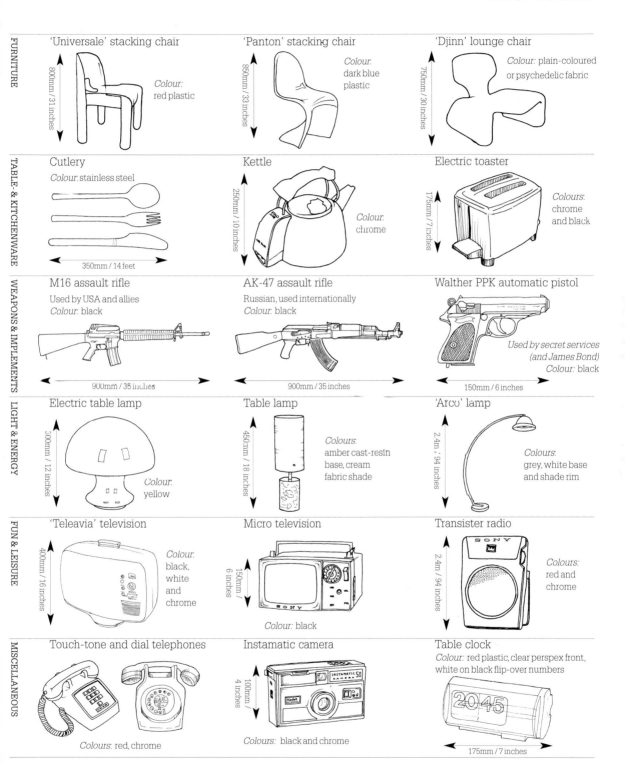

FURNITURE

'Universale' stacking chair
800mm / 31 inches
Colour: red plastic

'Panton' stacking chair
850mm / 33 inches
Colour: dark blue plastic

'Djinn' lounge chair
750mm / 30 inches
Colour: plain-coloured or psychedelic fabric

TABLE & KITCHENWARE

Cutlery
Colour: stainless steel
350mm / 14 feet

Kettle
250mm / 10 inches
Colour: chrome

Electric toaster
175mm / 7 inches
Colours: chrome and black

WEAPONS & IMPLEMENTS

M16 assault rifle
Used by USA and allies
Colour: black
900mm / 35 inches

AK-47 assault rifle
Russian, used internationally
Colour: black
900mm / 35 inches

Walther PPK automatic pistol
Used by secret services (and James Bond)
Colour: black
150mm / 6 inches

LIGHT & ENERGY

Electric table lamp
300mm / 12 inches
Colour: yellow

Table lamp
450mm / 18 inches
Colours: amber cast-resin base, cream fabric shade

'Arco' lamp
2.4m / 94 inches
Colours: grey, white base and shade rim

FUN & LEISURE

'Teleavia' television
400mm / 16 inches
Colour: black, white and chrome

Micro television
150mm / 6 inches
Colour: black

Transister radio
2.4m / 94 inches
Colours: red and chrome

MISCELLANEOUS

Touch-tone and dial telephones
Colours: red, chrome

Instamatic camera
100mm / 4 inches
Colours: black and chrome

Table clock
Colour: red plastic, clear perspex front, white on black flip-over numbers
175mm / 7 inches

The 1960s

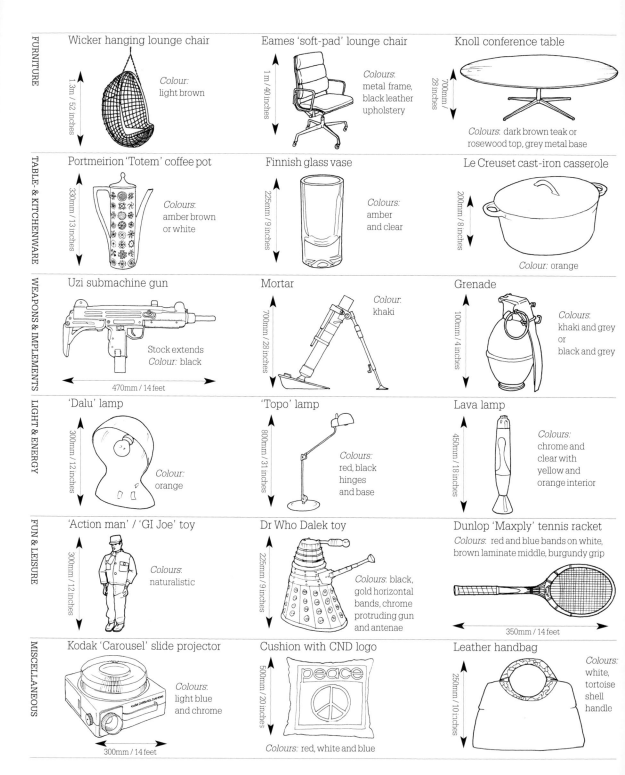

FURNITURE

Wicker hanging lounge chair
1.3m / 52 inches
Colour: light brown

Eames 'soft-pad' lounge chair
1 m / 40 inches
Colours: metal frame, black leather upholstery

Knoll conference table
700mm / 28 inches
Colours: dark brown teak or rosewood top, grey metal base

TABLE- & KITCHENWARE

Portmeirion 'Totem' coffee pot
330mm / 13 inches
Colours: amber brown or white

Finnish glass vase
225mm / 9 inches
Colours: amber and clear

Le Creuset cast-iron casserole
200mm / 8 inches
Colour: orange

WEAPONS & IMPLEMENTS

Uzi submachine gun
Stock extends
Colour: black
470mm / 14 feet

Mortar
700mm / 28 inches
Colour: khaki

Grenade
100mm / 4 inches
Colours: khaki and grey or black and grey

LIGHT & ENERGY

'Dalu' lamp
300mm / 12 inches
Colour: orange

'Topo' lamp
800mm / 31 inches
Colours: red, black hinges and base

Lava lamp
450mm / 18 inches
Colours: chrome and clear with yellow and orange interior

FUN & LEISURE

'Action man' / 'GI Joe' toy
300mm / 12 inches
Colours: naturalistic

Dr Who Dalek toy
225mm / 9 inches
Colours: black, gold horizontal bands, chrome protruding gun and antenae

Dunlop 'Maxply' tennis racket
Colours: red and blue bands on white, brown laminate middle, burgundy grip
350mm / 14 feet

MISCELLANEOUS

Kodak 'Carousel' slide projector
Colours: light blue and chrome
300mm / 14 feet

Cushion with CND logo
500mm / 20 inches
peace
Colours: red, white and blue

Leather handbag
250mm / 10 inches
Colours: white, tortoise shell handle

The 1970s

Riding high

Concorde crossed the Atlantic at supersonic speed, Queen Elizabeth II celebrated her Silver Jubilee and the first test-tube baby arrived. The decade saw advances in civil rights in the US, a strong feminist movement, heightened concern for the environment, and more distant space exploration.

Backdrop to the 1970s

Drama and theatre

The war in Vietnam inspired strong feeling in the US and Europe and many post-war playwrights wrote documentary dramas that explored the moral obligations of individuals – to themselves and to society.

In Europe there were many new interpretations of classical plays often with bold scenography, expressing ideas through action and the use of space. However, by the end of the decade there was a return to naturalism in both drama and art; the focus was on ordinary events and characters, and the language fragmentary, just like everyday conversation. Settings became more realistic again but, depending on the style of the play, the atmosphere was sometimes nightmarish.

In plays by Stephen Poliakoff, social realism was combined with very dark humour. An almost sinister humour could also be seen in the very different works by Alan Ayckbourn, Mike Leigh, Michael Frayn, Alan Bleasdale and Dennis Potter.

While far greater realism in sets was explored, the use of light and projection, symbolic pools of colour and optical illusion reflected the abstract art movements.

Plays set in 1970s include:

Absurd Person Singular – Alan Ayckbourn

American Buffalo – David Mamet

Aristocrats – Brian Friel

Bedroom Farce – Alan Ayckbourn

Cracks – Martin Sherman

A Chorus Line – musical by J Kirkwood, N Dante, M Hamlisch and E Kleban

Epsom Downs – Howard Brenton

The Freedom of the City – Brian Friel

Happy Families – John Godber

Miss Saigon – musical by A Boublil, C-M Schonberg and R Mally Jnr.

The Real Thing – Tom Stoppard

Rents – Michael Wilcox

Why Not Stay for Breakfast? – Gene Stone and Ray Cooney

Lifestyle

There was high inflation as well as economic uncertainty. Life expectancy rose to about 67 for men and 74 for women.

Decimilisation arrived in 1971.

In 1972, the British Museum hosted Tutankhamun exhibition, leading to a great interest in all things Egyptian.

Streaking nude in public became a fad; wife-swapping hit the headlines.

Home

Long-pile shag carpets were fitted in rooms decorated with a much wider choice of paint colours.

Fitted kitchens were now more common. Televisions were often housed in cabinets and colour TVs became a little more affordable, although by no means commonplace in the early part of the decade.

Laura Ashley revived Edwardian and Victorian country styles with flower sprigs and neat patterns on fabric, wallpaper, furnishings and clothes.

In 1971, the new North Sea oil rigs were drilling but the promise of cheaper fuel remained elusive. Meanwhile, in 1972, the miners strike lead to power cuts and all homes were well stocked with candles.

Art and literature

Pop Art was still represented by artists such as Andy Warhol and David Hockney but there was a gradual renewal of respect for traditional and historical art and architecture. Meanwhile, many books explored man's alienation from his spiritual roots through authors such as John Updike – and Jonathan Livingston's *Seagull*, which had a strong cult following.

Children and toys

Barbie Doll, Action Man and Lego were still highly popular toys. The board game, Trivial Pursuit, arrived in 1979. Star Wars figures, Rubik's cube, and smiley-face stickers arrived.

More homes had second cars now but many mothers still pushed quite large prams into town to shop. Baby gear, clothes and toys were available at specialist shops like Mothercare.

Food

Frozen and prepackaged meals saved time in the kitchen. There were many more ethnic foods available, as well as ethnic restaurants – and generally increased choice with foods formerly seen as exotic, such as melons and avacados. Young couples now hosted dinner parties.

Wrapped, sliced bread, prepared baby foods and 'ready-made' cakes eased the lives of many working wives – although most mothers still stayed at home until children were of school age. There were many more supermarkets now, even in outlying smaller towns.

Fashion

Following hippie and Beatle fashions, men sported shoulder-length hair and wore flared bellbottoms. Hot pants, platform shoes, clogs, T-shirts, tank tops, kaftans and gypsy dresses were popular. Long dresses were worn as casual clothing and generally fabrics became lighter as central heating and cars meant less exposure to the cold. Through this decade, fabric and haberdashery prices gradually rose as 'off-the-peg' garments became cheaper so fewer people made their own clothes.

Technology and medicine

Apollo 17 brought back samples of rock and soil from the moon, while unmanned space probes explored Jupiter, Mars, Saturn, Uranus, and Venus. US and USSR spacecraft linked up in space to conduct joint experiments.

The floppy disc appeared in the US in 1970, and the microprocessor chip followed soon after. The first low-priced TV games, and videocassette recorders revolutionised home entertainment, just as Jumbo jets revolutionized commercial flight and doubled passenger capacity.

In medicine, ultrasound diagnosis techniques developed. Genetic engineering was now possible but under ethical examination and the first test tube baby was born, developed from an artificially inseminated egg.

Politics and people

The Vietnam War continued to divide opinion. There were more women in politics and a rising divorce rate. The drug scene became a more prominent issue. The Watergate investigation lead to impeachment proceedings against President Nixon who was forced to resign. In 1973, an Arab oil embargo created severe shortages; energy prices rose sharply.

Popular music

The Beatles went their separate ways and Elvis Presley died (in '77). Pop music included soft rock, hard rock, punk rock, and country music. Disco dancing arrived in force! Artists included the Bee Gees, David Bowie, Fleetwood Mac, Elton John, Led Zeppelin, John Lennon, Pink Floyd, Rod Stewart, The Who, the Carpenters and Bob Marley.

Movies regained popularity with special effects in blockbusters such as *Star Wars, Towering Inferno, Earthquake, The Poseidon Adventure* and *Jaws*. Other successes included *Rocky, The Godfather, The Exorcist, Kramer vs. Kramer, Grease,* and *Saturday Night Fever.*

Television brought the conflict in Vietnam and the Watergate hearings into the homes of millions. *Sesame Street* introduced new learning techniques while *Blue Peter* remained a BBC perennial. *The Magic Roundabout* developed a cult following from adults and children alike – as did *Tiswas.*

Holidays and leisure

Foreign holidays became even cheaper; Spain was especially popular for the young but many families camped in France.

Historic background

1970
End of civil war in Biafra.
India invades Pakistan.

1971
Idi Amin seizes power in Uganda.

1973
US completes withdrawal from Vietnam.

1974
President Nixon resigns.
1st cooperative space mission between US and Soviet Union.

1975
Franco dies.
Communist forces capture Saigon, ending Vietnam War.
Suez Canal reopens.

1975-79
Unmanned space exploration of Venus, Mars and Jupiter.

1976
Apple introduce Apple II personal computer.

1977
1st elections in Pakistan.

1978
Smallpox eradicated.
First 'invitro' (test-tube) birth.

1979
Vietnamese take Phnom Penh.
Idi Amin overthrown.
Somalia and Ethiopia at war.
Southern Rhodesia now Zimbabwe.
Militant students seize US Embassy in Teheran.

The 1970s

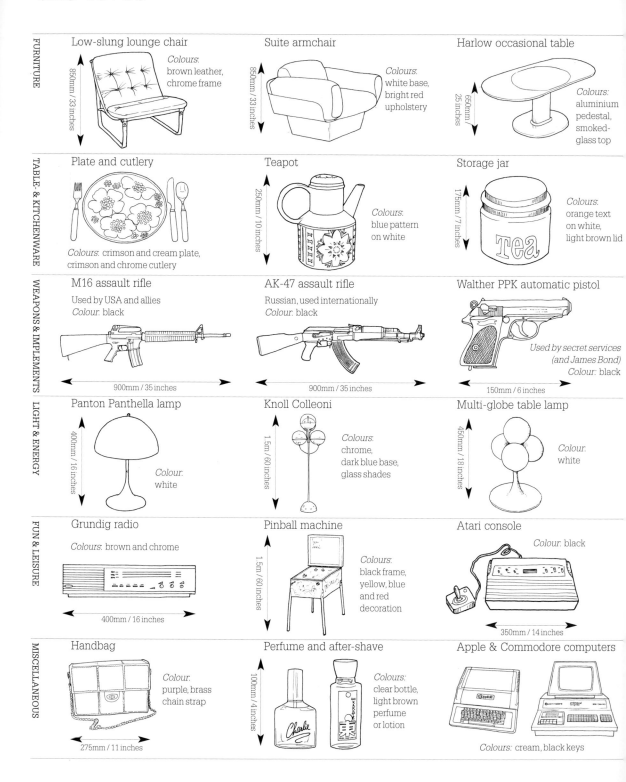

FURNITURE

Low-slung lounge chair
850mm / 33 inches

Colours: brown leather, chrome frame

Suite armchair

Colours: white base, bright red upholstery
850mm / 33 inches

Harlow occasional table
650mm / 25 inches

Colours: aluminium pedestal, smoked-glass top

TABLE- & KITCHENWARE

Plate and cutlery

Colours: crimson and cream plate, crimson and chrome cutlery

Teapot
250mm / 10 inches

Colours: blue pattern on white

Storage jar
175mm / 7 inches

Tea

Colours: orange text on white, light brown lid

WEAPONS & IMPLEMENTS

M16 assault rifle
Used by USA and allies
Colour: black

900mm / 35 inches

AK-47 assault rifle
Russian, used internationally
Colour: black

900mm / 35 inches

Walther PPK automatic pistol

Used by secret services (and James Bond)
Colour: black
150mm / 6 inches

LIGHT & ENERGY

Panton Panthella lamp
400mm / 16 inches

Colour: white

Knoll Colleoni
1.5m / 60 inches

Colours: chrome, dark blue base, glass shades

Multi-globe table lamp
450mm / 18 inches

Colour: white

FUN & LEISURE

Grundig radio
Colours: brown and chrome

400mm / 16 inches

Pinball machine
1.5m / 60 inches

Colours: black frame, yellow, blue and red decoration

Atari console
Colour: black

350mm / 14 inches

MISCELLANEOUS

Handbag

Colour: purple, brass chain strap

275mm / 11 inches

Perfume and after-shave
100mm / 4 inches

Charlie

Colours: clear bottle, light brown perfume or lotion

Apple & Commodore computers

Colours: cream, black keys

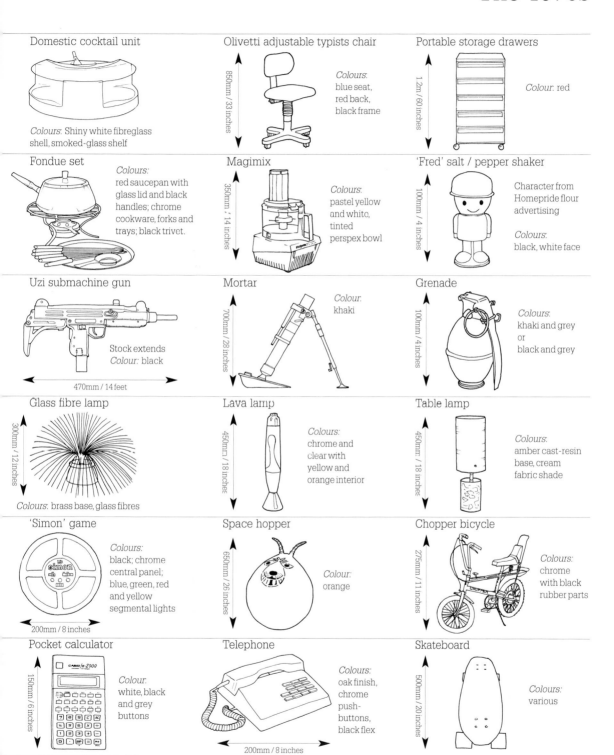

Domestic cocktail unit

Colours: Shiny white fibreglass shell, smoked-glass shelf

Olivetti adjustable typists chair

850mm / 33 inches

Colours: blue seat, red back, black frame

Portable storage drawers

1.2m / 60 inches

Colour: red

Fondue set

Colours: red saucepan with glass lid and black handles; chrome cookware, forks and trays; black trivet.

Magimix

350mm / 14 inches

Colours: pastel yellow and white, tinted perspex bowl

'Fred' salt / pepper shaker

100mm / 4 inches

Character from Homepride flour advertising

Colours: black, white face

Uzi submachine gun

Stock extends
Colour: black

470mm / 14 feet

Mortar

700mm / 28 inches

Colour: khaki

Grenade

100mm / 4 inches

Colours: khaki and grey or black and grey

Glass fibre lamp

300mm / 12 inches

Colours: brass base, glass fibres

Lava lamp

450mm / 18 inches

Colours: chrome and clear with yellow and orange interior

Table lamp

450mm / 18 inches

Colours: amber cast-resin base, cream fabric shade

'Simon' game

Colours: black; chrome central panel; blue, green, red and yellow segmental lights

200mm / 8 inches

Space hopper

650mm / 26 inches

Colour: orange

Chopper bicycle

275mm / 11 inches

Colours: chrome with black rubber parts

Pocket calculator

150mm / 6 inches

Colour: white, black and grey buttons

Telephone

Colours: oak finish, chrome push-buttons, black flex

200mm / 8 inches

Skateboard

500mm / 20 inches

Colours: various

1980s and 1990s

The digital age

The first space shuttle was launched, the Cold War ended and global warming became an issue. The youth culture lost impetus and people lived longer. Equal opportunities for women and gay issues impacted on society and Aids became an international threat. Personal computers, video recorders and the Internet arrived. As 1999 ended, there were Millennium celebrations around the globe.

Backdrop to the 1980s and 1990s

Drama and theatre

The need to compete with cinema, television and sophisticated camera effects led to experimentation. Now special knowledge was needed by theatre technical staff; computers became ever more advanced and expertise more specialized – certainly in the professional theatre.

Computer memory could store and replicate complicated arrangements, coordinating sound, light and pyrotechnics as scenographic boundaries became blurred. Now laser beams, holograms, fibre optics, projection and batteries of lamps could supply a great intensity of light. Multimedia became part of the scenic 'fabric'. However, the new systems were expensive and many amateur productions still relied on more mechanical means.

Many 18th-century theatres were restored. The classic proscenium arch theatre was still most common but experimental theatre stimulated new architecture – high raked seating or thrust stages, or theatre in the round – in real Roman arenas, or purpose-built open-air theatres like the replicated *Globe* in London. Some theatres could mutate from conventional seating to become theatre in the round – by revolving sections of seating.

Meanwhile, outdoor performances flourished in parks and historic sites in summer, while street theatre and festivals reinstated the travelling player's role worldwide. Amateur theatre thrived, as did semi-professional little theatres. Churches played host to plays or musicals with a religious flavour.

In the US, non-profit professional theatres shared productions, artists and costs and provided a source for serious dramatic plays that eventually moved to Broadway, where, despite rising costs, audiences continued to grow.

Plays set in 1980-1990s include:

Angels in America – Perestroika

A Chorus of Disapproval – Alan Ayckbourn

An Evening with Gary Lineker – Arthur Smith and Chris England

The Full Monty – Simon Beaufoy

Hapgood – Tom Stoppard

Love Valour Compassion – Terrence McNally

Rent Rock – update of *La Boheme* by Jonathan Larson

Three Tall Women – E Albee

Way Upstream – Alan Ayckbourn

Business and farming

Western economy boomed; income climbed by over 20%. Old industries died; new technologies flourished. As the Berlin Wall fell, the USSR opened up to private enterprise and eastern bloc countries sought liberation. Everywhere, the divide between rich and poor grew. Unemployment rose to levels unknown since the 1930s. In the UK, Thatcherism promoted privatization and consumerism. Hostile takeovers and mega-mergers spawned new billionaires, like USA's Donald Trump. Discount air fares increased independent foreign travel and flights across the Atlantic were cheaper. Farming was hit by BSE and Foot and Mouth Disease; combine harvesters became the norm.

Fashion

The 80s look was tailored with wide shoulders. Power dressing for women meant jackets, shoulder pads, and masculine style suits. Princess Di (UK) and Joan Collins and Nancy Reagan (US) became fashion icons. Clothes were decorated with beadwork and costume jewellery.

The 80s saw the shimmery shift dress in vivid fuchsia pinks and royal blues, batwing sleeves, cowl collars in knitwear, track suits, sneakers and legwarmers, the all in one body (the teddy) and French knickers. 1980s hairstyles involved masses of mousse and gel. Tanning salons thrived. In the 90s, as working from home became common, so did casual gear and comfort dressing.

Entertainment and toys

The 80s was the last great decade for the pop single. Live performances, such as Live Aid, took place before huge audiences in sports stadiums. Pop artists included Adam Ant, George Michael and Madonna. Rap arrived in the late 80s and 90s. Meanwhile, the compact disc (CD) revolutionized the music industry, and camcorders arrived.

Television's *Dynasty* and *Dallas* had a huge following. Children's programmes included the *Moomins, Jigsaw,* the *Flumps* and *Rainbow*. Talkshows proliferated, cable and satellite television were born. Movies included *Tootsie, E. T., Beverly Hills Cop, Out of Africa, Back to the Future, Good Morning Vietnam, Fatal Attraction* and *The Terminator*. Sell-out musicals included *Cats, Starlight Express, The Phantom of the Opera* and *Les Miserables*. Bestselling books included the launch of the Harry

Backdrop to the 1980s and 1990s

Potter series and titles by Stephen King and Danielle Steele.

Windsurfing and sail boarding became popular sports. Now video and computer games competed with Rubik's cubes. Collectibles were big news and included E.T. items, Cabbage Patch dolls, Barbies (now also Hispanic, Black or Asian) and Beanie Babies. Bouncy castles appeared at parties and fetes.

Family life and women's roles

The size of the average household dropped and more people lived alone for longer. Couples now often lived together, whether formally married or not and had fewer children later in life. Divorce, separation and single-parent families increased. Most women now worked full-time, even those with young children. The two-earner family was more common as more women gained degrees and powerful positions in business and politics – with a PM in the UK and a presidential candidate in the US.

Homes, food and furniture

Convenience, frozen or chilled foods and nouvelle cuisine became popular, as did pasta. McDonald's and pizza parlours spread while fast-food outlets provided sandwiches (with prawn mayonnaise the bestseller), pies and pasties.

Fitted kitchens now had microwaves, built-in ovens and hobs, plus white goods hidden behind cupboard doors. Homes often had an office or studio. Antiques were popular and the three-piece suite was replaced by mix-and-match sofas, chairs and corner seating. Polished wooden floors, wicker storage boxes, scatter rugs and futons gained momentum – as did low-voltage dimming lights

and fixtures on rails or uprights. Garden barbecues were popular.

Health and crime

AIDS was suddenly a huge threat as vast numbers died in Africa and many gays and drug users lived under the HIV 'timebomb'. Drug addiction increased crime and prisons overflowed as violent crimes increased. Crack arrived in 1985 and by 1990, cocaine addiction rose. Despite all this, people now lived longer: life expectancy was about 69.9 for men and 77.6 for women. There was a huge focus on health, diet and exercise with aerobics, health clubs and fitness equipment.

Shopping and auctions

Small supermarkets were replaced by out-of-town chain stores, superstores and shopping malls. IKEA offered a huge choice of home and office furniture. In 1980, plastic milk bottles appeared. Credit cards became a way of life. Labels became important for the young. Meanwhile, auctions of famous art works drew record prices as Van Gogh's *Irises* for $53.9 million.

Science and technology

Personal computers were now used in homes, offices, and schools. The Internet arrived in force towards the end of the millennium and was to have a huge impact. Major advances in genetics led to the 1988 funding of the Human Genome Project. Cloning became an issue and Viagra arrived.

Historic background

1980
Iraq-Iran War.

1982
War in Falkland Islands.

1984
AIDS recognised.

1986
Nuclear disaster at Chernobyl.

1986
Space shuttle *Challenger* explodes.

1987
Treaty ends Cold War. (Berlin Wall comes down in 1989)

1990
Yeltsin is Russian President.
Germany united.
Nelson Mandela freed.

1990-91
Gulf War.

1991
Hubble Telescope launched.
USSR's formal end.

1992
Civil war in former Yugoslavia.

1994
Channel tunnel opens.
Mandela President of Sth. Africa.
Civil War in Chechniya.

1996
Taliban capture Afghanistan.
TWA Flight 800 explodes.

1997
US *Pathfinder* lands on Mars.

1998
Northern Ireland peace.

1999
President Clinton impeached.
War in Kosovo
Floods in India.

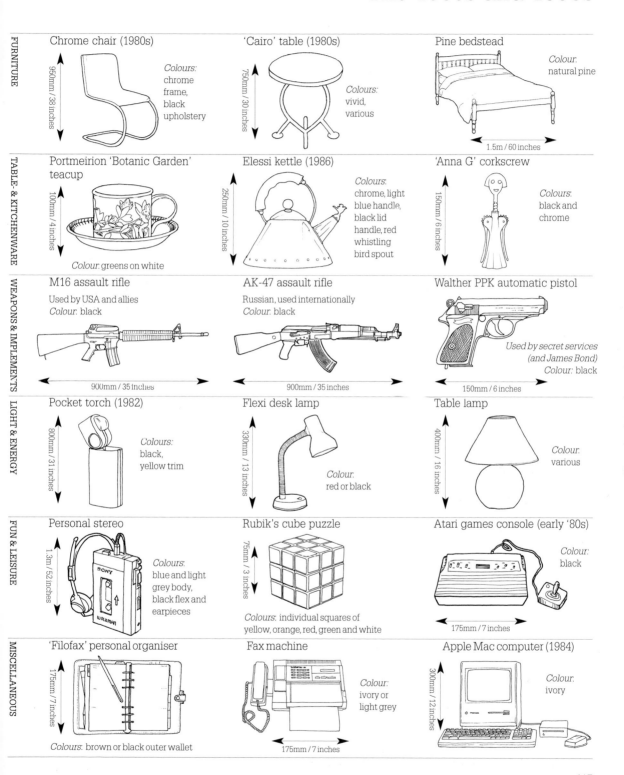

FURNITURE

Chrome chair (1980s)
950mm / 38 inches
Colours: chrome frame, black upholstery

'Cairo' table (1980s)
750mm / 30 inches
Colours: vivid, various

Pine bedstead
Colour: natural pine
1.5m / 60 inches

TABLE & KITCHENWARE

Portmeirion 'Botanic Garden' teacup
100mm / 4 inches
Colour: greens on white

Elessi kettle (1986)
250mm / 10 inches
Colours: chrome, light blue handle, black lid handle, red whistling bird spout

'Anna G' corkscrew
150mm / 6 inches
Colours: black and chrome

WEAPONS & IMPLEMENTS

M16 assault rifle
Used by USA and allies
Colour: black
900mm / 35 inches

AK-47 assault rifle
Russian, used internationally
Colour: black
900mm / 35 inches

Walther PPK automatic pistol
Used by secret services (and James Bond)
Colour: black
150mm / 6 inches

LIGHT & ENERGY

Pocket torch (1982)
800mm / 31 inches
Colours: black, yellow trim

Flexi desk lamp
330mm / 13 inches
Colour: red or black

Table lamp
400mm / 16 inches
Colour: various

FUN & LEISURE

Personal stereo
1.3m / 52 inches
Colours: blue and light grey body, black flex and earpieces

Rubik's cube puzzle
75mm / 3 inches
Colours: individual squares of yellow, orange, red, green and white

Atari games console (early '80s)
Colour: black
175mm / 7 inches

MISCELLANEOUS

'Filofax' personal organiser
175mm / 7 inches
Colours: brown or black outer wallet

Fax machine
Colour: ivory or light grey
175mm / 7 inches

Apple Mac computer (1984)
300mm / 12 inches
Colour: ivory

The 1980s and 1990s

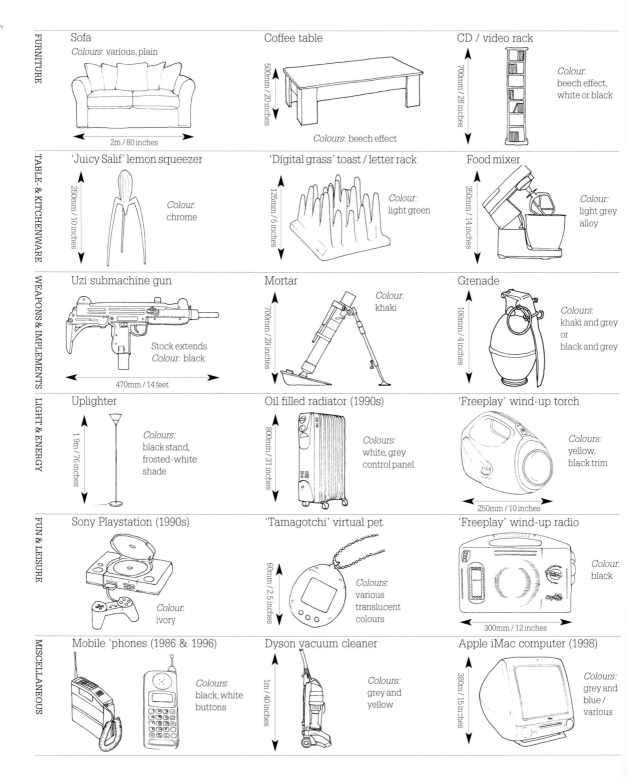

FURNITURE

Sofa
Colours: various, plain
2m / 80 inches

Coffee table
500mm / 20 inches
Colours: beech effect

CD / video rack
700mm / 28 inches
Colour: beech effect, white or black

TABLE & KITCHENWARE

'Juicy Salif' lemon squeezer
250mm / 10 inches
Colour: chrome

'Digital grass' toast / letter rack
125mm / 5 inches
Colour: light green

Food mixer
350mm / 14 inches
Colour: light grey alloy

WEAPONS & IMPLEMENTS

Uzi submachine gun
Stock extends
Colour: black
470mm / 14 feet

Mortar
700mm / 28 inches
Colour: khaki

Grenade
100mm / 4 inches
Colours: khaki and grey or black and grey

LIGHT & ENERGY

Uplighter
1.9m / 76 inches
Colours: black stand, frosted-white shade

Oil filled radiator (1990s)
800mm / 31 inches
Colours: white, grey control panel

'Freeplay' wind-up torch
Colours: yellow, black trim
250mm / 10 inches

FUN & LEISURE

Sony Playstation (1990s)
Colour: ivory

'Tamagotchi' virtual pet
60mm / 2.5 inches
Colours: various translucent colours

'Freeplay' wind-up radio
Colour: black
300mm / 12 inches

MISCELLANEOUS

Mobile 'phones (1986 & 1996)
Colours: black, white buttons

Dyson vacuum cleaner
1m / 40 inches
Colours: grey and yellow

Apple iMac computer (1998)
380m / 15 inches
Colours: grey and blue / various

Special types of plays

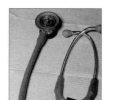

- Gardens
- Wild West
- Biblical
- Fairy tale and pantomime
- The Orient
- Institutions
- Shopping and offices
- Hotels, pubs and restaurants
- Farms and cottages
- Grand homes

This section of the book looks at special settings, rather than specific historical periods. Much will depend upon individual play directions and, in certain cases, may involve just a single scene or act, rather than an entire play. As with the first section of the book, the items selected can be only a representation of a much wider range of possibilities but should serve to focus ideas and provide a 'kick start' to finding the appropriate props.

Gardens

Gardens might be present-day or historic; they could be rambling cottage gardens, formal landscapes, a modern surburban backdrop or a fantastic garden such as in *Alice Through the Looking Glass*. Shakespeare depicted many gardens in his plays as well as wilder woodland settings. So the props will need to reflect this great variety and will range from fountains, birdbaths and urns to garden spades. A wide variety of seats and garden tables exist and it will be important to check the period and style of garden to ensure an appropriate choice of garden furniture. Plants in pots may be the responsibility of props or sets, but, in any case, the two departments must ensure close co-ordination.

Plays with scenes set in the garden or countryside

Alice Through the Looking Glass – adapted from Lewis Carroll by C Dane and R Addinsell

Brideshead Revisited – adapted from Evelyn Waugh by Roger Parsley

The Cherry Orchard – Chekhov

Fall – James Saunders

The Gazebo – Alec Coppel

The Importance of Being Earnest – Oscar Wilde

A Midsummer Night's Dream – William Shakespeare

Romeo and Juliet – William Shakespeare

Round and Round the Garden – Alan Ayckbourn

Lawnmower, early 1900s

Lawnmower, late 1900s

Wheelbarrow, early 20th century

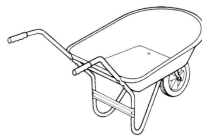
Wheelbarrow, late 20th century

Hose reel, early 20th century

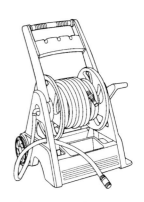
Hose reel, late 20th century

Traditional lawn shears

Motorised strimmer

Gardens

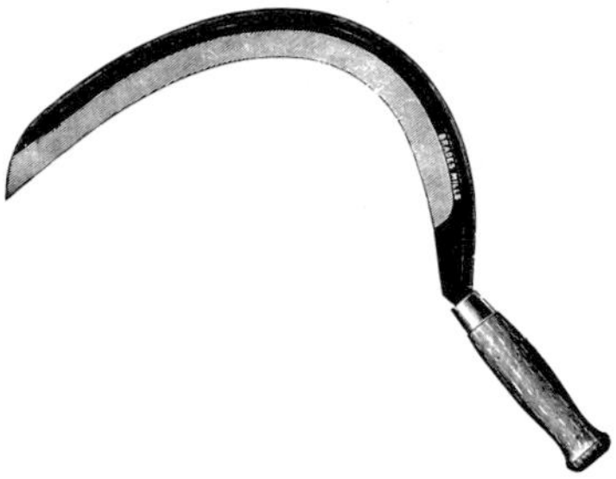

Reap hook

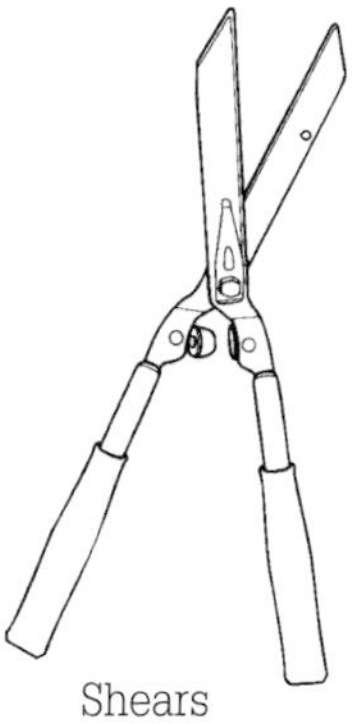

Shears

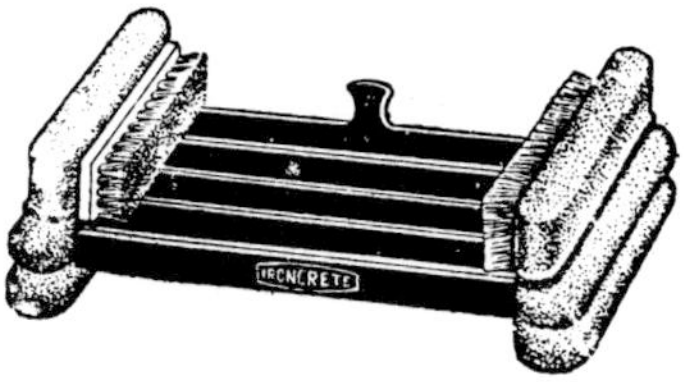

Boot scraper

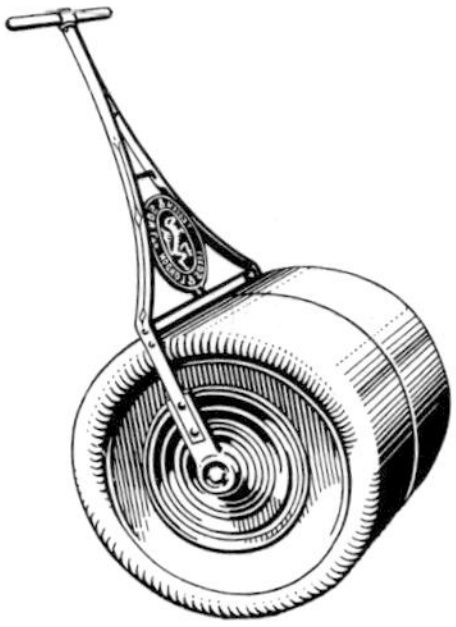

Roller

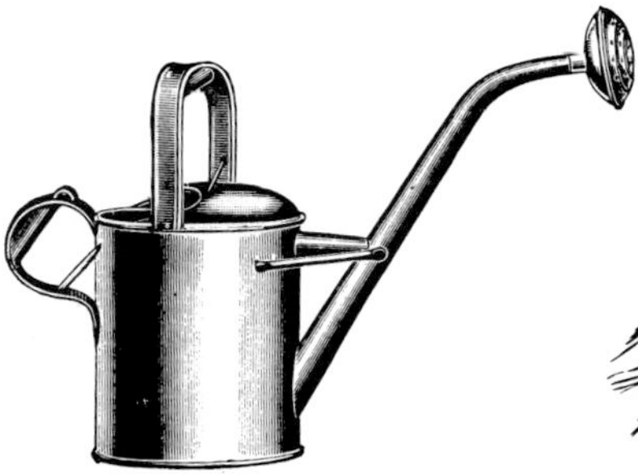

Watering can

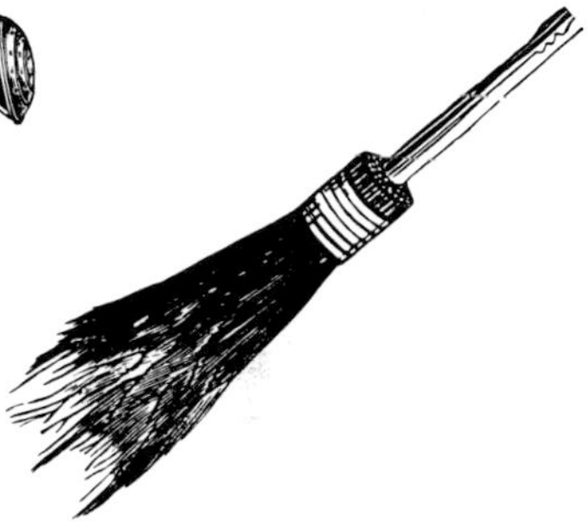

Birch broom

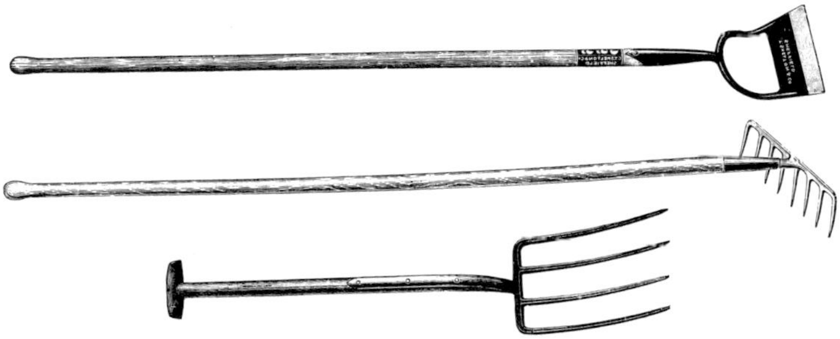

Dutch hoe, rake and digging fork

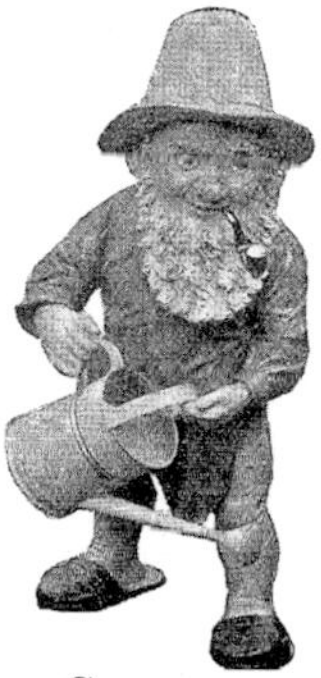

Gnome

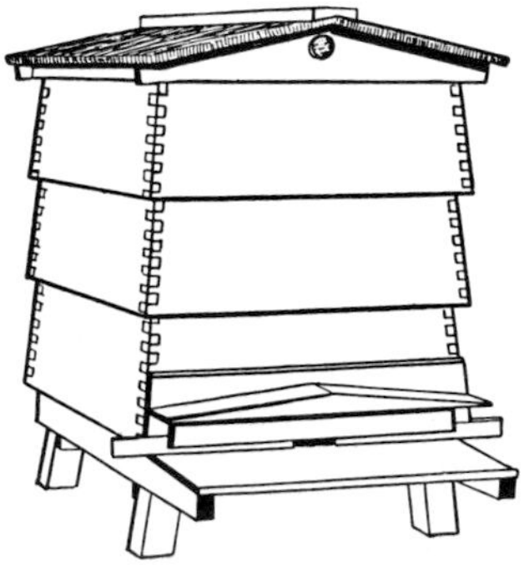

Bee hive

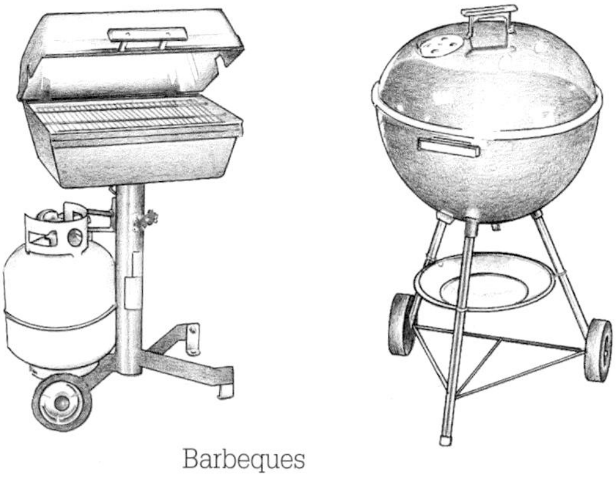

Barbeques

Gardens

Traditional wrought iron and pitch pine seat

Traditional teak seat

Traditional beech
and jute deck chair

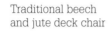

Papasan seating, 1980s

Rattan table and chairs, 1970s

Upholstered patio furniture

Timber patio furniture

Gardens: bird tables, seats, urns and statuary

Wild West

A wide variety of plays demand Wild West props, from weapons like Colt revolvers to bar items found in saloons and all the saddles and equine paraphernalia. The spectrum includes Native American settings too, so tomahawks, bows and arrows, totem poles and peace pipes may need to be investigated.

It is also worth a glance back at, say, the 1870-99 historical section, or whenever the play is set, to check out further possibilities.

Plays with Wild West settings:

Annie Get your Gun – musical by Irving Berlin and Herbert and Dorothy Fields

Calamity Jane – musical adapted for stage by Charles K Freeman, Sammy Fain and Paul Francis Webster

Hiawatha – Michael Bogdanov

Destry Rides Again – musical adapted from Max Brand by Harold Rome and Leonard Gershe

Oklahoma – Rodgers and Hammerstein

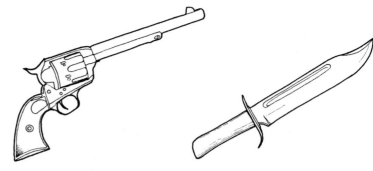

.45 Colt Peacemaker revolver

Bowie knife

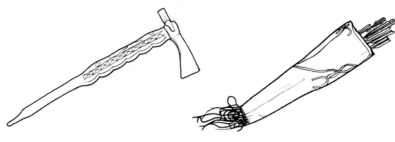

Tomahawk

Native American quiver

Native American knife

Native American bow

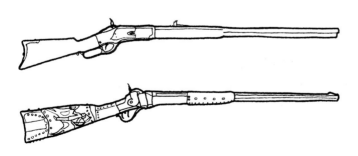

Winchester 1873 .44 rifle (top) and Native American rifle

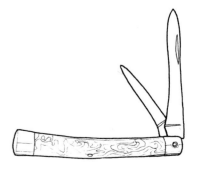

Penknife

Holster

Gattling gun

Spur

Badges

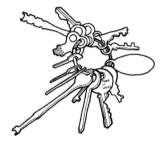

Sheriff's gaol keys

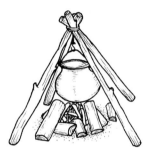

Campfire

Hunter's horn

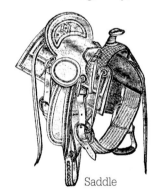

Saddle

Horse bit

Stirrup

Grooming brush

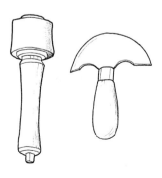

Saddlemaker's maul / crescent knife

Wild West

Sisal rope for cattle roping

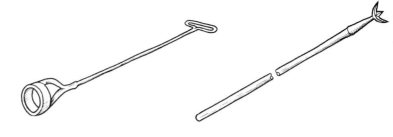

Branding iron

Gardian's trident

Birchbark canoe

Camulet

Rocking chair

Heavy canvas bedroll

Tobacco

Chuck box

Wooden pail

Coffee pot

Large cooking pot

Tin mug

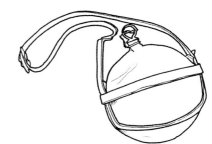

Water container

Skillet

Saloon whisky glass

Water barrel

Biblical

Biblical stories can be presented in many ways – from the child's nativity play to adult serious interpretation or medieval miracle plays. Whatever the approach, the Bible has ever been a rich source of drama and artistic interpretation – and has kept theatre alive during several periods when it was otherwise suppressed.

Plays with Biblical scenes or settings include:

Amahl and the Night Visitors – Opera by Gian Carlo Menotti

Boy with a Cart – Christopher Fry

Business of Good Government – Nativity play by John Arden Margaretta D'Arcy

Firstborn – Christopher Fry
(see also Ancient Egypt pages 8-14)

Godspell – John-Michael Tebelak and Stephen Schwartz

Jesus Christ Superstar – Andrew Lloyd Webber and Tim Rice

Joseph and his Amazing Technicolour Dreamcoat – Andrew Lloyd Webber and Tim Rice *(see also Ancient Egypt pages 8-14)*

Mysteries – Tony Harrison

Prelude – F E M Agnew

Second Easter – Norman Holland

Soldier and the Woman – Elaine Morgan

Son of Man – Dennis Potter

Victory of the Cross – passion play by M Creagh-Henry

Biblical dates (approximate)

2000-1750 BC Middle Bronze Age.

1800 BC Abraham and Patriarchs.

1440 or **1290 BC** Exodus: Moses and Joshua.

200-1150 BC Iron Age begins.

1050 BC Israelite monarchy begins: Samuel, Saul.

1000 BC David, Nathan.

922 BC Division of the Kingdom: Rehoboam, Jeroboam I.

850 BC Ahab and Jezebel; Elijah and Elisha.

750 BC Rise of Assyria: Amos, Hosea, Jeroboam II.

721 BC Fall of Samaria, end of Northern Kingdom: Ahaz, Isaiah.

701 BC Assyrian invasion of Judah, deliverance from Sennacherib: Hezekiah, Isaiah, Micah.

621 BC Josiah's reforms

605 BC Rise of Babylonian empire: Jeremiah, Habakkuk.

598 BC Israelites deported to Babylon: Jeremiah, Ezekiel.

586 BC Jerusalem destroyed; deportation and exile: Jeremiah, Ezekiel.

586-332 BC Babylonian and Persian Periods.

538 BC Overthrow of Babylonian Empire by Persians; return from exile: Cyrus.

520 BC Jerusalem temple rebuilt: Haggai, Zechariah, Zerubbabel.

450 BC Reforms of Ezra; Judaism begins: Nehemiah, Malachi.

332-152 BC Hellenistic Period.

323 BC Alexander the Great dies: Seleucids, Ptolomies.

167 BC Maccabean Revolt; Judas Macabbee, Book of Daniel.

63 BC Roman control of Palestine under the Pompey.

37 BC-324 AD Roman Period.

5-3 BC Herod the Great: Jesus born.

27-30 BC Death and resurrection of Jesus.

33-60 BC Ministry of Paul.

45 BC Council of Jerusalem: Christianity breaks from Judaism.

50 BC First New Testament writings: 1 and 2 Thessalonians, Paul, Barnabus, Silas.

60-70 BC First Gospel written by Mark; death of Paul.

70 BC Destruction of Jerusalem by Roman general, Titus.

90 BC Last New Testament writings: Gospel of John, Johannine literature.

135 BC Last Jewish revolt against Rome; Jews expelled from Palestine.

Patriarchal goblet

Pottery yoghurt maker, Patriarch period

Patriarchal gold chalice

Caananite stool

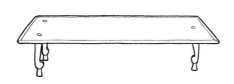

Caananite low wooden table

Small table stand

Small pottery dipper, bronze age

Canaanite pottery goblet

Bronze wine filter

Bronze battle axe, 3rd Millennium BC

Late bronze dagger

Canaanite pottery jug, early bronze age

Biblical

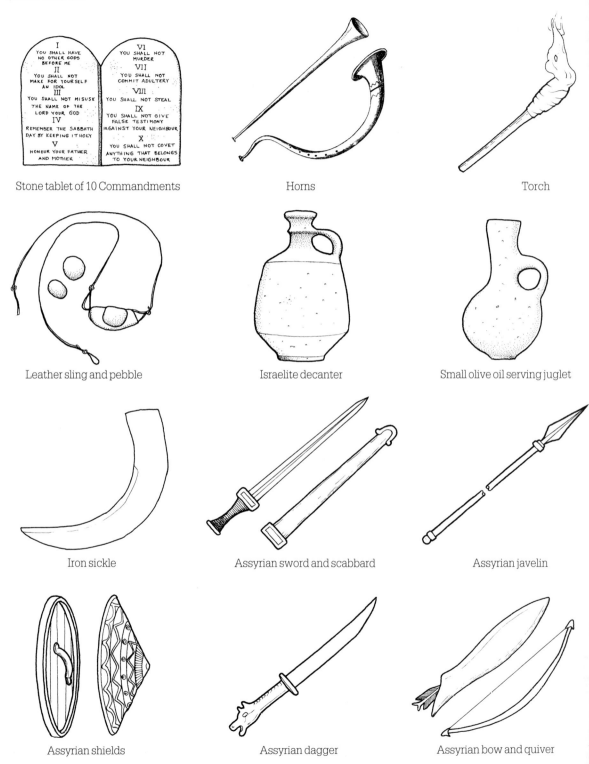

Stone tablet of 10 Commandments

I YOU SHALL HAVE NO OTHER GODS BEFORE ME
II YOU SHALL NOT MAKE FOR YOURSELF AN IDOL
III YOU SHALL NOT MISUSE THE NAME OF THE LORD YOUR GOD
IV REMEMBER THE SABBATH DAY BY KEEPING IT HOLY
V HONOUR YOUR FATHER AND MOTHER
VI YOU SHALL NOT MURDER
VII YOU SHALL NOT COMMIT ADULTERY
VIII YOU SHALL NOT STEAL
IX YOU SHALL NOT GIVE FALSE TESTIMONY AGAINST YOUR NEIGHBOUR
X YOU SHALL NOT COVET ANYTHING THAT BELONGS TO YOUR NEIGHBOUR

Horns

Torch

Leather sling and pebble

Israelite decanter

Small olive oil serving juglet

Iron sickle

Assyrian sword and scabbard

Assyrian javelin

Assyrian shields

Assyrian dagger

Assyrian bow and quiver

Menorah

Torah

Ark

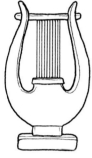

Harp

Bronze lamp, 6th century

Ivory comb

Shepherd's crook

Manger crib

Gold, Frankincense and Myrrh

Bread loaves

Bronze altar, Roman period

Stone burial box, Roman period

Fairy tale and pantomine

These shows for children provide a glorious opportunity for imaginative props and escapism. In particular, pantomimes are an excuse for bold humour and large-scale props.

Fairy tales, pantomimes and other plays for children include:

Aladdin – numerous versions

Beauty and the Beast – several versions, including the Walt Disney musical

Cinderella – numerous versions

Dick Whittington – numerous versions

Goldilocks – numerous versions

Grimm Tales – adapted from the Brothers Grimm by Carol Ann Duffy and Tim Supple

Jack and the Beanstalk – numerous versions

The Lion, the Witch and the Wardrobe – adapted from C S Lewis by Glyn Robbins

Little Red Riding Hood – numerous versions

Peter and the Wolf – adapted from Prokofiev's musical story: several versions

Pied Piper – numerous versions

Puss in Boots – numerous versions

Sleeping Beauty – numerous versions

Snow Queen – adapted from Hans Christian Andersen by Ron Nicol

Snow White and the Seven Dwarfs – numerous versions

Toad of Toad Hall – adapted from Kenneth Grahame's *Wind in the Willows* by A A Milne and H Fraser-Simson

Wizard of Oz – several versions adapted from L Frank Baum

The Water Babies – adapted from Charles Kingsley by Willis Hall and John Cooper

Cartoon-style well

Wand

Flute

Cartoon-style tea set

Aladdin's lamp

Magic mirror

Mirror

Fairy tale and pantomime

Cartoon-style rustic bed *(Snow White)*

Victorian bed *(Red Riding Hood)*

Canopy bed *(Sleeping Beauty, Frog Prince)*

Covered wicker basket

Spinning wheel

Pumpkin

Bucket

Broom

Clock

Laundry

Axe

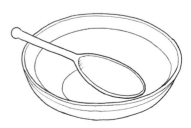

Wooden bowl and spoon

Fairy tale and pantomime

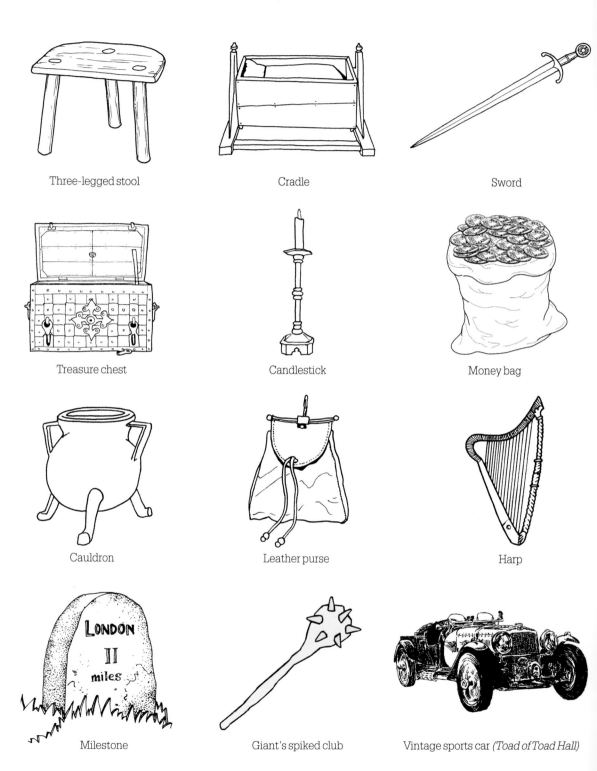

Three-legged stool

Cradle

Sword

Treasure chest

Candlestick

Money bag

Cauldron

Leather purse

Harp

Milestone

Giant's spiked club

Vintage sports car *(Toad of Toad Hall)*

THE ORIENT AND FAR EAST

A good number of plays set in the Orient are pure escapism, for the magical East has inspired many a fairy tale and romantic story; often the geographical and national barriers become blurred. Some musicals require a more accurate vision of these far climes while war dramas and the like will certainly need some greater definition.

Adding Chinese brushwork or Oriental script to an item with appropriate contours, such as a bowl or vase, will help to indicate an oriental origin.

Plays with an Oriental or Eastern setting include:

Aladdin – numerous versions

Chu Chin Chow – musical by Oscar Asche and Frederick Norton

Flower Drum Song – musical by Rodgers and Hammerstein

The Imperial Nightingale – Nicholas Stuart Gray

The King and I – musical by Rodgers and Hammerstein

M. Butterfly – David Henry Hwang

Madame Butterfly – opera by Puccini

Made in Bangkok – Anthony Minghella

Miss Saigon – musical by Alain Boublil, C M Schonberg & R Mally Jnr.

15th-century Ming vase

16th-century Ming bowl

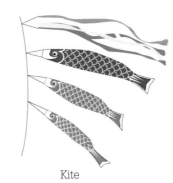

Rice bowl

Lantern

Kite

Kite

Lamp

Sake bottles

The Orient

Wok

Chopsticks

Dinner

Chinese for the four seasons: spring, summer, autumn and winter

Spinning top

Dolls

Instrument

Masks

Writing set

Gong

INSTITUTIONS

Religious settings (that include churches, monasteries, abbeys and convents), schools and hospitals are all 'institutions' but are very different settings that will need props that vary greatly according to the historical period and particular focus of the chosen play. Those illustrated here can only be a brief selection of items but the specific historical sections in the earlier section of this book may also merit a perusal.

Plays with scenes set in religious institutions include:

Becket, or the Honour of God – John Anouilh

The Devils – adapted from Aldous Huxley by John Whiting

Mistress of Novices – John Kerr

Nunsense II: the Second Coming – Dan Goggin

Once a Catholic – Mary O'Malley

The Sound of Music – Rodgers and Hammerstein

Chalices

Bible and rosary

Open Bible and candle

Communion set

Elaborate cross

Covered altar

Font

Altar

Organ

Institutions

Plays with scenes set in hospitals include:

National Health – Peter Nichols

One Flew over the Cuckoo's Nest – adapted from K Kesey by Dale Wasserman

Whose Life is it Anyway? – Brian Clark

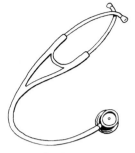

Stethoscope

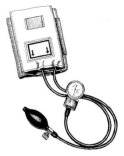

Blood pressure cuff

Thermometer

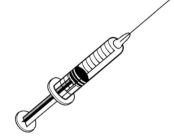

Syringe

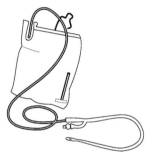

Urinary catheter and bag

Crutches

Walker

Wheelchair

Hospital bed

Bed pan

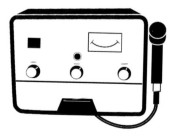

Ultrasound machine

Plays with scenes set in schools and colleges include:

The Browning Version – Terence Ratigan

Class Enemy – Nigel Williams

Daisy Pulls It Off – Denise Deegan

Forty Years On – Alan Bennett

The Happiest Days of Your Life – John Dighton

The Prime of Miss Jean Brodie – Jay Presson Allen

Shadowlands – William Nicholson

The Student Prince – Sigmund Romberg and Dorothy Donnelly

Desk

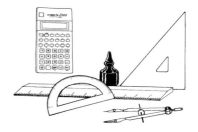

Desk equipment

Quill and ink pot

Diploma

Mortar board

Blackboard

Globe

Stop-watch

Pommel horse

Lacrosse crosse and tennis racket

Shopping and offices

These are all usually very busy sets that require a good number of props, whether books, fruit or antiques, to establish the venue. The degree of detail required will depend, of course, on whether the set is for the play's duration, an act, or just a scene – and as to whether the props are essential elements of the plot or simply to establish location and period.

Plays with scenes set in shops, markets or offices include:

84, Charing Cross Road – adapted from Helene Hanff by James Roose-Evans (set in a bookshop)

American Buffalo – David Mamey (set in a Chicago junk shop)

Half a Sixpence – adapted from H.G. Wells' *Kipps* by B Cross and D Heneker (begins in a drapers' shop)

Hobson's Choice – Harold Brighouse (set in a boot shop)

Imaginary Lines – Reggie Oliver (a flat and a bookshop)

Man Alive – John Dighton (window dressing and wax dummies)

My Fair Lady – adapted from Bernard Shaw's *Pygmalion* by Lerner and Loewe (scenes in Covent Garden market)

The Office Party – John Godber

Office Suite – Alan Bennett

Staircase – Charles Dyer (set in a barber's shop)

Sweeney Todd – many versions (some scenes set in a barber's shop)

Cash register, late 1800s

Cash register, late 1900s

Weighing scales, mid 1900s

Traditional sack of rice

Tinned goods, early 1900s

Sweets candies container

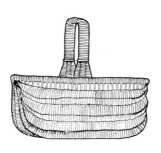

Wicker shopping basket

Shopping trolley

Telephones, 1920s & 1930s

Telephones, 1960s & 1970s

Typewriters, early and late 1900s

Desk, late 1800s

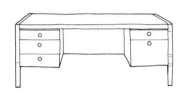

Desk, late 1900s

Drawing board

Chair

Filing cabinet

Anglepoise desk lamp

Stack of paper

Adding machine, 1970s

Computer, 1990s

Hotels, pubs and restaurants

These are places to eat, drink and sleep, public places rather than homes and, in most cases, the props will be less personal than they would be in a home setting. A busy restaurant will require altogether different elements from a quiet hotel bedroom and some props, such as luggage, will need to reflect the personal choices of the characters.

Plays with scenes in:

Hotels

Hotel Paradiso – Georges Feydeau and Maurice Desvallieres

Bedfull of Foreigners – Dave Freeman

Fish out of Water – Derek Benfield

Plaza Suite – Neil Simon

The Hotel in Amsterdam – J Osborne

Private Lives – Noël Coward

Waters of the Moon – N C Hunter

Pubs, inns and bars

Oliver – musical, adapted from Charles Dickens by Lionel Bart, David Merrick and Donald Albery

The Student Prince – Sigmund Romberg and Dorothy Donnelly

Restaurants and cafés:

Between Mouthfuls (from *Confusions*) – Alan Ayckbourn

The Café – James Saunders

Café Society – Ayshe Raif

Luggage trolley

Luggage

Champagne in ice bucket

Coffee maker

Billiard table

Cocktail glasses

Soda syphon

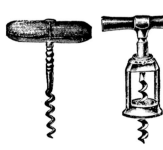

Corkscrews

Barrel

Traditional tankards

Beers

Whisky

Jukebox

Slot machine

Darts

Wine glass

Glass decanter

Silver dish cover

Traditional fiddle-pattern cutlery

Plain modern cutlery

Farms and cottages

These more humble country homes feature in numerous plays, set in every period from medieval times, and the props will generally be a many-faceted mix of styles and periods. Farm settings may involve some specific pieces of farm equipment or tools, and cottage contents will depend on whether this is a simple peasant's abode or a present-day country retreat.

Plays with scenes in farms and cottages include:

Adam Bede – adapted from George Eliot by Geoffrey Beevers

Animal Farm – adapted from George Orwell by Nelson Bond (or Peter Hall)

The Camel's Back – Arnold Helsby

Cider with Rosie – adapted from Laurie Lee by James Roose-Evans

Cold Comfort Farm – adapted from Stella Gibbons by Paul Doust

The Darling Buds of May – H E Bates

Extremities – William Mastrosimone

Five Finger Exercise – Peter Shaffer

The Gypsy's Revenge – Michael Lambe

Larkrise – adapted from Flora Thompson by Keith Dewhurst

Robin Redbreast – John Bowen

Tess of the d'Urbervilles – adapted from Thomas Hardy by Michael Fry

Whistle Down the Wind – Andrew Lloyd Webber and Jim Steinman

Early comb-back Windsor chair

Later Windsor chair

Rocking chair

Settle

Stool

Bed

Barrel churn

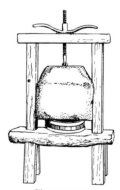

Cheese press

Farms and cottages

Plunger churn

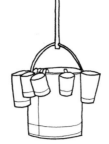

Dairy / milkmaid's pail

Wooden pail

Metal milk churn

Scotch hands (butter shaper)

Sheep shears

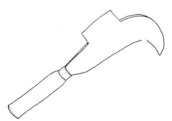

Bill hook

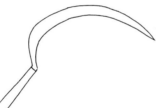

Scythe

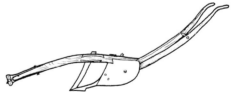

Horse-drawn plough

Shepherd's crook

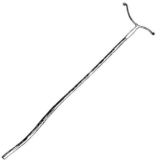

Sheep dipping paddle

Wooden hay rake

Farms and cottages

Grooming brush

Rushlight holder

Paraffin hurricane lamp

Victorian oil lamp

Candlestick

Inglenook cooking pot

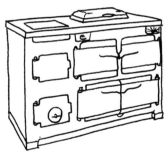

Mid-20th-century range cooker

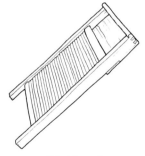

Washboard

Wicker basket

Rustic cutlery

Cornishware jug

Jug and ewer

GRAND HOMES

As with the Orient, the props for plays set in palaces, castles, stately homes and mansions may be escapist – or may need a more academic approach. This depends on whether the production is a serious slice of history, such as *Crown Matrimonial* or one with a less factual approach such as the *House of Dracula*.

In either case, these settings all have their place in history and the earlier sections of the book may be useful to refer to for prop specifics. Each individual play will make its own demands, of course, such as Yorick's skull in *Hamlet* – and safe swords for the fight scenes.

Plays with scenes in grand homes include:

Palaces

Balmoral – Michael Frayn

Camelot – Frederick Loewe and Alan Jay Lerner

Crown Matrimonial – Royce Ryton

The Madness of George III – Alan Bennett

A Man for All Seasons – Robert Bolt

Richard III (and many other histories) – William Shakespeare

Castles

Hamlet – William Shakespeare

House of Dracula – Martin Downing

House of Frankenstein – Martin Downing

The Lion in Winter – James Goldman

Stately homes and mansions

Anastasia – Marcelle Maurette

Arcadia – Tom Stoppard

Mansfield Park – adapted from Jane Austen by Willis Hall

Sleuth – Anthony Shaffer

A Tomb with a View – Norman Robbins

Medieval throne

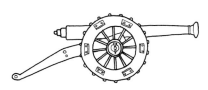

Cannon, 1500s

Crown

Candelabra

Heraldic banner

Knight's armour

Ornate chair, 1500s

Grand homes

Cradle

Four-poster bed, 1500s

Chair, 1600s

Chair, early 1700s

Settee, 1700s

Harpsichord

Drinking glasses, 1700s & 1800s

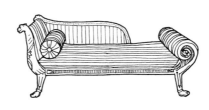

Grecian-style couch, early 1800s

Candelabrum, 1800s

Lady's fan, 1800s

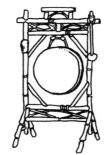

Dinner gong, early 1900s

Armchair, early 1900s

UK

A + M Hire Ltd
The Royals
Victoria Rd
London NW10 6ND
T 020 8233 1500
F 020 8233 1550
E mark@amhire.com

Albemarle of London
74 Mortimer Street
London W1N 7DF

Allprops
Unit 2 – 3
Acton Central Industrial
Estate
2a Rosemont Road
London W3 9LR
T 020 8993 1625
F 020 8993 7570

The Border Studio:
Riverside Mill
Level Crossing Road
Selkirk TD7 5EQ
T 01750 20237
F 01750 20313
E info@borderstudio.com

British Harlequin Plc
Bankside House
Vale Road
Tonbridge
Kent TN9 1SJ

Castle Gibson
106A Upper Street
London N1 1QN
T 020 7704 0927
F 020 7704 0927
E castlegibsonshop
@lineone.net

**China & Company
Props Hire**
2c Macfarlane Road
London W12 7JY
T 020 8740 9588
F 020 8740 8873
E p-anton@dircon.co.uk

Fab n Funky
18-20 Brunel Road
Acton
London W3 7XR
T 020 8746 7746
F 020 8743 2662
E inquiries
@fabnfunky.co.uk
W www.fabnfunky.co.uk

Farley
1-17 Brunel Road
London W3 7XR
T 020 8749 9925
F 020 8749 8372
E props@farley.co.uk
W www.farley.co.uk

H & R Hire
14 Wendell Road
London W12 9RT
T 020 8743 1452
F 020 8746 0018

Hip Props Ltd
Unit 5
98 Victoria Road
London NW10 6NB
T 020 8961 0070
F 020 8961 3375
E info@hipprops.com
W www.hipprops.com

Hopscotch
1-4 Bethune Road
London NW10 6NJ
T 020 8965 9909
F 020 8965 8107
E props@superhire.co.uk

Lacquer Chest
75 Kensington Church
Street
London W8 4BG
T 020 7938 2070
F 020 7376 0223

Men At Work
90-95 Waterside Centre
Trumpers Way
Hanwell
London W7 2QD
T 020 8574 6915
F 020 8571 6505
E enquiries
@menatwork.co.uk
W www.menatwork.co.uk

Motion Picture Props
18A Redlands Court
London Road
River, Near Dover
Kent CT17 0TW
T 01304 824 477
E enquiries@
motion-pictureprops.com
W www.motion-
picture-props.com

**Newman Hire
Company Ltd**
16 The Vale
Acton
London W3 7SB
T 020 8743 0741- 5
F 020 8749 3513
E info@newman-
hire.co.uk

Old Times Furnishing
Unit 1
Powergate
Volt Avenue
London NW10 6PW
T 020 8961 1452
F 020 8961 1462
E inquiries
@oldtimesuk.com

**Period Props and
Lighting**
17-23 Stirling Road
London W3 8DJ
T 020 8992 6901
F 020 8993 4637
E pplprops@supanet.com
W www.periodprops
andlighting.co.uk

**Picture Props
Company Ltd**
Brunel House
12 - 16 Brunel Road
London W3 7XR
T 020 8749 2433
F 020 8740 5846

Printed Word, The
1-3 Telford Way
London W3 7XR
T 020 8740 8804
F 020 8740 1253
E printedword
@dsl.pipex.com

Props Galore
15-17 Brunel Road
London W3 7XR
T 020 8746 1222
F 020 8354 1866

Scene Two Hire
18 - 20 Brunel Road
London W3 7XR
T 020 8740 5544
F 020 8743 2662
E inquiries
@scene2hire.co.uk
W www.scene2hire.co.uk

Set Pieces
Unit 1
Powergate
Volt Avenue
London NW10 6PW
T 020 8838 1100
F 020 8838 2200
E inquiries
@setpieces.com

Stuart Learmonth
Unit 24
Acton Park Industrial
Estate
The Vale
Acton
London W3 7PE
T 020 8749 3100
F 020 8749 3111

Superhire
1-4 Bethune Road
London NW10 6NJ
T 020 8965 9909
F 020 8965 8107
E props@superhire.co.uk
W www.superhire.co.uk

Tables Laid
Church Farm
Ashchurch
Gloucestershire GL20 8JU
T 01684 297 999
F 01684 291 201
E tableslaid@ision.co.uk
W www.tableslaid.co.uk

Talking Props
10 Mitre Way
London W10 6AU
T 020 8964 6699
F 020 8964 6698
E info@talkingprops.co.uk
W www.talkingprops.
co.uk

Theatre Props
8 Blenheim Crescent
Broughton Adtley
Leicestershire LE9 6QL

Theme Traders
The Stadium
Oaklands Road
Cricklewood
London NW2 6DL
T 020 8452 8518
F 020 8450 7322
E proproom
@themetraders.com
W www.
themetraders.com

Trevor Howsam
7 Bethune Road
London NW10 6NH
T 020 8838 6166
F 020 8838 6167

Vivelle Ltd
Victoria House
Croft Street
Widnes
Cheshire WA8 0NQ
T 0151 423 6273
F 0151 495 1438
E vivelle@globalnet.co.uk

USA

**Kuttner Prop
Rentals Inc**
601 W 26th St
Ste 330
New York 10001
T 212 242 7969
F 212 242 1293

**PDI-Props Displays
& Interiors**
132 W 18th St
6-7th Ave
New York 10011
T 212 620 3840
F 212 620 5472

Props for Today
330 W 34th St
12th Floor
8-9th Ave
New York 10001
T 212 244 9600
F 212 244 1053

Props NYC
Pier 40
2nd Floor South
New York 10014
T 212 352 0101
F 212 741 8552

Theatrical Props
562 Route 17M
Ste 8
Monroe
New York 10950
T 212 691 3359
F 845 783 9471

Periods and styles

	Style	Principal woods	British monarchs	British periods	French periods
1500	Gothic 1500-1620	Oak period to c.1700 but 1750 in the provinces		Tudor-Gothic	
1510					
1520					
1530					
1540					
1550					
1560			Elizabeth I 1558-1603	Elizabethan	Renaissance
1570					
1580					
1590					
1600			James I 1603-25	Jacobean	
1610					Louis XIII 1610-43
1620	Baroque c.1620-1700		Charles I 1625-49	Carolean	
1630					
1640					Louis XIV 1643-1715
1650			Commonwealth 1649-60	Cromwellian	
1660			Charles II 1660-85	Restoration	
1670					
1680					
1690	Rococo c.1695-1760	Walnut period c.1690-1735	James II 1685-88 / William & Mary 1688-94	William & Mary	
1700			William III 1694-1702	William III	
1710			Anne 1702-14	Queen Anne	Régence 1715-23
1720			George I 1714-27	Early Georgian	Louis XV 1723-74
1730			George II 1727-1760		
1740	Neo classical c.1755-1805	Early mahogany period c.1735-70 / Satinwood 1740-1800			
1750					
1760			George III 1760-1820	Georgian	
1770		Late mahogany period c.1770-1850			Louis XVI 1774-93
1780					
1790					Directoire 1793-99
1800	Empire c.1799-1815				Empire 1799-1815
1810	Regency c.1812-30	Rosewood 1810-50		Regency	Restauration 1815-30
1820			George IV 1820-30		Charles X 1820-30
1830	Eclectic c.1830-80		William IV 1830-37	William IV	Louis Philippe 1830-48
1840		Walnut 1840-60	Victoria 1837-1901	Victorian	
1850					2nd Empire 1852-70
1860					
1870					3rd Republic 1871-1940
1880	Arts & Crafts c.1880-1900	Rosewood 1880-1900 / Satinwood 1880-1920			
1890	Art Nouveau c.1890-1920				
1900			Edward VII 1901-10	Edwardian	
1910					
1920					

Periods and styles

German periods	Italian periods	Low countries	Spain/Portugal	USA periods	
Renaissance to c.1650	Cinquecento 1500-1600 High Renaissance 1500-1630	Renaissance	Renaissance		**1500**
					1510
					1520
					1530
					1540
			Plateresque		1550
	Baroque 1560-1700				1560
					1570
					1580
		Baroque			1590
				Early Colonial	**1600**
					1610
					1620
					1630
			Herrara		1640
Renaissance/ Baroque c.1650-1700					1650
					1660
			Chirriguera		1670
					1680
				William & Mary	1690
Baroque c.1700-30	Rococo			Dutch Colonial Queen Anne	**1700**
			Churrigueresque		1710
					1720
Rococo c.1730-60		Rococo			1730
					1740
Neo-classicism c.1750-1800	Venetian			American Chippendale	1750
					1760
					1770
					1780
	Empire			Early Federal 1790-1810	1790
Empire c.1800-15		Empire		American Directoire 1798-1804	**1800**
Biedermeier c.1815-48		Neo-Gothic	Fernandino 1814-33	American Empire 1804-15	1810
		Rococo revival		Later Federal 1810-30	1820
Revivale c.1830-80			Isabellino 1833-1870		1830
		Historical renaissance		Victorian	1840
					1850
					1860
					1870
Jugendstil c.1880-1920 and Biedermeier 1880-1920	Gusto Floreale				1880
		Art Nouveau		Art Nouveau c.1890-1920	1890
					1900
					1910
	Stile Liberty				1920

British rulers

Rulers of England

Saxons

Egbert	827-839
Ethelwulf	839-858
Ethelbald	858-860
Ethelbert	860-865
Elthelred I	865-871
Alfred the Great	871-899
Edward the Elder	899-924
Athelstan	924-939
Edmund	939-946
Edred	946-955
Edwy	955-959
Edgar	959-978
Edward the Martyr	975-975
Ethelred the Unready	978-1016
Edmund Ironside	1016

Danes

Canute	1016-1035
Harold I Harefoot	1035-1040
Hardicanute	1040-1042

Saxons

Edward the Confessor	1042-1066
Harold I	1066

House of Normandy

William the Conqueror	1066-1087
William II	1087-1100
Henry I	1100-1135
Stephen	1135-1154

House of Plantagenet

Henry II	1154-1189
Richard I	1189-1199
John	1199-1216
Henry III	1216-1272
Edward I	1272-1307
Edward II	1307-1327
Edward III	1327-1377
Richard II	1377-1399

House of Lancaster

Henry IV	1399-1413
Henry V	1413-1422
Henry VI	1422-1461

House of York

Edward IV	1461-1483
Edward V	1483
Richard III	1483-1485

House of Tudor

Henry VII	1485-1509
Henry VIII	1509-1547
Edward VI	1547-1553
Mary I	1553-1558
Elizabeth I	1558-1603

Rulers of Scotland (to 1603)

Malcolm II	1005-1034
Duncan I	1034-1040
Macbeth	1040-1057
Malcolm II Canmore	1058-1094
Donald Bane	1093-1094
Duncan II	1094
Donald Bane (restored)	1094-1097
Edgar	1097-1107
Alexander I	1107-1124
David I	1124-1153
Malcolm IV	1153-1165
William the Lion	1165-1214
Alexander II	1214-1249
Alexander III	1249-1286
Margaret of Norway	1286-1290
Interregnum	1290-1292
John Balliol	1292-1296
Interregnum	1296-1306
Robert I (Bruce)	1306-1329
David II	1329-1371

House of Stuart

Robert II	1372-1390
Robert III	1390-1406
James I	1406-1437
James II	1437-1460
James III	1460-1488
James IV	1488-1513
James V	1513-1542
Mary	1542-1567
James VI	1567-1625

(Became James I of England in 1603)

Rulers of Wales (to 1282)

Wales was usually divided into separate
kingdoms or principalities. Five important
rulers ruled the whole (or most) of Wales:

Rhodri Mawr	820-878
Hywel Dda	890-950
Gruffudd ap Llywelyn	1007-1063
Llywelyn the Great	1173-1240
Llywelyn the Last	1246-1282

(defeated by English King Edward I, 1282)

Rulers of Britain

House of Stuart

James I	1603-1625
Charles I	1625-1649
Commonwealth	1649-1660

House of Stuart (Restored)

Charles II	1660-1685
James II	1685-1688
William III and Mary II	1689-1694
William III	1694-1702
Anne	1702-1714

House of Hanover

George I	1714-1727
George II	1727-1760
George III	1760-1820
George IV	1820-1830
William IV	1830-1837
Victoria	1837-1901

House of Saxe-Coburg

Edward VII	1901-1910

House of Windsor

George V	1910-1936
Edward VIII	1936
George VI	1936-1952
Elizabeth II	1952-____

Prime ministers and presidents

British Prime Ministers

Sir Robert Walpole	1721-1742
Earl of Wilmington	1742-1743
Henry Pelham	1743-1754
Duke of Newcastle	1754-1756
Duke of Devonshire	1756-1757
Duke of Newcastle	1757-1762
Earl of Bute	1762-1763
George Grenville	1763-1765
Marquess of Rockingham	1765-1766
Earl of Chatham	1766-1767
Duke of Grafton	1767-1770
Lord North	1770-1782
Marquess of Rockingham	1782
Earl of Shelburne	1782-1783
Duke of Portland	1783
William Pitt	1783-1801
Henry Addington	1801-1804
William Pitt	1804-1806
Lord Grenville	1806-1807
Duke of Portland	1807-1809
Spencer Perceval	1809 1812
Earl of Liverpool	1812-1827
George Canning	1827
Viscount Goderich	1827-1828
Duke of Wellington	1828-1830
Earl Grey	1830-1834
Viscount Melbourne	1834
Sir Robert Peel	1834-1835
Viscount Melbourne	1835-1841
Sir Robert Peel	1841-1846
Lord John Russell	1846-1852
Earl of Derby	1852
Earl of Aberdeen	1852-1855
Viscount Palmerston	1855-1858
Earl of Derby	1858-1859
Viscount Palmerston	1859-1865
Earl Russell	1865-1866
Earl of Derby	1866-1868
Benjamin Disraeli	1868
William Gladstone	1868-1874
Benjamin Disraeli	1874-1880
William Gladstone	1880-1885
Marquess of Salisbury	1885-1886
William Gladstone	1886
Marquess of Salisbury	1886-1892
William Gladstone	1892-1894
Earl of Roseby	1894-1895
Marquess of Salisbury	1895-1902
Arthur Balfour	1902-1905
Sir H Campbell-Bannerman	1905-1908
Herbert Asquith	1908-1916
David Lloyd-George	1916-1922
Andrew Bonar Law	1922-1923
Stanley Baldwin	1923-1924
J Ramsay MacDonald	1924
Stanley Baldwin	1924-1929
J Ramsay MacDonald	1929-1935
Stanley Baldwin	1935-1937
Neville Chamberlain	1937-1940
Winston Churchill	1940-1945
Clement Attlee	1945-1951
Sir Winston Churchill	1951-1955
Sir Anthony Eden	1955-1957
Harold Macmillan	1957-1963
Sir Alec Douglas-Home	1963-1964
Harold Wilson	1964-1970
Edward Heath	1970-1974
Harold Wilson	1974-1976
James Callaghan	1976-1979
Margaret Thatcher	1979-1990
John Major	1990-1997
Tony Blair	1997-____

American Presidents

George Washington	1789-1797
John Adams	1797-1801
Thomas Jefferson	1801-1809
James Madison	1809-1817
James Monroe	1817-1825
John Quincy Adams	1825-1829
Andrew Jackson	1829-1837
Martin van Buren	1837-1841
William H Harrison	1841
John Tyler	1841-1845
James K Polk	1845-1849
Zachary Taylor	1849-1850
Millard Fillmore	1850-1853
Franklin Pierce	1853-1857
James Buchanan	1857-1861
Abraham Lincoln	1861-1865
Andrew Johnson	1865-1869
Ulysses S Grant	1869-1877
Rutherford B Hayes	1877-1881
James A Garfield	1881
Chester A Arthur	1881-1885
Grover Cleveland	1885-1889
Benjamin Harrison	1889-1893
Grover Cleveland	1893-1897
William McKinley	1897-1901
Theodore Roosevelt	1901-1909
William H Taft	1909-1913
Woodrow Wilson	1913-1921
Warren G Harding	1921-1923
Calvin Coolridge	1923-1929
Herbert C Hoover	1929-1933
Franklin D Roosevelt	1933-1945
Harry S Truman	1945-1953
Dwight D Eisenhower	1953-1961
John F Kennedy	1961-1963
Lyndon B Johnson	1963-1969
Richard M Nixon	1969-1974
Gerald R Ford	1974-1977
Jimmy Carter	1977-1981
Ronald Reagan	1981-1989
George Bush (Snr)	1989-1993
Bill Clinton	1993-2001
George Bush (Jnr)	2001-____

Bibliography

Airne, C W
The Story of Prehistoric and Roman Britain Told in Pictures
Thomas Hope and Sankey Hudson Ltd

Andrews, John
Furniture
Antique Collectors' Club (UK) 1995

Atterbury, Paul
Victorians at Home and Abroad
V&A Publications (UK) 2001

Bender, Lionel
Eyewitness Guides: Inventions
Dorling Kindersley (UK) 1992

Bridgeman, Roger
Eyewitness Guides: Technology
Dorling Kindersley (UK) 1995

Byam, Michele
Eyewitness Guides: Arms and Armour
Dorling Kindersley (UK) 1988

Cole, Alison
Eyewitness Guides: Renaissance
Dorling Kindersley (UK) 1994

Coote, Roger
The Anglo Saxons
Wayland (UK) 1993

Davies, Gill
The Complete Stage Planning Kit
A & C Black UK 2003

Davies, Gill
Create Your Own Stage Effects
A & C Black (UK) 1999
Watson Guptill (USA) 1999

Davies, Gill
Create Your Own Stage Make-up
A & C Black (UK) 2001
Watson Guptill (USA) 2001

Davies, Gill
Create Your Own Stage Production
A & C Black (UK) 2000
Watson Guptill (USA) 2000

Davies, Gill
Staging a Pantomime
A & C Black (UK) 1995

Davies, Gill
Stage Source Book Sets
A & C Black (UK) 2004

De Castres, Elizabeth
The Observer's Book of Silver
Frederick Warne (UK) 1980

Feild, Rachael
Collectors Guide to Buying Antique Furniture
Greenwich Editions (UK) 1998

Foote, P G and Wilson, D M
The Viking Achievement
Sidgwick and Jackson (UK) 1970, 1979

Forman, Joan
The Romans
Macdonald Educational (UK) 1975

Fry, Plantagenet Somerset
History of the World
Dorling Kindersley (UK) 1994

Funcken, Liliane and Fred
Arms and Uniforms
Ward Lock (UK) 1972

Gardiner, Juliet
From the Bomb to the Beatles
Collins and Brown (UK) 1999

Govier, Jacquie
Create Your Own Stage Props
A & C Black (UK) 1984
Prentice Hall Inc. (USA) 1984

Govier, Jacquie and Davies, Gill
Create Your Own Stage Costumes
A & C Black (UK), 1996
Heinemann. (USA) 1996

Hammond, Tim
Eyewitness Guides: Sport
Dorling Kindersley (UK) 1988

Hart, George
Eyewitness Guides: Ancient Egypt
Dorling Kindersley (UK) 1990

Haywood, John
The Romans
Oxford University Press (UK) 1994, 2001 (US) 1996

Higgins, Katherine
Collecting the 1970s
Miller's (UK) 2001

James, Simon
Eyewitness Guides: Ancient Rome
Dorling Kindersley (UK) 1990

Jenkins, J Geraint
Life and Tradition in Rural Wales
J M Dent and Sons (UK) 1976

Langley, Andrew
Eyewitness Guides: Medieval Life
Dorling Kindersley (UK) 1996

Margeson, Susan
Eyewitness Guides: Viking
Dorling Kindersley (UK) 1994

Marsh, Madeleine
Collecting the 1960s
Miller's (UK) 1999

Massey, Anne
Interior Design of the 20th Century
Thomas and Hudson (UK) 2001

Matthews, Rupert
Eyewitness Guides: Explorer
Dorling Kindersley (UK) 1991

Murdoch, David
Eyewitness Guides: Cowboy
Dorling Kindersley (UK) 1993

Parsons, Martin
Air Raids: Britain at War
Wayland (UK) 1999

Payne, Christopher
Collecting Furniture
Miller's (UK) 1995

Payton, Mary and Geoffrey
The Observer's Book of Glass
Frederick Warne (UK) 1976

Payton, Mary and Geoffrey
The Observer's Book of Pottery and Porcelain
Frederick Warne (UK) 1973

Pearson, Anne
Eyewitness Guides: Ancient Greece
Dorling Kindersley (UK) 1992

Porter, Valerie
Life Behind the Cottage Door
Whittet Books (UK) 1992

Reid, William
Weapons Through the Ages
Peerage Books (UK) 1984

Sparke, Jenny
The Design Source Book
Macdonald (UK) 1986

Thomas, Terry
Create Your Own Stage Sets
A & C Black (UK) 1985
Prentice Hall Inc. (USA) 1985
Watson Guptill (USA) 1999

Tubb, Jonathan
Bible Lands
Dorling Kindersley (UK) 1991

Wood, Richard
Bedrooms Through the Ages
Wayland (UK) 1999

Wright, Michael (Editor)
Treasures in Your Home
Reader's Digest Association (UK) 1993

Twentieth Century Design series:

Jones, Helen
'40s and '50s: War and Post-War Years
Heinemann Library (UK) 1999

Bingham, Julia
'60s: The Plastic Age
Heinemann Library (UK) 1999

Gaff, Jackie
'70s and '80s: The High-Tech Age
Heinemann Library (UK) 1999

Gaff, Jackie
1900-1920: The Birth of Modernism
Heinemann Library (UK) 1999

Ford, Hannah
The '90s: The Digital Age
Hcinemann Library (UK) 1999

Index

84 Charing Cross Road 140

A

Abacus 19
Absurd Person Singular 110
Action man 106, 110
Adam Bede 68, 144
Adding machine 141
Admiral Chrichton, The 82
Adze 12, 34
Aftershave 112
Agnew, F E M 128
Aida 9
Aide-mémoirè 71
Airship 90
Aladdin 132, 135
Albee, Edward 105, 115
Alchemist, The 48
Alexandra 83
Alfie 105
Alice through the Looking Glass 120
All's Fair 95
Allice 96
Altar 131, 137
Amadeus 55
Amahl and the Night Visitors 128
American Buffalo 110, 140
Amin, Idi 111
Amphora 20
Amundsen 83
An Evening with Gary Lineker 115
An Inspector Calls 82
Anastasia 89, 147
And A Nightingale Sang 95
Anderson, Elizabeth Garrett 76
Andirons 60, 72
Angels in America 115
Anglo Saxon box 33
Animal farm 144
Animals, The 106
Ankh 11
Annie get your Gun 124
Anouilh, Jean 36, 100, 137
Anthony and Cleopatra 8, 22
Apartheid 90
Apollo 17, 111
Apple computers 112
Arcadia 95
Arden, John 128
Aristocrats 110

Aristophanies 16
Ark 131
Armchair 50, 64, 77, 78, 84, 85, 92, 97, 102, 112, 148
Armour 147
Arsenic and Old Lace 95
Art & design 76
Art & literature 110
Art and leisure 106
Art Deco 89
Art Nouveau 74, 76, 78, 79, 82
Art 76
Arts & Crafts 76, 77, 82
Asche, Oscar 135
Ashtray 93, 98
Atari console 112, 117
Atom bombs 98, 102
Atom 90
Auctions 116
Auschwitz 96
Axes 11, 31, 46, 129, 133
Ayckbourn, Alan 110, 115, 120, 142

B

Bacchae, The 16
Back to the Future 115
Backstaff 51
Badges 125
Bag, leather 33
Bakelite 89, 91, 95, 103
Balmoral 147
Banner 147
Barbeques 121
Barbie doll 106, 110
Barnard, Christian 106
Barnum 68
Baroque 82
Barrel 143
Barrie, J M 82
Bart, Lionel 100
Bartholomew Fair 48
Basket 12, 97, 102, 133, 140, 146
Bassey, Shirley 106
Bates, H E 100, 144
Bath 73, 75, 80, 86
Bathrooms 75
Bauhaus 89
Bayonets 57
Beach Boys, The 106
Beardley, Audrey 82
Beatles 105
Beaufoy, Simon 115

Beauty and the Beast 132
Beaux Stratagem, The 55
Becket 137
Bed pan 138
Bed waggon 73
Bedful of Foreigners 142
Bedroll 126
Bedroom farce 100
Beds 12, 25 30, 32, 39, 44, 51, 58, 72, 79, 85, 92, 98, 117, 133, 138, 144, 148
Bee Gees 111
Bee hive 121
Beer syphoning vessel 11
Beer 143
Beggar's opera, The 55
Bell 57, 76
Bellows 34
Bench 27
Benfield, Derek 142
Bennett, Alan 55, 100, 139, 140, 147
Bernstein, Leonard 100
Between Mouthfuls 142
Beverley Hills Cop 115
Beyond the Horizon 89
Bible and rosary 137
Biblical 119, 128, 29, 130, 131
Bicycle 80, 113
Bikini Atoll 96
Bill Haley and the Comets 101
Bill hook 73, 80, 145
Billiard table 142
Billy Liar 100
Birch broom 121
Biunial magic lantern 79
Black, Cilla 106
Blackboard 139
Bleasdale, Alan 110
Blithe Spirit 95
Blood pressure cuff 138
Blue Murder 105
Blue Remembered Hills 95
Boeing 90, 247
Boer war 76
Bogdanov, Michael 124
Bolt, Robert 82, 147
Bomb 97
Bookcase 73
Bookshelf 98
Bookstand 86, 87
Boone, Pat 101
Boot scraper 120
Booth, William 76
Bottles 25, 50, 51, 57, 72
Bottom's Dream 41
Bow 33, 124, 30
Bowen, John 144

Bowie knife 124
Bowie, David 111
Bowl and spoon 46, 53, 133
Bowls 14, 31, 135
Boy with a Cart 29, 128
Boyfriend, The 89
Branding iron 126
Brazier 19, 25
Bread 131
Breadbin 92
Brecht, Bertolt 22, 82, 95
Brenton, Howard 110
Brideshead Revisited 95, 120
Brighouse, Harold 140
Brinsley Sheridan, Richard 55
Britannicus 22
Broadway Bound 95
Broadway 89, 100
Broom 133
Browning Version, The 139
Brylcreem 103
Buckets 33, 57, 58, 66, 133
Burial box 131
Burrows, Abe 75
Business and farming 115
Business of Good Government 128
Bust bodice 83
Bustle 76

C

Cabaret 89
Cabinets 73, 79, 86
Caesar and Cleopatra 22
Café Society 142
Café, The 142
Calamity Jane 124
Calculator 113
Camel's back, The 144
Camelot 29, 147
Camera 72, 78, 85, 92, 93, 107
Camille 68
Campfire 45, 51, 59, 125
Camulet 126
Can Can 75
Candelabra 44, 147
Candelabrum 64, 70, 148
Candle holder 38, 43
Candlesticks 38, 43, 50, 57, 58, 64, 71, 77, 91, 134, 137
Cannon 144, 147
Cannonade 59, 65

Canoe 126
Car 134
Carpenter's drill bow 13
Carpenter's saw 13
Carpenters, The 111
Cased glass lustre 79
Cash register 140
Castro 101, 65
Cat Among the Pigeons 100
Catapult bolts 25
Cats 115
Caucasian Chalk Circle 95
Cauldron 33, 38, 46, 134
Cause Célèbre 89
Cezanne 76
Chairs 11, 14, 18, 24, 30, 38, 43, 50, 51, 57, 64, 70, 71, 78, 84, 91, 97, 98, 101, 103, 107, 108, 112, 113, 117, 141, 144, 147, 148
Chalice 38, 129, 137
Chamber pot 39
Chambers, John 29
Champagne 142
Charleston 88
Charley's Aunt 75
Cheese press 144, 120
Cherry Orchard, The 75, 120
Chess set 79
Chests 34, 45, 46, 53, 58, 59
Children & toys 110
Chiltern Hundreds, The 95
Chinese lettering 136
Chisels 13, 26
Chodorov 75
Chloroform inhaler 77
Chopsticks 136
Chorus Line, A 110
Chorus of Disapproval, A 115
Christie, Agatha 9, 89
Christmas Carol, A 68
Chu Chin Chow 135
Chuck box 126
Churn 144, 145
Cider with Rosie 44
Cigarette holder 93
Cinderella 132
City of Angels 95
Clark, Brian 138
Class Enemy 139
Claudel 75
Cliff, Claris 89
Clink, The 41
Clock 64, 91, 92, 107, 133
Closet 75

Index

Clothes press 60
Clothes 29, 63
Clothing and appearance 22, 29, 42
Club 134
Coal scuttle 73, 80, 92, 97
Cocktail cabinet 93
Cocktail unit 113
Coffee maker 142
Coffee pot 59, 78, 108, 126
Coffer 53
Coffins and tombs 9
Coins 18, 31
Coke bottle 85
Cold Comfort Farm 89, 144
Cold war 94, 104, 114
Collaborators 100
Colt peacemaker 77, 86, 124
Combs 13, 24, 34, 131
Common market 101, 106
Communion set 45, 137
Compass 44
Computer 141
Computer, Apple 112, 117
Computer, Apple iMac 118
Computer, Commodore 112
Concorde 106, 109
Congreve, William 55
Conran, Terence 106
Cooker 86, 92, 98, 146
Cooking pan 33
Cooking pot 34, 45, 51, 59, 66, 72, 126, 146
Cooper, Susie 89
Coppel, Alec 120
Coriolanus 22
Corkscrew 117, 142
Coronation 100
Corpse! 89
Corsets 83
Cosmetic 12, 14, 20
Cottages 119, 144, 145
Couch 19, 24, 65, 148
Count Dracula 75
Country Wife 48
Coward, Noel 89, 95, 142
Cracks 110
Cradle 1, 34, 39, 45, 148
Cranaquin 39
Crazy Gang 95
Creagh-Henry, M 28
Crescent knife, saddlemaker's 125
Crib 85
Crime and weapons 49

Crook 13, 46, 131, 145
Cross 137
Crosstaff 51
Crown Matrimonial 89, 147
Crown 46, 147
Crucible, The 48
Crutches 138
Cupboard 39, 46, 52
Cups and beakers 12, 18, 19, 24, 25, 32, 44, 71, 117
Cushion 108
Custer 76
Cutlass 52
Cutlery 58, 66, 107, 112, 143, 146
Cyrano de Bergerac 48

D

D'Arcy, Margarette 128
Dachau 90
Daggers 12, 19, 24, 39, 129
Daisy Pulls it Off 89, 139
Dallas 115
Dame of Sark, The 95
Dark Ages, The 28-33, 34
Darling Buds of May, The 100, 144
Darts 143
Date display 92
Daviot, Gordon 36
Day, Doris 101
Death of a Salesman 95
Death on the Nile 9
Decanter 57, 77, 85, 91, 130, 143
Decimilisation 110
Deck chair 122
Deegan, Denise 89, 139
Deep Blue Sea, The 100
Delaney, Shelagh 100
Design 76
Desk equipment 139
Desk 139, 141
Destry Rides Again 124
Desvallieres, M 82, 142
Devils 48
Devils, The 137
Diary of Anne Frank, The 95
Dick Whittington 132
Dickens, Charles 75
Digging fork 121
Dighton, John 95, 139, 140
Digital age 114
Dinky toys 106
Dinner parties 83

Dinner 136
Dior 96
Diploma 139
Dipper 129
Disc player 78
Discus 19
Dish cover 143
Dish 80
Dividers 27
DIY 96
Dolls 136
Donnelly, Dorothy 139, 142
Downing, Martin 147
Doyle, Sir Arthur Conan 75
Dr Finlay's Casebook 106
Dr Who 106
Drama 82
Drawing board 141
Dress and hygiene 17
Dresser 86
Dresser, The 95
Dressing table set 93
Dressing table 73, 91
Drinking vessels 31
Duchess of Malfi, The 48
Dutch hoe 121
Dyer, Charles 140
Dynasty 115

E

E.T. 115
Ear trumpet 73
Earhart 90
Earthquake 111
East Lynne 68
Eastman 76
Edison 76
Education Act 76
Education 22, 76
Edward VII 82, 83
Edward VIII 88, 90
Egypt 8-14, 90
Eiffel Tower 76
Einstein 83
Electric light bulbs 76
Electric lighting 75, 78, 82
Elizabeth II 99, 101, 109
Emancipation 81
Embalming/mummifying table 14
Empire State Building 90
Empire 82
Employment 76
Empress of India 76
England, Chris 115
Ensemble theatre 105

Entertainment and games 42
Entertainment and leisure 17, 23, 100
Entertainment and toys 115
Entertainment 48
Epsom downs 110
Euripedes 16
Everest 101
Everley Brothers, The 101
Ewer 51
Exorcist, The 111
Expressionist 82
Extremities 144

F

Fairy tale 119, 132, 133, 134
Faith, Adam 106
Fall 120
Family life 48, 116
Fan 64, 72, 148
Farming and food 30
Farms and cottages 119, 144, 145
Farquhar, George 55
Fascist 90
Fashion 76, 83, 96, 101, 105, 111, 115
Fatal Attraction 115
Fax machine 117
Ferdinand, Archduke 83
Festival of Britain 100
Festival theatre 75
Feydeau, George 82, 142
Figurine 87
Filing cabinet 141
Filofax 117
Fings Aint Wot They used T'be 100
Fire grate 34
Fire trivet 59
Fire 93, 98, 103
Fireiron 73, 80
Fireplace shovels 60
Fireplace tongs 60
First theatres 16
Firstborn 9
Fish out of Water 142
Five Finger Exercise 100, 144
Flare Path 95
Flask 26, 39, 51, 65
Flea in her Ear, A 82
Fleetwood Mac 111
Floor polisher 87, 92
Flower Drum Song 135
Flumps, the 115

Fly whisk 14
Fondue set 113
Font 137
Food 55, 76, 101, 110
Food and drink 9, 17, 22, 30, 49, 116, 149
Food and health 76
Food containers 11, 14
Food mixer 97, 102, 118
Foot rule 27
Football 77, 92
Footstool 102
Ford 83
Ford, John 48
Forks 52
Forrest 75
Forty Years On 139
Fountain 27
Franco, General 111
Frankincense 131
Frankenstein 62
Frayn, Michael 110, 147
Freedom of the City, The 110
Freeman, Dave 142
Front Page, The 89
Fry, Christopher 9, 16, 29, 36, 48, 128
Full Monty, The 115
Funny Thing Happened on the Way to the Forum, A 22

G

Gagarin, Yuri 106
Galsworthy 7,
Games 11, 24, 26, 31, 32, 34, 45, 46, 51, 58, 113, 117, 136
Gandhi 90
Gaol keys 125
Gardens 119, 120, 121, 122, 123
Gas heater 102
Gas lighting 75
Gas mask case 97
Gas masks 97
Gaslight 75
Gate, The 89
Gattling gun 71, 78, 125
Gay, John 55
George V 83
George VI 90, 96, 101
Gerry and the Pacemakers 106
Ghelderode, Michel de 100

Index

Gigi 82
Gilbert & Sullivan 75
Giraudoux, Jean 100
Gladius 24
Glaive 38
Glass Menagerie 95
Glass rummer 64
Glasses 51, 57, 91, 93, 126, 142, 143, 148
Globe 66, 139
Gnome 121
Goblet 70, 77, 129
Godber, John 110, 140
Godfather 111
Godspell 128
Goggin, Dan 137
Gogol 75
Gold 9, 131
Goldilocks 132
Goldman, James 36, 147
Goldsmith, Oliver 55
Gong 84, 136, 148
Good Morning Vietnam 115
Goodbye Iphigenia 16
Gordon, Peter 105
Götterdämmerung 29
Government Inspector, The 75
Gramophone 76, 82, 90, 91
Grand homes 119, 146-48
Grand opera 75
Grater 27
Gray, Simon 105
Grease 100, 111
Great Depression 88
Great Waltz, The 75
Greece 15-20
Greek ornament, ancient 20
Greenwood, Duncan 100
Grenade 86, 108, 113, 118
Gridiron 26, 33
Grimm Tales 132
Grooming brush 125, 146
Guillotine 60
Gun, 'tommy' 91
Guthrie, Tyrone 89
Gypsy's Revenge, The 144

H

Habitat 106
Hair dryer 103
Hair 105
Half a Sixpence 140
Hall, W 100
Hall, Willis 95

Hallstand 87
Hamilton, Patrick 75
Hamlet 147
Hammer 51
Hammerstein, Oscar 89, 95, 124, 135, 137
Christopher 55, 105
Hancock's Half Hour 106
Hand bell 57
Handbag 103, 108, 112
Handcuffs 51, 59
Hapgood 115
Happiest Days of Your Life, The 95, 139
Happy Families 110
Hardy, Thomas 75
Harp 11, 131, 134
Harpoon 14
Harpsichord 148
Harrison, Tony 128
Harwood, Ronald 95
Hauptmann 75
Hay Fever 89
Headrest 14
Health and medicine 56, 76
Health and crime 116
Hearth 39
Hecht, Ben 89
Hedda Gaber 75
Heinz 76
Heiress, The 68
Helmets 19, 20, 32, 33, 65, 72, 85, 98
Hendrix, Jimi 106
Henry VII 41
Henry VIII 41
Hiawatha 124
Hieroglyphic alphabet 14
Hilary, Sir Edmund 101
Hip flask 86
Hiroshima 94, 96
Hitler 90, 96
Hobson's Choice 140
Hockney, David 110
Holidays & leisure 111
Holland, Norman 128
Holster 70, 78, 125
Homes 10, 110, 116
Home, William Douglas 95, 100
Homecoming, The 105
Homelife 23, 62, 95
Homes 49, 56, 75, 89, 100, 116
Honour of God, The 137
Horn book 43
Horn 125, 130
Horse bit 125
Hose reel 120
Hot water bottle 73, 80
Hotel in Amsterdam 142

Hotel Paradiso 82, 142
Hotels 119, 142, 143
Hound of the Baskervilles, The 75
House of Dracula 147
House of Frankenstein 147
Houses 105
Hunter, N C 142
Hutch 45
Hwang, David Henry 135
Hygiene 17

I

Ibsen, Henrik 62, 75
Ice skate 33
Imaginary Lines 140
Imperial Nightingale 135
Importance of Being Earnest, The 7, 120
Impressionism 74
Incense burner 12, 20
Inglenook andirons 72
Inkpot 25, 43, 139
Inkstand 60
Inkwells 39
Institutions 119, 137, 138, 139
Inventions 76
Iolanthe 75
Iron curtain 96
Iron 80, 93
Irving, Sir Henry 75

J

Jack and the Beanstalk 132
Jack the Ripper 75, 76
Jane Eyre 68
Jar stand 13
Jars 19, 24, 45
Javelin 24, 130
Jaws 111
Jeffreys, Stephen 41, 48
Jekyll and Hyde 68
Jellicoe, Ann 105
Jesus Christ Superstar 128
Jewel box 70
Jewellery 10
Jigsaw 115
John, Elton 9, 111
Jones, Tom 106
Jonson, Ben 48
Joseph and His Amazing Technicolour Dreamcoat 9, 128
Journey's End 82

Jug & ewer 79, 85, 146
Juglet 130
Jugs 20, 33 38, 43 44, 45, 46, 64, 66, 70, 72, 79, 85, 92, 97, 103, 129, 146
Jukebox 143
Julius Caesar 22
Jumbo jets 111
Jumping weights 19
Juno and the Paycock 89

K

Kaleidoscope 71
Kander and Ebb 89
Keg 39, 45
Kennedy, J F 104
Kerr, John 137
Kesselring, Joseph 95
Kettle 66, 73, 80, 84, 107, 117
Keys 33
King and I, The 135
King Henry IV, First part of 36
King Henry IV, 2nd part of 36
King Henry VI, First part of 36
King Henry VI, 2nd part of 36
King Henry 36
King John 36
King Richard II 36
King Richard III 36
King, Martin Luther 104
King, Philip 95
Kingdom of Earth 105
King's seal 13
Kinks, The 106
Kite 135
Knack, The 105
Knife box 59
Knife, stone 124
Knives 12, 27, 34, 38, 44, 52
Knoll Colleoni 112
Kodak 76
Komisarjevski 88
Korean war 101
Korngold 75
Kramer v Kramer 111
Kylix 18

L

La Ronde 82
La Turista 105
Lacrosse crosse 139

Ladle 14, 34, 46
Lady Audley's Secret 68
Lady Chatterley's Lover 106
Lady's netting vice 73
Lady's Not for Burning 36
Laine, Frankie 101
Lambe, Michael 144
Lamp stands 25
Lamps 24, 31, 58, 65, 70, 75, 77, 78, 79, 84, 85, 91, 97, 102, 107, 108, 112, 113, 117, 131, 132, 135, 141, 146
Land army 95
Lantern 38, 43, 51, 70, 135
Lark Rise 75, 144
Lark 36
Larson, Jonathan 115
Lasers 106
Laundry 133
Laura Ashley 110
Lawn shears 120
Lawnmower 120
Lawrence, D H 106
Le Creuset 108
League of Nations 90, 96
Led Zeppelin 111
Lego 106, 110
Leigh, Mike 110
Leisure 9, 17, 23, 29, 82
Lemon squeezer 118
Lennon, John 111
Lerner, Jay 29, 36, 147
Les Liasons Dangereuses 55
Les Miserables 62, 115
Letter casket 43
Letter of Resignation 105
Letter rack 118
Letters 9
Levy, Benn W 16
Libertine, The 48
Library globe 66
Lillo, George 55
Lindbergh 90
Lindisfarne Gospels 32
Linnebach 82
Lion in Winter, The 36, 147
Lion, the Witch and the Wardrobe, The 132
Little Red Riding Hood 132
Living Doll 101
Livingstone, Jonathan 110
Lloyd Webber, Andrew 128, 144
Lock up Your Daughters 55

Index

Loewe, Frederick 29, 36, 147
London Merchant, The 55
London 76
Long and the Short and the Tall, The 95
Long March, The 90
Look Back in Anger 100
Lorna Doone 48
Lost in Yonkers 95
Love of the Nightingale 16
Love, Valour, Compassion 115
Lowboy 59
Luggage trolley 142
Luggage 142
Lulu 106
Lusitania 83
Luther 41
Lysistrata 16

M

M. Butterfly 135
MacArthur, Charles 89
MacEwan Green, George 16
Machine gun 79, 84, 97, 102
Mackintosh, Charles Rennie 76, 78, 80
Madame Butterfly 135
Made in Bangkok 135
Madness of George III 55, 147
Maeterlinck 75
Magic lantern 79
Magic Roundabout 111
Magimix 113
Magistrate, The 75
Magnifying glass 50
Man Alive 140
Man for All Seasons, A 41, 147
Manet 76
Manger 131
Mangle 87, 98, 103
Mannlicher rifle 77
Mansfield Park 62, 147
Map 87
Marley, Bob 111
Marney, David 140
Marriage 23, 82
Marshall Aid 96
Martino, Al 101
Mary Stuart 41
Masks 20, 26, 136
Massinger, Philip 22

Mastrosimone, William 144
Matchgirls, The 75
Mattock 25
Maughan, Somerset 89
Maul, saddlemaker's 125
Maurette, Marcelle 89
Maurier, Daphne du 100
McCarthy, Senator 101
McNally, Terrence 115
Measles vaccine 106
Meat chopper 79
Medea 16
Medicine jar 45
Medicine 49, 56, 69, 111
Menorah 131
Menotti, Gian Carlo 128
Microchip 101
Microphone 103
Microscope 65
Middle Ages, The 35, 36, 37, 38, 39
Midsummer's Night Dream, A 120
Mighella, Anthony 36
Milestone 134
Milk bottle 103
Millar, Ronald 36
Miller, Arthur 48, 95
Minghella, Anthony 135
Mirrors 11, 18, 24, 132
Misanthrope, The 48
Miss Saigon 110, 135
Mistress of Novices 137
Mitchell, Julian 36
Mobile telephone 118
Model T 83
Modernism 89
Moka express 102
Molière 48
Monet 76
Money and coins 106
Money bag 134
Month in the Country, A 68
Moomins 115
Moon, Gerald 89
Morecombe and Wise 106
Morgan, Elaine 128
Morning Star, The 95
Morris, William 76
Morse key 70
Mortar and pestle 25
Mortar board 39
Mortar 108, 113, 118
Mortimer, John 100
Mother, The 82
Mothercare 110
Motor car 76, 81
Mug 39, 65, 70, 71, 103, 126
Mummy case 11

Murder of Maria Marten 62
Music cabinet 87
Music hall 82
Music stand 80
Musical instruments 11, 12, 18, 19, 25, 31, 38, 39, 43, 44, 51, 59, 60, 64, 66, 73, 84, 92, 136, 137, 148
Musket 44, 57, 64
Mussolini 96
My Cousin Rachel 68
My Fair Lady 82, 140
Myrrh 131
Mysteries 128

N

Nagasaki 96
National Health 138
NATO 96
Naughton, Bill 105
Navigational dividers 44
Nazi 90, 96
Never Called me Mother 68
Nicholas II, Czar 83
Nichols, Peter 95, 105, 138
Nicholson, William 100, 139
Night of the Iguana 95
Nixon, President 111
Norman, Frank 100
North pole 83
Northanger Abbey 62
Norton, Frederick 135
Nunsense II: the Second Coming 137
Nuremburg trials 96
Nursery basin 79

O

O'Casey, Sean 89
Offices 119, 140, 141
O'Malley, Mary 100, 137
O'Neill, Eugene 75, 89
Oak press 46
Oedipus at Colonus 16
Oedipus the King 16
Office Party, The 140
Office Suite 140
Oil lamps 11, 18, 24, 31, 66, 70, 146
Oil-filled radiator 118
Oklahoma 124
Oliver Twist 75
Oliver 142

Oliver, Regie 140
Once Upon a Catholic 100, 137
One Flew Over the Cuckoo's Nest 138
Open fires 13, 19, 26, 33, 45, 59
Opera glasses 85, 93
Organ 137
Orient, The 82, 119, 135, 136
Ornament, 17th C. 53
Osborne, J 41, 142
Osment, Philip 105
Ottoman 90
Out of Africa 115
Ovens 12
Owen, Bill 75

P

Pacific flight 90
Paddle 145
Pail 53, 73, 80, 126, 145
Painter's brush 14
Papal crook 46
Papal crown 46
Papasan seating 122
Paper 141
Parallel ruler 59
Parasol 65, 72
Paris 76
Partition of Palestine 96
Pasteur, Louis 76
Paterae 27
Pathe, C 83
Patio furniture 122
Patriarchal 129
Pearl Harbour 96
Peary 83
Peer Gynt 62
Pen 43
Penknife 124
Penny farthing 80
Perambulator 79, 85
Percolator 84
Perestroika 115
Perfume and bottles 19, 86, 112
Peron 96
Perry Mason 106
Personal stereo 117
Peter and the Wolf 132
Phantom of the Opera, The 115
Pharoahs, Age of 8
Phoenix too Frequent, A 16
Phonographs 69, 84
Piano 84, 90
Pickwick Papers 62

Picture of Dorien Grey, The 75
Pied Piper 132
Pilum 24
Pinball machine 112, 68
Pink Floyd 106, 111
Pinter 75, 105
Pipe and tobacco 97, 103
Pipe 87
Pirandello, Luigi 100
Pistol 50, 51, 58, 64, 65, 85, 91, 107, 112, 117
Plate rack 86
Plates 43, 53, 58, 78, 112
Play script 46
Playstation 118
Plaza Suite 142
Plough 66, 73, 80, 145
Plumbob 27
Pogo stick 103
Polaroid 96
Poliakoff, Stephen 110
Police rattle 78
Police revolver 78
Police truncheon 79
Police whistle 78
Polio vaccine 101
Politics 83, 111
Pommel horse 139
Poole, Alan 41
Popular music 111
Porter, Cole 75
Portraits 100
Poseidon Adventure, The 111
Pot 26
Potter, Dennis 95, 110, 128
Potty 20
Pouffe 103
Poverty 69
Prelude 128
Presley, Elvis 101
Press, Flemish oak 46
Presson Allen, Jay 89, 139
Pride and Prejudice 62
Priestley, J B 82
Prime of Miss Jean Brodie, The 139
Private Lives 89, 142
Privates on Parade 95
Prohibition 88, 90
Proxinoscope 79
Pubs 119, 142, 143
Puccini 135
Pugio 24
Pumpkin 133
Purse 38, 134
Puss in Boots 132

Index

Q

Quant, Mary 105
Quartermaine's Terms
  105
Quern stone 31
Quill 39, 43, 139
Quiver 33, 124, 130

R

Racine 22
Radio Luxembourg 100
Radio 91, 97, 100, 102,
  107, 112, 118
Raif, Ayshe 142
Rainbow 115
Rake 46, 53, 121, 145
Range cooker 79, 86, 146
Rape of the Belt 16
Rattan furniture 122
Rattigan, Terence 82, 89,
  95, 100, 139
Rattle, 11, 71, 78, 98
Razor 12, 102
Reading glass 50
Real Thing, The 110
Realism 82
Reap hook 121
Rebecca 95
Record player 102
Recruiting Officer, The
  55
Refrigerator 87, 93, 98
Regency 63
Renoir 76
Rent rock 115
Rents 110
Restaurants 119, 142,
  143
Revolution 83, 90
Revolver 70, 78
Rhinegold, The 29
Rice, Tim 128
Richard III 147
Richard of Bordeaux 36
Richard, Cliff 101
Rifle 44, 50, 71, 77, 84, 85,
  86, 91, 107, 112, 117
Rimes, Leanne 9
Rivals, The 55
Roasting spit 13, 32, 34,
  44
Robbins, Jerome 100
Robbins, Norman 147
Robert and Elizabeth 68
Robin Hood 36
Robin Redbreast 144
Rock and roll 99, 100, 101
Rocket launcher 97

Rocking chair 77, 126,
  144
Rocking horse 85
Rocky 111
Rococo 82, 90
Rodgers & Hammerstein
  89, 95, 124, 135, 137
Roller 121
Rolling pin 73
Rolling Stones, The 106
Roman Actor, The 22
Roman ornament,
  ancient 27
Romberg. Sigmund 139,
  142
Rome 21
Romeo and Juliet 120
Rommel 96
Rookery Nook 89
Roosevelt 90
Roots 100
Rope, sisal 126
*Rosencrantz and
  Guildenstern are Dead*
  41
Roses of Eyam 48
Ross 82
Rostrand, Edmund 48
*Round and Round the
  Garden* 120
Royal Hunt of the Sun 41
Rubik Cube 110, 117
Rugby ball 77
Rule 93
Runic alphabet stick 34
Rushlight holder 58, 71,
  146
Russell, Tony 75
Ryton, Royce 89, 147

S

Sack of rice 140
Saddle 125
Sake bottles 135
Salt/pepper pot 91
Salt/pepper shaker 113
Salvation Army 76
Sassoon, Vidal 105
Saturday Night Fever
  111
Sauce boat 60
Saucepan 26, 86
Saucer 71
Saunders, James 120,
  142
Savages 105
Savoy 75
Saw 13, 34
Scabbard 59, 130
Scales 25, 32, 98, 140

Scalextric 106
Scarlet Pimpernel, The
  55
Scent bottle 20, 26, 57, 80
Schiller, Friedrich 41
Schnitzler 82
School for Scandal, The
  55
Schwartz, Stephen 128
Science and medicine 49
Science and technology
  116
Scotch hands 145
Scott 83
Scribe's desk and
  document holder 13
Scythe 53, 145
Seagull, The 75
Seat 13, 24, 26, 32, 122
Second Easter 128
Second Reich 76
See How They Run 95
Seed drill 60
Senet game table 12
September Tide 100
Sesame Street 111
Settee 43, 58, 84, 148
Settle 58, 144
Sewing implements 26
Sewing machine 77
Shadowlands 100, 139
Shaduf 14
Shaffer, Anthony 147
Shaffer, Peter 41, 55, 100
Shakespeare, William 9,
  16, 22, 36, 41, 120, 147
Shaw, George Bernard 9,
  22, 82
She Stoops to Conquer
  55
Shears 26, 121, 145
Shepard, Sam 105
Sheraton 82
Sheriff, R C 82
Shields 12, 20, 32, 38, 60,
  130
Ship's wheel 84
Shopping 116, 119, 140,
  141
Shopping trolley 140
Shotgun 71
Showboat 88
Shrimpton, Jean 105
Shrine/casket 33
Sickles 11, 39, 130
Siegfried 29
Sigorsky, Ivor 90
Simon, Neil 95, 142
Single Spies 100
Sinn Fein 83
Sino-Japanese war 90
Sistrum 11

Skateboard 113
Skillet 52, 126
Skis 86
Sledge 34
Sleeping Beauty 132
Sleuth 147
Slide projector 108
Sling 130
Slot machine 143
Smallpox 111
Snow goggles 72
Snow Queen 132
*Snow White and the
  Seven Dwarfs* 132
Snuff box 58, 65, 70, 78
Snuffers 65
Soda syphon 142
Sofa 65, 71, 78, 92, 118
Soldier and the Woman
  128
Soldier's Altar 24
Someone Waiting 100
Son of Man 128
Sophocles 16
Sound of Music, The 137
South Pacific 95
South pole 83
Spanish civil war 90
Spears 18, 31
Spectacles 38
Spinning wheel 57, 66,
  133
Spirit level 93
Spoon rack 60
Spoons 27, 38, 46, 52, 53
Sport 82
Spring and Port Wine 105
Springfield, Dusty 106
Spur 125
Sputnik 101
Square 27
Staircase 140
Stalin 90
Stands 27
Stanislavsky 75
Star Wars 110, 111
Starlight Express 115
State of Revolution 82
Steinbeck, John 89
Steinman, Jim 144
Stereoscope 71
Stethoscope 71, 138
Stevenson, R L 75
Stewart, Rod 111
Stirrup pump 97
Stirrup 125
Stock market 90
Stoker, Bram 75
Stools 19, 25, 32, 43, 50,
  129, 134, 144
*Stop the World, I want to
  Get Off* 105

Stop watch 139
Stoppard, Tom 41, 82,
  110, 115, 147
Storage drawers 113
Storage jar 112
Stove 80, 86
Strainer 26
*Strange Case of Dr Jekyll
  and Mr Hyde* 75
Strimmer 120
Strindberg 75
Stuart Gray, Nicholas 135
Student Prince, The 139,
  142
Styles and trends 36, 89
Styli 25
Stylus, bone 19
Submachine gun 108,
  113, 118
Suez canal 101, 111
Suez war 101
Suffragettes 82
Sugar Loaf 52
Summer and Smoke 82
Sweeney Todd the Barber
  68
Sweeney Todd 140
Sweets container 140
Swords 11, 18, 19, 24, 31,
  38, 43, 52, 59, 60, 66, 72,
  130, 134, 136
Syringe 138

T

Table lamps 78, 107
Table stand 129
Tables 20, 25, 26, 33, 38,
  44, 52, 60, 64, 65, 66, 72,
  73, 79, 80, 86, 93, 103,
  108, 112, 117, 118, 129
Tablet 20, 130
Taking Sides 95
Tale of Two Cities, A 55,
  68
Talented Mr Ripley, The
  100
Tales of King Arthur 29
Tallboy chest 97
Tamagotchi virtual pet
  118
Tankards 32, 39, 43, 50,
  57, 143
Tape recorder 103
Taste of Honey, A 100
Taylor, C P 95
Taylor, Don 48
Tea set 32
Teapot 59, 65, 66, 72, 78,
  112
Teapoy 66

Index

Tebelak, John Michael 128

Technology 111

Telephone 91, 107, 113, 141

Telescope 58, 86

Television 90, 97, 100, 101, 102, 106, 107, 111

Telstar 106

Tennis racket 77, 87, 92, 108, 139

Tensing 101

Terminator, The 115

Tess of the d'Ubervilles 75, 144

Teutonic chest 33

Thark 89

The Plough and the Stars 82

The Way of the World 55

Theory of Relativity 83

Thermometer 138

This Happy Breed 89

Thomas, Brandon 75

Thomas, Dylan 100

Thomson, Flora 75

Thor, With Angels 29

Three Musketeers, The 48

Three Tall Women 115

Throne 11, 147

Tins 79, 140

Tis Pity She's A Whore 48

Tiswas 111

Toad of Toad Hall 132

Toaster 107

Toasting fork 45, 73

Tobacco pipe 50, 58

Tobacco pouch 45, 50

Tobacco 126

Toilet set 27

Tom Jones 55

Tomb with a View 147

Tommy gun 91

Tongs 26

Tooth cleaner 44

Tootsie 115

Top of the Pops 106

Torah 131

Torches 12, 19, 25, 32, 39, 44, 117, 118, 130

Towel rail 87

Towering Inferno 111

Toys 13, 14, 18, 20, 24, 27, 32, 33, 46, 50, 57, 65, 70, 87, 98, 101, 108, 113, 136

Transport 101, 105

Travel 23, 29, 56

Travers, Ben 89

Travesties 82

Treasure chest 134

Treasure Island 68

Treaty tablet 20

Trelawny of the 'Wells' 68

Trespass 95

Trial of Lucullus 22

Trident 126

Tripod 33

Trivial Pursuit 110

Troilus and Cressida 16

Trojan Women, The 16

Trotsky 90

Trowel 93

Truncheon 72, 79

Tupperware 102

Turf cutter 25

Turn of the Screw, The 75

Tutankhamun 90, 110

Twiggy 105

Two plants and a passion 36

Typewriter 78, 84, 93, 141

U

Ubu roi 75

Ultrasound machine 138

Umbrella stand 87

Under Milk Wood 100

Updike, John 110

Uplighter 118

Urinary catheter and bag 138

Urns 34, 87

V

Vacuum cleaner 87, 92, 102, 103, 118

Valkyrie, The 29

Vases 13, 24, 50, 80, 87, 93, 98, 108, 135

Vaudeville 82

Verdi 9

Vickery, Frank 95

Victoria, Queen 76, 83

Victory of the Cross 128

Vietnam war 106, 110, 111

Viking dancing god 33

Viking impact 30

Vivat! Vivat! Regina 41

W

Wagner, Richard 29, 75

Walker 138

Wand 132

War, 81, 83, 88, 90

Wardrobe 80, 93

Warhol, Andy 105, 110

Warming pan 66, 72

Wash bowl 46

Washbasin 75

Washboard 73, 86, 98, 146

Washing machine 92, 102

Washstand 86

Watch with Mother 100

Watch 45, 50, 60, 79, 87

Water 75

Water Babies, The 132

Water barrel 126

Water can 121

Water container 33, 126

Watergate 111

Waterhouse, K 100

Way of the World, The 55

Way Upstream 115

Wealthy lifestyle 63

Weapons 29, 33, 38, 39, 43, 44, 45, 46, 49, 50, 51, 57, 58, 59, 60, 64, 65, 70, 71, 72, 84, 85, 86, 91, 97, 98, 102, 107, 108, 112, 113

Weaving loom 32

Webster, John 48

Weighing balance 12

Weights 31

Well 132

Wertenbaker, Timberlake 16

Wesker, Arnold 100

West Side Story 100

What I Did in the Holidays 105

Wheelbarrow 120

Wheelchair 138

When We are Married 82

Whisky 143

Whistle down the Wind 144

Whistle 58, 71, 78

Whitemore, Hugh 105

Whiting, John 48

Who, The 106, 111

Who's Afraid of Virginia Woolf? 105

Whose Life is it Anyway? 138

Why Not Stay for Breakfast 110

Wicker basket 97, 102, 133, 140, 146

Wicker linen basket 77

Wilcox, Michael 110

Wild West 119, 124, 125, 126, 127

Wilde, Oscar 75

Williams, Emlyn 75, 89, 95, 100

Williams, Nigel 139

Williams, Tennessee 75, 82, 95, 105

Winchester rifle 77, 124

Wind of Heaven, The 75

Wine coaster 64

Wine cooler 60, 65

Wine filter 129

Wine jars/vessels 11, 18, 20, 60

Wine strainer, 19

Winslow Boy, The 82

Wizard of Oz 132

Wok 136

Woman in White 68

Women's role 48, 76, 82, 116

Woodstock 106

Wool spindle 18

World War I 83, 95

World War II 88, 94

Wright brothers 83

Wright 75

Writing set 136

Wycherley, William 48

X

X-Rays 76

Y

Yoghurt maker 129

You're a Good Man, Charlie Brown 105

Z

Z Cars 106

Zeppelin 83

Zulu war 76